The Covenant's Veil

ORTHODOX CHRISTIANITY AND CONTEMPORARY THOUGHT

SERIES EDITORS
Aristotle Papanikolaou and Ashley M. Purpura

This series consists of books that seek to bring Orthodox Christianity into an engagement with contemporary forms of thought. Its goal is to promote (1) historical studies in Orthodox Christianity that are interdisciplinary, employ a variety of methods, and speak to contemporary issues; and (2) constructive theological arguments in conversation with patristic sources and that focus on contemporary questions ranging from the traditional theological and philosophical themes of God and human identity to cultural, political, economic, and ethical concerns. The books in the series explore both the relevancy of Orthodox Christianity to contemporary challenges and the impact of contemporary modes of thought on Orthodox self-understandings.

The Covenant's Veil

Ethiopian Orthodox Tradition of Elaboration

Alexandra Sellassie Antohin

FORDHAM UNIVERSITY PRESS
New York • 2025

Copyright © 2025 Fordham University Press

All rights reserved. No part of this publication may be reproduced, stored in a retrieval system, or transmitted in any form or by any means—electronic, mechanical, photocopy, recording, or any other—except for brief quotations in printed reviews, without the prior permission of the publisher.

Fordham University Press has no responsibility for the persistence or accuracy of URLs for external or third-party Internet websites referred to in this publication and does not guarantee that any content on such websites is, or will remain, accurate or appropriate.

Fordham University Press also publishes its books in a variety of electronic formats. Some content that appears in print may not be available in electronic books.

Visit us online at www.fordhampress.com.

Library of Congress Cataloging-in-Publication Data available online at https://catalog.loc.gov.

Printed in the United States of America

27 26 25   5 4 3 2 1

First edition

Contents

	Preface	*vii*
	Notes on Transliteration	*xi*
	Introduction	1
1	Ethiopia's Story of the Covenant	21
2	Covenant as a Holographic Idea	38
3	The Liturgy and Stances of Giving Respect	55
4	Constructing Church Futures	72
5	*Mahaber* and the Blessing	93
6	Movements of Sacred Promise	119
	Conclusion	149
	Acknowledgments	*157*
	Glossary	*161*
	Notes	*165*
	Bibliography	*173*
	Index	*185*

Preface

This book is, at the surface level, an examination of what is most known about Ethiopia. It is a place where significant things happened in Jewish, Islamic, and Christian history. The legend of Queen Sheba, King Solomon, and their son Menelik I, who traveled from Jerusalem to Axum with the Ark of the Covenant, is one of those significant events. This book is about how that story is a gateway for understanding how Ethiopian Orthodox Christians develop and sustain their devotional culture.

At first, I did not want to write about Ethiopia and its covenant, a topic overexposed to the point of cliché. Moreover, the topic involves a closely guarded idea for Ethiopians, and probing too deeply would not be approved of. When sharing the germ of this idea with a member of the Ethiopian Orthodox Tewahedo Church in London, she exclaimed, "Don't tell them! Don't give it away!" This book is also about how spiritual knowledge, such as Ethiopian ideas about the covenant, are enriched and preserved by its devotees.

There are few comprehensive studies of Ethiopian Orthodox Christianity that detail the lived experiences of its devotees. Social scientific methods such as semistructured interviewing; daily field notes; and many months of observing and documenting ceremonies, ritual preparations, social and administrative gatherings, funerals, and weddings—anything and everything that had to do with participating in devotional life—were novel formats of learning for the priests, teachers, and occasional Church officials I built relationships with over the course of this project. There was also a healthy mistrust of and a protective barrier built to keep out scholastic traditions external to Orthodox Christian theological disciplines. An interaction with a Russian Orthodox priest, during one of my first encounters as a fieldworker, serves as an illustration. He advised me that you can't know the Church via the pursuit of study through intellectual traditions shaped by secularism or, worse, atheism. He felt it was far more worthwhile to love the Church. Faith is how you know.

Studying Orthodox Christianity anthropologically has been a project I've been engaged with for some time. My biography as a child of Ethiopian and Russian parents, both Orthodox Christians, played a significant part in my ability to signal my honest intentions, which is crucial if one wants to engage in the invasive activities of the fieldworker. When doing studies with lay communities in Magadan, a city in the Russian Far East, parishioners interpreted my presence as a way to get closer to Russian spirituality and hence my Russian roots. I took this narrative and ran with it. Later, I framed my fieldwork project in Ethiopia as personal: a desire to learn Amharic, my mother's language, and to build an individual, rather than inherited, relationship with family history. I selected a region that had been governed by my great-grandfather, Crown Prince Asfa Wossen, heir apparent to the last emperor of Ethiopia, Haile Sellassie I. Doing pilgrimages to the Gishen Mariam Church followed the tracks of the grandmother I never met who was baptized there. I attended Sunday school sessions with still a beginners' grasp of the language; the lead teacher reasoned that my exposure to the Church's teachings was the primary benefit and that comprehension would come because of faith.

Over ten years since my first steps as an ethnographer of Orthodox Christian devotional culture, I can say that these experiences have directly influenced my spiritual life and how I define myself as a multidiasporan. I was not "raised in the Church," as the Orthodox Christian idiom goes, and therefore am not well versed on the ins and outs of liturgical praxis. I was committed to offer myself as a resource for ethnographic inquiry. Being Orthodox on both sides opened up possibilities to explore structural connections and cultural variations and to navigate lay communities with familiarity. As a grad student, I got the impression from my academic circles that possessing this insider card was a golden opportunity. The reality was far more complicated and personally taxing. It was not the homecoming that I had prepared in my head. I grew up primarily in the United States, a place where refashioning identity and family backstories is what immigrants are encouraged to do. In my ancestral homelands, people were curious about this cultural hybridity of mine, but the focus was most often about what made me *different* from them. I would see this reverse gaze for what it was only many years later.

This book reflects a research approach that is sensitive to the cultural norms of Orthodox Christians and how I think they want their Church to be represented. I apply this level of care and attention because I want them to read this book and treat it as an asset to public scholarship. I also envision this effort as a way to bring interdisciplinary studies of Eastern Christianity into conversation with intellectual traditions rooted in Western Christian legacies of Euro-American audiences. In my view, it is possible to acknowledge and respect the historical, theological, and epistemological differences between these two Christianities (and their many trunks and branches) while also advocating for greater cultural fluency between these frameworks and the societies they implicate. The recent conflicts in Ukraine and Ethiopia and how issues such as nationalism, religion, identity, and belonging are presented for the general public, typically in stark, reductive contrasts between West and the Rest, only serve to prove this point.

I hope that the personal motivations behind this study offer a unique perspective, one that reflects certain realities and possible futures for Orthodox Christians. Their communities are more diverse than ever, more transnational, more culturally porous, with leadership that is younger in age and more inclusive to women. These trends showcase a religious lifeworld that is responsive to the movements and priorities of its believers, and one seeks to have the beauty of their tradition more deeply engaged with.

Notes on Transliteration

Amharic is a syllabic alphabet of 231 characters, with seven principal vowel sounds that pair with consonants (for example: አ – a (short), ኡ – u, ኢ – I, ኣ – a (wide), ኤ – aye, እ – i', ኦ – o). I follow a simplified transliteration of Amharic to correspond to the closest approximation of vowel sounds in the Latin alphabet, using a single apostrophe for an elongated sound and pronounced break between consonants and vowel sound.

Consonants and Stress Marks
q – explosive "k"
t' – explosive "t"
a'a – separation between characters (i.e., *sa'atat*)

Short Demonstration of Pronunciation
a *ma**h**aber* [like **ha**ppen]
u *s**u**baye* [like **u**lulate]
I *fitat* [like **ea**gle]
aye *hud**aday**e* [like **day**]
e' *fetena* [like **fe**ll]
I' *h**ig** [like **fig**]
o *t**a**bot* [like **o**pen]

Terms employed consistently in this book have been made plural in certain cases based on English grammar rules (i.e., *tabot* [ark] becomes *tabots* in plural), given the terms in analytical use and to make the foreign word more portable. When quoted in speech, these Amharic words correspond to their articulation (i.e., the plural of *mahaber* [association] is *mahaberoch*).

The dates of events in the Ethiopian Orthodox liturgical calendar were designed to correspond to the Ethiopian Orthodox Church calendrical system, with the Western (Gregorian) calendar cited in brackets.

: veil

Introduction

I start this introduction the way many Orthodox Christians typically approach the curious but uninitiated: by giving them a glimpse inside their church. On one occasion, Wondwossen, a deacon, offered me a detailed tour of Ba'ata Mariam in Addis Ababa, one of the oldest churches of the city. Its interior followed the traditional tripartite structure of the three concentric circles of an Ethiopian church. The *bete meqdes*, the holy of holies, a zone closed off by heavy satin curtains, is the location of the Eucharistic altar—entry is forbidden to anyone other than clergy. The *qeddest*, where the sacrament is distributed, is primarily reserved for the spiritually esteemed: monastics, elderly, and parents with their infants. The *qene mahelet*, the sound space of hymns, drums, and sistra, is populated during liturgy by celebrants who spill out into the church's courtyard. From this outer ring, Wondwossen recounted this church's importance as a center of traditional church schooling, a distinction typically reserved for monasteries in remote enclaves of islands and mountains. We take in the icons that line the walls and stop at St. Mary, *Emebetachin* ("Our Lady"). The depiction of this central religious figure is unmistakably Ethiopianized, from its complexion and features to the country's map overlaid upon her belly. As we stand by the painting, Wondwossen pauses, then states: "You know the ark is Mary's womb." By "ark," I understood him to mean the "Ark of the Covenant," the container that held the tablets of God's law as delivered to the Prophet Moses, commonly referred to as the Ten Commandments (Exodus 20:1–17). I assumed this because this Ark, *Tabota Tsion* in Amharic, is a foundational truth for Ethiopian Orthodox

Christians, who believe it was brought by their first emperor, Menelik I, in the tenth century BC and has remained on Ethiopian soil ever since. The deacon continues matter of factly: "Because Mary is Zion." At the time, I had a dim idea that what I was witnessing was a metaphoric structuring of a core theme of Ethiopian Orthodox Christianity. Wondwossen, a person of advanced knowledge of Ge'ez, the liturgical language, was equipped to parse out symbolic associations and discursive links to make these statements logically seamless. In this instance, he offered several metaphoric arrangements, equivalencies, and formulas at once. COVENANT IS ETHIOPIA, affirmed by the oft-cited passage "Ethiopia shall soon stretch her hands unto God" (Psalms 68:31). COVENANT IS MARY'S WOMB, verified by the adoration of Mary as the God-bearer, as well as by the material reality that the Ark of the Covenant's resting place is in the sanctuary of the Church of Mary of Zion in the holy city of Axum (Tigray, northern Ethiopia). COVENANT IS ZION, to be fulfilled as the "new Jerusalem," God's promise of eternal communion in His heavenly Kingdom.

Any one of these statements would be understood as a basic fact by most Ethiopian Orthodox believers and not as an especially nuanced theological idea. Wondwossen's explication, however, in his conversation with me, an outsider lacking intimate knowledge of these concepts, moved easily from one connection to another with a perceptible thrill in his voice. I began to recognize that enthusiasm as a special habit of practice and pedagogy. When people would tell me about their Orthodox church, it was often with a sense of wonder, discovery, and revelation. This inspirational sensibility was nurtured by a deeply held recognition of Ethiopia's status as the land of chosen people, a belief so commonplace that it serves as a type of national mantra. To have access to the church was to enter a densely packed spiritual reserve, a figurative space where the convention of elaboration extended to the laity, not just some distant mysticism of a cloistered priesthood trained to interpret and cite complex constructions of symbols, idioms, and narratives.

Ethiopia's story of the covenant represented perhaps one of its most robust genres of narrative engagement. To apprehend the complexity of this concept would require breaking through its edification as a grand narrative. It is hard to see beyond the historical and textual essences of the covenant claim. Ethiopia is biblically significant, mentioned thirty-eight times in the Bible and considered a land at the apex of Eden via the Nile (Genesis 2:13), one of the rivers of Paradise (Ghion). Ethiopia exists before all history; it is the "cradle of humankind" where the earliest hominids were found. These attributes of antiquity are eagerly incorporated into contemporary practices of talking about the Ethiopian Orthodox Church and faith, blending the present day with spiritual history, the real with the ideal.

The Ethiopian story of the covenant, I argue, follows patterns of elaboration that have preserved and perpetuated the covenant's dynamism as a living and active concept. These patterns are manifest in a web of devotional expressions whose exploration allows for novel insights and interpretations of Ethiopian Orthodoxy. By examining parts of Ethiopian Orthodox devotional culture, I propose that the Ethiopian Orthodox Church and its believers cite, illustrate, and envision the covenant's dynamism as a living and active concept through a matrix of relations to the Church and their faith, what I refer to as "covenant refractions." I propose five instances of Ethiopian Orthodox devotional expression where these refractions can be observed: (1) the public's partaking of the festivities of Timqet, the feast of Epiphany; (2) the individualized demonstrations of *temesgen* (thanksgiving) visible in liturgical and nonliturgical spaces; (3) the storytelling surrounding the histories of local arks (*tabots*) that are housed in every Ethiopian Orthodox church; (4) the spiritual kinship found in Orthodox lay associations; and (5) the vow making conducted during personalized customs of pilgrimage. I conducted this study in Dessie, a location with relatively newer Church communities, a city established in the late 1800s in a country that traces its formal adoption of Christianity to the fourth century. For this reason, it felt initially anachronistic to propose an argument centered on Ethiopia's most ancient story. Rather than dismiss Ethiopia's antique religiosity as external to the ethnographic method, these tropes feature as a centerpiece of this study.

This book considers this theological and devotional understanding and positions it as an axis to explore how Ethiopian Orthodox Christians live their faith. "The covenant idea" or covenant refractions are based on anthropological analysis and theorization from ethnographic observation and engagement with Ethiopian Orthodox belief and practices. Despite the vast scholarship on how Ethiopian Orthodox Christianity presents "covenant"—as historical narrative, as scriptural truth, as indigenous philosophical ethos—the interpretation presented in this work challenges the reader to adopt a novel understanding of this well-worn idea. I offer this exploration of the web of devotional expressions as a way to develop a new vocabulary for understanding the pattern of thought and quality of inspiration of Ethiopian Orthodox believers when they speak about the Church and their place in it.

Ethiopian Orthodox Veneration and Vitality

Many outside of Ethiopia are surprised to learn that Christianity was established there long before most of Western and Eastern Europe. Two shipwrecked Syrians, Aedesius and Frumentius—the latter would become patriarch of the Church of Alexandria—are credited with converting the Axumite king Ezana in the fourth century. From this time until 1959, Ethiopian Orthodox believers were under the ecclesiastical authority of the Church of Alexandria, led by the patriarch of the Egyptian Orthodox Church. For this reason, Ethiopia is still often referred to as "Coptic," which is problematic, given its contentious history with the Egyptian Orthodox Church over the centuries. While canonically united and administratively governed under the Patriarchate of Alexandria, Ethiopian Orthodox Christianity flourished independently; Egyptian involvement was primarily reserved for appointing bishops, who often were estranged from the districts they served and functioned as figureheads. The Egyptian bishops did control a powerful domain, the crowning of monarchs, which was one of the contributing factors for the gradual splintering of Coptic-appointed bishops with indigenous Ethiopian clergy. The process can be dated to the era of King Tewodros II (1855–1868) and culminated in Emperor Haile Sellassie I's successful efforts in 1959 to form the Ethiopian Orthodox Tewahedo Church (EOTC), independent from the Egyptian Church.[1] In contemporary speech, referring to Ethiopian Orthodox as Coptic is an efficient way to discover whether a domestic or foreign perspective is on display: In Amharic, one will more often hear the qualifier "*Gibsawi*" (Egyptian) than "Coptic" in reference to the Egyptian Church.[2] Furthermore, Ethiopian Orthodox Christians represent the demographic majority of the country's population,[3] as compared to Egypt, where Orthodox Christians make up less than 10 percent of society.

Several attributes distinguish Orthodox or Eastern Christians from Western Christians, such as Catholics, Protestants, and their denominations, particularly its canonical positions and theological interpretations, as well as the cultural, linguistic, and political factors that encourage independent institutional governance. The EOTC is grouped within the category of Oriental Orthodox churches, which includes Armenian, Egyptian, Eritrean, Malankara Syrian [Indian], and Syriac traditions. Because of the canonical disagreement at the Council of Chalcedon in AD 451, Oriental Orthodox churches have not been in communion[4] with the Eastern Orthodox churches, a classification that includes the Russian, Greek, Serbian, Romanian, Bulgarian, and Georgian patriarchates, to list the most populous ones. Ecumenical councils functioned as the fulcrum of power and influence between sociocultural zones, in addition to their importance of maintaining theological orthodoxy. For the Oriental Orthodox churches, the point of friction concerned the divinity and humanity of Christ and how to understand the presence of these natures in one person. The Alexandrian theologians and patriarchs of the fifth century asserted a doctrinal position that "Christ is one Lord, one Son, one nature, one hypostasis, one activity, and one will, i.e. He is the "one incarnate nature of the divine Logos" (Isak and Bibawy 2016, 273), which is classed as "Miaphysite Christology," following the formula attributed to St. Cyril of Alexandria, patriarch from 412 to 444. Hence, the "tewahedo" of the Ethiopian Orthodox Tewahedo Church, meaning "unity" in Ge'ez, underscores this doctrinal position of the indivisibility of the two natures that instigated this historic split. The drift between the two branches of Orthodox Christianity, Oriental and Eastern, calcified over the centuries. While contemporary Oriental and Eastern churches do participate in ecumenical activities in forums such as the World Council of Churches, the two branches of Orthodox Christianity remain institutionally separate.

These historical details often position Ethiopian Orthodox Christianity in a unique category, the antiquity of its Church tradition constituting a sort of virtual-reality experience of biblical times. Examples abound in travelogues and photo books of Ethiopia's northern circuit, comprising locations such as Axum, Gondar, and Lalibela. Such presentations can obscure the religion's contemporary presence in the lives of its believers, which compose approximately 44 percent of a country totaling 74 million by the last official census (Population Census Commission, FDRE 2008), though estimated to be closer to 112 million (United Nations, Department of Economic and Social Affairs, Population Division 2019). In addition to its demographic representation, Ethiopian Orthodox Christians are called by their faith to participate in an active liturgical calendar, including church attendance on significant feast days, extensive fasting regimes, and carrying out pilgrimages and devotional vows. As an ethnographer of Orthodox Christian traditions, I grouped these activities together as indicators of intense religiosity and concrete demonstrations of the dynamism of aged religion.

The phenomenology of devotional behaviors and articulations represents the bulk of this study's ethnographic material in order to open a pathway for better understanding the transformational impact of Ethiopian Orthodoxy for its adherents. I use the word "transformational" deliberately here. While many Orthodox Christians regard their faith as an unquestioning component of their cultural identity and heritage, Ethiopian Orthodox Christians' engagement with their Church is more comprehensive in comparison to many contemporary Christians. Feast-day celebrations are one context where I often observed how believers anticipate transformational impact. Previous studies of feast-day celebrations in Ethiopia have evaluated its political importance as a platform for national identity making (Kaplan 2008, Marcus 2008). Commemoration of a saint on their feast day is a monthly, biannual, or annual activity that generates mass participation in the liturgical service. The height of the program is the procession of the *tabot* of the saint outside of the sanctuary of the church, wrapped in ceremonial fabric and glorified through a specific genre of liturgical chant and devotional stances of veneration such as bowing and ululation. I participated in this program countless times, but one occasion best highlights the collective excitement and elated phenomenological experience common to Ethiopian Orthodox ceremony.

On October 24, the annual feast of Abune Aregawi is celebrated. This saint is significant for evangelizing early Axumite Ethiopia (fifth to sixth century) and for founding the important monastery of Debre Damo. Like most feast days, the subject of celebration is the saint and the miracles attributed to them and the blessings that are bestowed to all those who pray in their name. During this celebration, I was accompanied by a group of teenage girls from a local school in Dessie, a city approximately four hundred kilometers north of the capital. Standing in the courtyard of the church compound, we edged our way closer to the front of the church, out of the shade of the trees. Most people had arrived by the time the liturgy had concluded, when the procession commenced; on this occasion, the compound resembled a city park, with groups huddled on the patchy grass and a few men carrying children on their backs. Everyone was jubilant, and popular devotional songs (*mizmur*) were sung in full force. People braced themselves around the main doors—simultaneously pushing in to hear but also making way for the clergy, who were chanting the Psalms as they began to process out of the building. The principal chanter hovered on a series of half tones, and complete silence ensued.

This degree of undivided attention was in stark contrast to the frenetic energy at this very same location not thirty minutes earlier. Turning back to me, the girls added their commentary: "how great" (*endet girum new*), or "how exceedingly wonderful" (*bewenet asdenaqi new*), accentuated by one of the teenagers expressively touching her chest. "Why weren't you smiling?" they inquired.

This is a classic description of Ethiopian Orthodox religious experience and demonstrates the enduring ability of ritual forms to draw a community of people together. "Collective effervescence,"[5] a term coined by Emile Durkheim to characterize the vitality of social life through collective activities found in events and behaviors of worship, is an appropriate term to apply here. I was witnessing joy and enchantment in response to a ritual sequence repeated many times yet communicated to me as if it were experienced anew. The scene that played out was both commonplace and extraordinary. Moreover, these patterns of veneration and its affective qualities are ever-present and all-encompassing for Ethiopian Orthodox Christians. Activities and ritual forms that are typically classed as "traditional" behave dynamically for its participants. Such expressions of transformational impact form the core of what this book presents: the elaboration of tradition.

Templates of Lay Engagement

The lifeworld of Ethiopian Orthodox Christianity is vibrant, as the feast day of Abune Aregawi illustrated. The *tabot* serves as a key emblem for Ethiopian Orthodox Christian engagement and enchantment and makes these traditions have contemporary impact. A *tabot* is a prototype of its archetype, the Ark of the Covenant, described in Exodus 25:10–22 as made of acacia wood and overlaid with gold and built to contain the Ten Commandments. They function as the consecrating element of a church: without a *tabot*, a church ceases to be. Its liturgical function is to perform the sacrament of Holy Communion, parallel to the *antimension*, a ceremonial cloth representative of the shroud, in other Orthodox traditions (Raes 1951). All *tabots* move out of their sanctuaries at least once a year, except for the *Tabota Tsion* in Axum.[6] A church normally has multiple *tabots*, with each dedicated to a different holy figure. This feature of localized saint veneration, discussed in more detail in Chapter 2, has influenced the ways that *tabots* behave as stand-ins for local parish identity and as "a refraction" of the saint or holy personage's personality and essence (Hoben 1973). However, this book is not a study of the *tabot*. For one thing, Ethiopian Orthodox Christians never speak of it as a stand-alone idea or as a material—to do so is actually regarded as taboo. Instead, its significance and articulation come alive in its devotional context. Therefore, I treat "veneration" as the consistent phenomenon to observe and learn from: This term[7] is preferred by Orthodox Christians to describe their devotional actions and responses to holy presence in their life.

The body of the ethnographic material is dedicated to describing the variations embedded in devotional context. I refer to these as templates of lay engagement. I categorize five archetypes of activities: celebrating a major feast day, everyday churchgoing, telling and sharing miracle stories, participating in mutual-aid societies, and fulfilling a vow as a pilgrim.

Locating lay engagement can often start by observing the impact of the local church and the activities it inspires. A church's liturgical program or service can average approximately three to four hours, with attendees ebbing and flowing across its duration. For these reasons, it can be a challenging task to describe patterns of common believers' worship, prayer, charity, faith-driven engagement, and other actions during liturgical time/space. The concentric circles of the round Ethiopian Orthodox church architecture (see Chapter 2) can serve a useful visual analogy for conceiving of the fluidity of interactions, particularly for celebrants participating outside the church building. Lots of my fieldwork time was spent standing or crouching on the grounds of the compound, that is, the space between the church walls and the outer gates. There I was able to observe individualized worship expressions such as reading from the devotional prayer books or moving and pausing along the walls of the church to prostrate and carry out a more outward expression of humility.

The liturgical calendar of the Ethiopian Orthodox Tewahedo Church is an important factor that shapes lay participation. In addition to commemorations plotted throughout the year, there is also a calendar of monthly feast days. Participation in these feast days depends on the popularity of the saint and if their *tabot* is housed in a particular church (for example, St. Mary, St. Gabriel, and St. Michael are among the most celebrated). The cycles of fasting are structured around major feast seasons such as the Feast of the Nativity of Jesus and Feast of the Holy Resurrection:

On average, this amounts to about 250 days in a year. Keeping the fast is often a supreme mark of devotional seriousness, with children old enough to maintain the regime eager to participate. Hart's (1993) ethnography of Greek Orthodox village life observed how the liturgical calendar helps formalize and sharpen for believers their consciousness of saints as intercessors, either through name-day celebrations or their importance to local history. Liturgical calendars are also important for marking agricultural time: The Feast of the Holy Cross, which follows the Ethiopian new year on September 11, is a festival rich with fertility symbolism. Since Ethiopia is still a largely rural country that relies on small-scale agriculture for many citizens' livelihood, these aspects of calendrical time continue to be relevant. As Ethiopia becomes more urban, industrialized, and wage-labor focused, it becomes increasingly challenging to adhere to a commemorative calendar, but many do.

Within the category of lay engagement, I include movements, gestures, and ordered patterns of liturgical time/space as actions that encompass Orthodox devotional culture. For Ethiopian Orthodox, the call to worship, such as the sensation of hearing *qidase* (liturgy), is nearly a social reflex. This might include greeting the church at all given hours of the day, accompanied by a display of surrender manifested in motions at various points of its exterior and matched by formalized prayers or statements of personal petition. I observed that these acts are done individually and publicly and contain a cyclical quality of repetition, what Rappaport regards as the "obvious aspects of ritual" (1979) or what Houseman and Severi elaborate as "ceremonial behavior in terms of special 'procedures' or characteristic morphological features: conventionality, repetition, fragmentation or 'parcelling,' fixity, framedness, condensation or fusion of meaning, numinous experience, etc." (1998, 181). The associated posture of paying respect is a specific, individualized approach that is intentional, reflexive, and manifest in bodily posture: It is itself conceptualized as sacred. I propose to think of these movements of paying respect as a clear template of devotional action and as an entry point for better understanding how common believers structure their everyday life to be attuned to liturgical time/space.

The defining qualities of Orthodox aesthetics or material ecology are rooted in individualized customs of prayer and intercession. Ethiopia's remote Orthodox monasteries and their monastics have been well studied (Newman 1998; Persoon 2002, 2003; Wright 2004) and offer rich ethnographic details about devotional acts such as pilgrimage and vow making.

More mundane spaces of devotional regime making are found in the home, such as Paxson's (2005) description of how the icon corner or red corner in Russian cultural life emphasizes the overlap of symbolic forces in the material composition of the home, where portraits of Soviet premiers, keepsakes, votive glasses of vodka, candles, miscellaneous auspicious objects, and icons rest on a shelf or ledge. It is a syncretic space, a potent, focalizing point, and the place to localize prayer. It also demonstrates how materials and media, such as quotations from Scripture as popular sticker decals on Ethiopian public transport vehicles (Mihretie 2015), permit devotional attention to extend beyond Church time/space or locations of concentrated piety.

The activities of mutual-aid societies, *mahabers*, or the equivalent term "brotherhood" or "sisterhood" in broader Orthodox Christian contexts, or confraternities,[8] in Catholic contexts, represent another key template of lay activity. *Mahabers* are groups with small to large membership that meet regularly, typically on a monthly basis, usually to collect funds for mutual assistance or for projects that support churches and monasteries. They are benefactors that feed the poor or traveling pilgrims, fundraise for their local parishes and affiliated projects, and act as the main spokespeople of financial assistance, moral support, and promoters of community relations. The authority that *mahabers* wield in local parish relations indicates their position as dynamic institutions for how Orthodox Christian sociality is cultivated. These "spiritual kin" operate within "political, national, and transnational frames to build and define community relations, and down into and between the intimate affects, spaces, and bodies of persons" (Wellman et al. 2017, 3). Certain group structures, such as the *tsewa* (chalice) *mahaber*, mirrored the exemplars of Christ's disciples by their set number of twelve members per group, underscoring the dimensionality/reflexivity of the iconographic in Orthodox Christianity, the exemplary as possessing an embedded gravity of liturgical interaction (Hann and Goltz 2010, 12).

Refracting the Covenant Idea

I propose to focus attention to the devotional contexts of Ethiopian Orthodox Christians in order to better understand the ground that orients ideas such as covenant. Covenant is broadly defined as a bond of protection and mutual responsibility between a supreme being and a prescribed group. It can, though not always, have theological implications and direct applications to specific rites and responses. However, in Ethiopia's case, covenant is an idea that also extends into cultural and political zones. As Chapter 1 presents, it is most dominantly linked to the narratives built around the claim that the Ark of the Covenant exists in Ethiopia. This book seeks to widen the lens and draw together a working theory from Ethiopian Orthodox patterns of interaction.

"Covenant refractions" is a framing device I use to identify resemblances and similes for this theological idea. I present ethnography that groups together devotion activities such as *mahaber* rituals of communing and processions of *tabots* on feast days. It also covers habits of making vows, presenting oneself at church, and telling stories of saints and their covenants. Thinking about the covenant concept as refracting—the bending motion of points coming into contact with a common surface—is a way to conceive of how these points expose a methodology of coherence, what I theorize as the Ethiopian Orthodox method of elaboration.

Covenant as a central focus of theorization is a rare project in Ethiopian studies, with one recent exception. Mohammed Girma's *Understanding Religion and Social Change in Ethiopia: Towards a Hermeneutic of Covenant* (2012) situates covenant thinking in the contemporary political context of ethnic federalism and the secular state. Covenant has been historically tied to ideologies of "Ethiopianness," particularly in the ways the Ethiopian monarchs have tied their divine election to a narrative of chosen people and national exceptionalism (see Chapter 1 for a fuller review of this literature). The book articulates an objective of applied practice grounded in the political theology that informs Girma's analysis: "How is it possible to transform and retool covenant-thinking in such a way that it can be a tool to negotiate between continuity and change" (xviii). With a state long detached from the Orthodox Church, the future of the covenant idea and its relevance in an increasingly multireligious society, along with the political pressures of ethnic fragmentation, is a salient question to ask for all scholars of Ethiopia, given the prevalence of covenant narratives domestically and internationally.

This book's argument, based on ethnographic documentation and anthropological analysis, falls within debates on social complexity and on how the inner workings of cultural frameworks or cosmologies retain their form. I have found inspiration from works that propose heuristic tools for theorizing the "premises" for how cultural ideas are structured and maintained. The diversity of this concept emerged by asking a question: "What if we treated rituals (and objects) in their own right?"(Lévi-Strauss, in Handelman

2004). For instance, to take *qidase* (liturgy) as only literal or textual (i.e., symbolic translation) or phenomenological would severely limit the possibilities of envisioning a localized methodology of maintaining and inscribing cultural values such as obligation, respect, and protection. Covenant refractions is my proposed method of studying relationships between relations, in this case the way that one dominant idea, the covenant in Ethiopia, has expanded out into the devotional culture of Ethiopian Orthodox Christians. I make reference to theoretical mentions of refraction as developed in anthropological thought and specifically include linguistic theory (e.g., Durkheim 1982, Pritchard 1956, Herzfeld 1987, Bakhtin 1981). In Ethiopian studies, Levine's *Wax and God* (1965) represents a parallel project of studying cultural sophistication through the practice of embedding rich hidden meaning through skilled linguistic masking: the gold inside the wax. Vocabularies, idioms, genres, and tropes of cultural value and expression point to the complexity, the depth, the chains of associations that anthropological analysis is uniquely positioned to address.

I consider the habits of elaboration by devotees as governed by what academic sciences refer to as a conceptual framework or cosmology. I also make efforts to reference with care concepts indigenous to Orthodox Christianity. Orthodox Christian theological discourse often describes its faith as grounded in Scripture, the Teachings of Church Fathers, and Tradition. St. Basil the Great[9] offers a description that many reference as Tradition:

> Concerning the teachings of the Church, whether publicly proclaimed (*kerygma*) or reserved to members of the household of faith (*dogmata*), we have received some from written sources, while others have been given to us secretly, through apostolic tradition. Both sources have equal force in true religion. . . . For instance (to take the first and most common example), where is the written teaching that we should sign with the sign of the Cross those who, trusting in the Name of Our Lord Jesus Christ, are to be enrolled as catechumens? Which book teaches us to pray facing the East? Have any saints left for us in writing the words to be used in the invocation over the Eucharistic bread and the cup of blessing? As everyone knows, we are not content in the liturgy simply to recite the words recorded by St. Paul or the Gospels, but we add other words both before and after,

words of great importance for this mystery. We have received these words from unwritten teaching.

(Basil the Great, 98–99)

I have often heard Holy Tradition, as it is also referred to, phrased as the inheritance of Orthodox believers over the course of the Church's history, dating back to apostolic times. This concept of inherited truth encoded into devotional ways of being or stances also effectively contained and mediated this most crucial element of the Church. As St. Basil adds farther down the page, much of the Church's received knowledge is difficult and obscure. A common perspective from Orthodox clergy is to guard against ungrounded and unmediated interpretation, which jeopardizes the preservation of the tradition and in fact corrupts it.

Covenant refractions within Ethiopian Orthodox devotional culture not only demonstrate the established pattern of magnifying spiritual importance through symbolic similes and analogic pairings but performs a vital function for keeping traditional knowledge alive and current. The ability of the covenant idea to refract allows the perpetuation of the cultural value while simultaneously keeping it encased in its originating context, in this case, inside the Scriptures and Holy Tradition. The Ethiopian idea of covenant, as preserved by the Ethiopian Orthodox Church, acts similarly to how du Boulay (2009) describes the fractal qualities of sacred time as they operate in Greek Orthodox village life. It is a nesting of cycles, from major liturgical seasons such as Easter and Christmas to the more microscale of the liturgy of the hours (*s'atat*) that temporalize the life of Christ. While these rites might appear repetitive, they are actually opportunities for re-presentation, "a mode of sacred time where eternal truths become visible" (128). What du Boulay calls the "vital symbiosis" of reference and resources available in the Orthodox lifeworld is the nexus point for observing the dynamism of tradition.

Organizing ideas and behaviors on or about worship as "refractions" of the covenant idea serves a heuristic purpose: to consider how the actions and articulations of believers connect to foundational ideas of the EOTC. My intention is to initiate a rethinking of templates of lay engagement, particularly its ritualized and thus seemingly static qualities, as a key vehicle for keeping traditions vitalized.

Before embarking on this book's main ethnographic chapters, let me emphasize how I define this study's field and ethnographic context. This book is based on research that was carried out primarily in Dessie from 2010 to 2012 but also includes material from time spent in Addis Ababa over the following years. For the sake of clarifying my argument and interpretative framework, I present a limited frame: templates of lay engagement that serve as archetypal behavior that can be applied to any parish church in Ethiopia or in the Ethiopian diaspora abroad. Therefore, what I present here is not a holistic study of local life in a situated place and time, the more standard methodology of ethnography (see Antohin 2014 for a political and social history of Dessie). This is partly motivated by my comparative aims to make a more radical assemblage though the extractability of constitutive parts (Marcus and Saka 2006, 102), a suitable analytical approach. In Orthodox Christian discourse, the field context I am studying is the universal Church. Here, I incorporate a more conceptual and idealized understanding common to Orthodox Christians as "a personality conscious of being in a superpersonal spiritual unity, in a unity with a spiritual organism, within the Body of Christ, i.e. the Church" (Berdyaev 1952). I have chosen to arrange the ethnography synchronically to make a diachronic point. I will let the subsequent chapters testify to this ambition.

Devotional Culture as Lived Religion

This study represents eighteen months of ethnographic research in urban Ethiopia, primarily in Dessie, a city of nearly a quarter-million people and the regional capital of South Wollo (north-central Ethiopia). I selected this locale for several reasons, principally for the multiple ways it disrupted the ideal types of Orthodox Christian representation (see Preface). The region and city are demographically heterogeneous, with approximately equal numbers of Orthodox Christians and Muslims, and it was established relatively recently by Ethiopian standards (the late 1800s). It is a transport and market hub between the capital city, Addis Ababa, and the next biggest city, Mekele, in the Tigray region of northwestern Ethiopia). It is well known for its multiethnic, multireligious composition; for its historical relevance to the Italian occupation era; and as a site of the famines that spurred revolution and the overthrow of Emperor Haile Sellassie I in 1974. Early in my fieldwork I was confident that because Dessie's attributes did not align neatly with the reputation of the Christian centers of Gojjam, Gondar, and Northern Tigray, principally because of its recent founding as a city, my research would more flexibly be able to explore an urban outlook, informed by my understanding that traditionalist features diminish in "modernizing" locales such as cities given increased pressures to keep pace with the country's development aspirations. Dessie's location offered a context of intense church-building projects, accompanied by a competitive zeal with a well-established Muslim and a growing Pentecostal Christian presence in the city that reflected the national Church's diminishing position as the hegemonic religious authority.

The fieldwork focused on representing lay participation of Ethiopian Orthodox Christians, the praxis and media of the "common believers"[10] that make up their devotional culture. The project was designed to follow points in the liturgical calendar, the fast and feast seasons, in order to analyze two principal themes: first, to present the experiences of devotees with as much attention as possible to their diversity and plurality, with a focus on commemorations as one reliable way of observing flows of activity; second, to chart the capacities of tradition-based domains, such as the routines of going to church, to inspire individual creativity and expression. My position as an ethnographer was one of a sympathetic coreligionist and compatriot—I am baptized Russian Orthodox and have Ethiopian ancestry. My background allowed for my behaviors to be interpreted somewhat naturally. It became far more acceptable why I wanted or was allowed to go to Gishen, a pilgrimage site eighty kilometers away from the city, when I explained that my grandmother was baptized there, because it was a personal and comprehensible story for my fellow pilgrims. This factor of being a quasi-insider influenced my movements and alliances with the Orthodox Church locally. Initial introductions to Dessie were facilitated by family who had connections to the South Wollo diocese and patriarchate office in Addis. To have a network of personal contacts was both an advantage but also established certain expectations that I would be presenting the Church in a positive light.

Explaining the central axis of my studies was a consistent challenge, given that the Church was seldom a subject of ethnography. In discussing how to present the Church as a living tradition with Yohannes, a well-versed lay member, for example, I spoke about the spheres of activities I researched, such as my activities with *mahabers* (membership-based devotional groups), the phenomenon of pilgrimage, and individuals' sacramental lives. While these were all noteworthy topics to explore, Yohannes figuratively waved these preoccupations aside and asked: "Do you want to know why we go to church?" He told me that it is "our duty" (*giddeta*) as Christians, first and foremost, to "give thanks" (*temesgen*) every day, for "the gifts of Holy Spirit and to honor the house of God." To understand why Ethiopian Orthodox Christians go to church with such intensity and steadfast endurance is to comprehend that they are paying respect, what I emphasize as part of a constellation of orientations contained within Orthodox Christian veneration. This behavior is exhibited in the metaphysical posture of *mesalem*, the act of crossing oneself and greeting (i.e., kissing, genuflection) the doors of the church, an intimate custom that involves more than a nod of recognition to the church in one's nearby vicinity. The stress on the reflective gesture by making the sign of the cross, in similar testimonies of the facts of the faith by Greek Orthodox Christians (Hart 1994), was punctuated by Hart's informant's disposition to "abandon all other ideas of significance" (267). In the Ethiopian context, the unceasing, reflexive act of giving thanks signaled a particular regime of practice between Christians and their Church, of acknowledging always.

This book is not a comprehensive presentation of a fieldworker's holistic documentation of a place in time. I arrange the ethnography in such a way that it presents a more stable picture than reality. I make a deliberate choice to select and isolate specific activities to argue for a patterned methodology of Ethiopian Orthodox elaboration. I propose that the devotional culture of Ethiopian Orthodox Christians is exhibited through these "templates" of lay engagement and function as a reservoir of influences on people's everyday lives. I work with the lived religion approach, described by Orsi (2002 [1985]) as "the study of lived religion [that] situates all religious creativity within culture and approaches all religion as lived experience, theology no less than lighting a candle for a troubled one; spirituality as well as other, less culturally sanctioned forms of religious experience" (xix). Hence, a lived religion approach privileges lay articulations of a faith tradition and in some ways eschews top-down presentations of religion (e.g., how historians or clerics may describe doctrine). This study also treats Ethiopian Orthodox Christians as part of a "living tradition" drawing from Makris's (2007) articulation of Islam in the Middle East and North Africa as both "a unified tradition possessing a global vision that aspires to go beyond cultural and other specificities, but at the same time as a dynamic tradition that is locally shaped and continually reinterpreted in terms of specific idioms grounded on history" (1). Given the plural nature of covenant in Ethiopian Orthodoxy as a past and future concept filtered through the present, the primacy of discourse that is lived as well as located in ideal time/space will be a necessary balance to achieve.

Organization of the Book

The book explores the ways Ethiopian Orthodox Christians express their devotional lives. I do this using the methods of ethnographic description and inquiry, with reference to Ethiopian Orthodox Christian theological teachings and historical writings. The majority of the chapters are focused on deep description of lay participation in order to build a fuller social context of common believers. This is a perspective that is generally lacking in Ethiopian religious studies and the social sciences. Categories such as "devotional culture" and "templates of lay engagement" are created to help make this analytical focus more visible. There is another analytical rationale for these classifications, as well. I present each of the five "templates" as connecting to a pattern that I began to notice and found significant enough to bring out. Ideas and symbols of "the covenant" are commonly located in Jewish and Christian Scripture. In this book, I propose that we consider the vast integration of the covenant idea in multiple instances of devotional culture as reflective of a development indigenous to Ethiopian Orthodox Christianity. I have arranged the ethnographic material to make the case that the covenant can be located in many formations: a foundational liturgical and theological principle, a persuasive local and national narrative, a personal habit of promise making. This is a work of anthropology: Its interpretation is guided by disciplinary influences external to Orthodox Christianity's own discipline of reasoning and interpretation.

I take another interpretive liberty with this book's argument. To help illustrate the elaboration and diverse applications of the covenant idea, I suggest thinking about them as refractions, much like the surfaces of a prism. For one, I hope this encourages readers to orient to the material in a nonlinear way and to provoke thinking about "templates of lay engagement" as overlapping with one another. And while I seek to eschew a hierarchy of meaning, the prism metaphor does initiate the conceptual importance of an axis point. For Ethiopian Orthodox Christians, the axis is their tenets of the faith as contained and sustained by the Church. In Chapter 1, I provide context to the liturgical and historical narratives that form common understandings about the covenant. I survey popular variations of the covenant idea that operate as frames of reference for Ethiopian Orthodox Christians. The goal is not to provide a unified definition but to chart its diversity of applications. Presenting a collection of instantiations functions as supporting evidence for the complexity of this term. The chapter's objective is to set the stage for how the covenant, particularly the *tabot*, lives in popular imagination and operates as a space to modulate intimacy and distance to divine presence, which the rest of the book seeks to establish.

Chapter 2 examines a major way that common believers encounter a covenant refraction: the *tabot* on Timqet (Epiphany). Its procession during this feast day is an important setting for observing several key frames of reference. I argue that liturgical chant establishes a way for believers to apprehend with their senses the presence attributed to holy figures such as saints. Timqet is described ethnographically in order to outline the multiple perspectives of participants and to showcase how this specific type of ritual context brings a locale's many Church communities together. Chapter 3 considers the rhythm of more mundane time in the liturgical calendar in order to explore how church space influences devotional actions. Detailing this less acknowledged and more invisible domain of lay engagement is essential for understanding behaviors such as paying respect and orienting to liturgy that is detached from *qurban*, the sacrament of the Eucharist. This focus helps better qualify what makes Ethiopian Orthodox Christians "religious," an existing perception in popular (and Western) media. If religiosity for many believers is not through the sacrament and all its bodily and spiritual requirements, what does it look like for lay people? I pay attention to how people attend *leqso bet* (the funeral house), another highly observed custom, in order to examine how obligation takes on a positive value, akin to an honor. Both these chapters provide rich discourse about the covenant, grounded in the Ethiopian Orthodox Christian liturgical canon.

Chapter 4 is dedicated to unpacking how common believers talk, or don't talk, about *tabots* as animating spiritual forces in their lives and local histories. These items are never regarded as objects but as a direct holy presence of the saint, *Emebetachin* (Mary, Mother of God), or dimension of the Godhead that the *tabots* are dedicated to. I argue that they are vessels for discourse about the intimate role of the Holy in believers' lives. Stories of miracles and protest are attributed to individual *tabots* and can reflect the struggles and conditions of those who pray to them. Every church also possesses more than one *tabot* in its sanctuary, which inspired my probing more deeply about how they are not only agentive but also multiple. How are Church communities mobilized by a *tabot* that cures or a *tabot* that compels the faithful to build a church in their name? In this discussion, I juxtapose the intensity of church construction projects during the time of research in order to consider how the refracting elements of the Ethiopian covenant idea contribute to parish expansion and an emerging economic class of church benefactors.

Chapter 5 presents another template of lay engagement: the *mahaber*, a category that spans mutual-aid societies to brotherhoods and sisterhoods. These associations provide a vital space for leadership and participation and help build kin relationships within an Orthodox Christian cultural framework. Member roles and activities also offer a window into devotional life outside the Church, particularly as it impacts charitable works. Certain *mahabers* mirror key elements of Orthodox Christian symbolism that relate directly to the covenant as Eucharist, which motivated me to explore this domain as another potential refraction. Preparing and eating food together produces a type of social communion and spiritually charged space. I propose that these customs of reciprocity confer blessings on the givers and receivers and create authority for lay members as mobilizers of charitable works.

Chapter 6 is an opportunity to consider how the Ethiopian covenant idea as proposed here refracts into multiple facets of a pilgrim's journey. I present an ethnography of oath making at Gishen Mariam, a circuit of churches on a remote mountain top that is renowned for its relic of the True Cross. What brings people to make a vow and what brings them back after its completion, often annually, are questions that shape this popular lay activity. The chapter draws out Orthodox Christian liturgical and cultural themes and seeks to create connected threads to pilgrims' articulations and prayers of thanksgiving. The history of the relic likewise has key narrative similarities to how the covenant and *tabot* stories are told and circulated. The argument ponders what these patterns do—and the space it creates—for pilgrims or other independently led lay activities. The Gishen pilgrimage showcases the devotional inspiration of its participants and permits us to examine popular understandings of the teachings of the Church and the ways that devotional culture creates and encourages the propagation of Holy Tradition.

The Conclusion revisits the key terms of this study in light of the increased political fragmentation of the Church and Ethiopian society.

Ethiopia's story of the covenant, while it may not command the same unifying effect as it once did, is one of the more consistent symbols of identity and cultural value. I reflect on what I consider an enduring dilemma for faith traditions like Ethiopian Orthodox Christianity: How will their spiritual heritage serve as a space for inclusion, one that does not homogenize distinctions such as local histories, languages, and ethnicities?

CHAPTER

1

Ethiopia's Story of the Covenant

This chapter proposes key points of reference for how covenant is understood in Ethiopia as well as by audiences attracted to and intrigued about its narrative of exceptionalism. I consider how the narrative of Ethiopia as the resting place of the Ark behaves as a site of gazing both out and in. How do tropes of Ethiopia as a land of a "biblically rooted way of life" contribute to a local consciousness that shapes Ethiopian articulations of itself as a place of spiritual significance? I seek to establish that the covenant is a concept that expands beyond the Ethiopian narrative of religious and political exceptionalism. This chapter will reground the covenant in its liturgical context and introduce ways it can be contained within an Orthodox Christian understanding of Tradition. This will be important for evaluating and engaging with the subsequent ethnographic chapters, which present facets of covenant that are embedded in templates of lay engagement.

My central objective is not to define covenant but to point out the dominant outlines of Ethiopia's covenant idea and its representation in Orthodox Christian cultural discourse, Western academic perspectives, and global popular imagination. The following chapters will continue to contribute to this body of knowledge and take it to new analytical directions. I aspire to plausibly argue and demonstrate that covenant refractions are indications of the elaborative qualities of Ethiopian Orthodoxy and its Church. The ultimate aim will be to consider how the patterns of elaboration carry over and simultaneously live with other important hallmarks of Ethiopian Orthodox devotional culture.

The Covenant and Ethiopian Exceptionalism

On a basic level, covenant, *kidan* in Amharic, means an agreement, stemming from the root *takayada*: to enter into a pact or bond with another by contract, such as the sacrament of marriage (Kane 1990). Other examples from the Amharic lexicon can refer to legal oaths (*kal kidan*) and relationships (e.g., adopted children—*yekal kidan lij*; allies of World War II—*yekalkidan ageroch*) as well as "wicked people" who are not bound by an oath or have not taken Communion (*kalachew lekalkidan afechew leqwarban yaltegaba*). From the context of Jewish and Christian texts, covenant is a mutual relationship of honor and responsibility, a theologically developed idea of protection as expressed through the narrative of "chosen people." *Yekidan Muse* (the covenant as revealed to the Prophet Moses) refers to the event of Egzeiabher (God) offering to protect the "children of Israel," which was conditional upon following moral laws and proscriptions.

Kidan is a recognizable term for Ethiopian Orthodox Christians, primarily as a testament of promise making between God and His people. However, it does not encompass the meanings and references to its political, cultural, and liturgical contexts; hence this book's choice to refer to this discourse as covenant refractions. The physical container (the ark or *tabot*) that holds the tablets as received by the prophet Moses on Mt. Sinai has a uniquely Ethiopian history. The basic sequence of the legend is as follows: Queen Sheba, or Makeda in Amharic, hears of the reputed wisdom and noble character of King Solomon of Israel and decides to set out to meet him. Sheba travels from Ethiopia to Jerusalem and in the course of their meeting engages in a seductive play of wits. She forges a romantic alliance and births a son, Menelik, and they both return to Ethiopia. After passing his youth away from Solomon, his father, Menelik is reacquainted with him in Jerusalem and upon his return home to Ethiopia brings with him the Ark of the Covenant (the *Tabota Tsion*).[1] Ethiopian Orthodox Christians maintain that the Ark is located in the chapel of the Church of Mary of Zion in Axum, though it has rested in other locations in Ethiopia throughout the centuries. This story is often depicted as a multiframed storyboard in the Orthodox iconographic form (Figure 1) and represents a dominant reference point of the Ethiopian covenant idea.

The legend of Queen Sheba, King Solomon, and their son Menelik is sourced from a fourteenth-century text called the Kebre Negest (Glory of the Kings). The work has a murky provenance: It is either a Coptic or an

Figure 1. The Kebre Negest legend (a ceiling mural at Ghion Hotel) that recounts the story of Queen Sheba's trip to Jerusalem and the subsequent journey of the Ark of the Covenant to Ethiopia.

Ethiopian text based on Coptic and Arabic traditions (Marrassini 2007, 367). Academic scholarship consistently regards this royal chronicle as an instrumental document for what is referred to as the "restoration of the Solomonic dynasty." The Zagwe kings (tenth to thirteenth century) were overthrown by Yekuno Amlak, who traced ancestry to Menelik I. For these reasons, the Ethiopian story of the covenant through the Ark of the Covenant legend, and where it is sourced, is shaped by the close relationship between Church and state and is part of the national narrative of Ethiopia's Amhara and Tigrean kings and queens.

This political dimension of Ethiopia's covenant idea has prompted scholars to view covenant as a symbol to edify the status quo of the country's ruling elite. Chronicles have served similar uses in other national histories—see, for example, the Matter of Britain, the body of medieval literature where King Arthur legends are sourced. Ethiopia's story of the Ark of the Covenant, as sourced from the Kebre Negest, contributes to a broader discourse of national or religious exceptionalism. For political philosophy, the concept of a chosen people governed by moral righteousness and bonded by divine protection is found in many societies (Walzer 1985), from the Dutch Reformed Church in South Africa to the Church of Latter-Day Saints in the United States (Smith 2003).

However, the scholarly attention to its political utility may have the effect of dismissing the theological magnitude of this claim, specifically the two-way direction of being a "covenantal people." From this Church's perspective, not only is it important to explain how people come to have a covenant but also, perhaps more importantly, how to keep one. In the reasoning of Abune Yesehaq, patriarch in exile (1974–1994), a close reading of Scripture (1 Kings 11) shows that "in the last years of his life, King Solomon 'did not keep what the Lord had commanded'" (Yesehaq 1991, 3). The suggestion here is that this most sacred item was not in the hands of the righteous. Is this a way to present the actions of Menelik in a positive light, that is, not stealing the Ark but rather having it arrive at its intended home? This crucial distinction is most clear when people talk about the *Tabota Tsion* "resting" in Axum (*ezeh new yarefew*) rather than being a possession. This semantic emphasis is important and can be interpreted as an argument against the ways that foreigners understand the covenant narrative as a historical claim.

The narrative of exceptionalism has been attached to Ethiopia, or "Abyssinia," the name used more dominantly before the nineteenth century, for some time. Ethiopia's deep religious history supports the narrative of exceptionalism beyond its territories. The kingdom of Axum adopted Christianity in the fourth century, around the same time as Constantinople and many centuries before societies on the European continent. During this era, Ethiopian Orthodox Christianity cultivated a written liturgical language (Geez) and a tradition of Church schooling and scholasticism that developed with more sophistication over the course of highland Ethiopian history. It is known for building architecturally inventive churches out of rock cliffs in Lalibela and part of Tigray, unique to the northern and north-central parts of the region. The Church was the steward of a rare translation of the Book of Enoch, an apocryphal text that vanished from the other branches of Christianity and has inspired attention from scholars of scriptural studies. In short, it is a significant place and continues to capture the interests of a diverse array of interlocutors.

The exceptionalism narrative is active also in ways independent of its Christian legacy. From the global historical perspective, Ethiopia has been a shining example of an African civilization whose political power triumphed into the modern era. Several features support this reputation. It is cited as the only indigenous African country not successfully colonized by European nations.[2] Its rulers garnered international respect: Emperor Menelik II (1889–1913) and Ethiopian armies thwarted Italian colonial ambitions in 1892; Haile Sellassie I's (1930–1974) League of Nations address was a prescient warning about the fascist tide that would seize Europe in the 1940s. Haile Sellassie is also one of the architects of the Organization of African Unity, now the African Union, headquartered in Addis Ababa. These historical details from recent modern history all contribute to Ethiopia's prominence as a fount of African self-determination and of Pan-Africanism.

So what to make of these articulations of covenant as a local Ethiopian concept and powerful national symbol for many Ethiopians? As a historical claim, it permits envisioning Ethiopia as the "new Jerusalem." This understanding is supported in popular speech and media by an active mining of citations from Holy Scripture (see Figure 2), the most famous being: "Ethiopia shall soon stretch her hands unto God" (Psalms 68:31). It is also a potent piece of nation building and, from contemporary perspectives that are critical of highland Ethiopia, a successful form of propaganda. By and large, the Kebre Negest has been the source text for establishing many of the popular reference points described here. It continues to have contemporary impact, particularly for religious movements such as Rastafarianism, whose

Figure 2. "Ethiopia shall soon stretch her hands unto God," as inscribed to the right of the painting. Kechine Medhane Alem (Addis Ababa).

followers maintain that Haile Sellassie I, the 225th descendent of King Solomon and Queen Sheba, is their messiah. This serves as one indication that Ethiopia's story of the covenant remains influential to a public outside Ethiopia.

Ethiopian Christianity through the Looking Glass

A dominant trend in Ethiopian studies, particularly with European and American scholars, is to present the region as a fulcrum of religious history and a place to observe a biblically rooted way of life. Edward Ullendorff's *Ethiopia and the Bible* (1968) is a popular source that showcases this trend, though it is by no means the only one: Its introduction functions as a bibliography of supporting scholarship. A central fascination of this literature is to explain the characteristics of Ethiopian Orthodox Christianity that contain certain "Old Testament" qualities, chief among these being male circumcision, dietary laws such as the prohibition of pork, and observing Saturday as a day of rest. The first thirty pages of the book reviews the record of firsthand accounts from travelers from the thirteenth century onward and is positioned to support what Ullendorff argues for: evidence of the "Judaizing trends into the life of the Ethiopian nation and church" (27) to support a diffusionist thesis. The focus on linguistic and ethnoreligious categories is consistent with the methodological approaches of linguists, philologists (historians of languages), and "Orientalists" of the nineteenth and twentieth century. One issue with characterizing Ethiopian ethnic groups of the Axumite kingdom as Judaicized is that it ascribes cultural innovation as introductions from Jewish people. Scholarship on Jewish and Ethiopian migrations offers several theories about how and when contact took place on the South Arabian peninsula, their likely meeting point, but a basic understanding of Israelite history would acknowledge their presence in the Old Kingdom of Egypt (2700–2200 BC). There is no reason to assume that the cultural movements could not have traveled north to south, as Kebede (2003) suggests. Scholars of religions and theology would mostly have a developed consciousness and knowledge of these histories and geographies.[3] But the casual enthusiast of ancient history, one kind of reader of "Orientalist scholarship," would likely not.

And therein lies the detrimental ramifications of what Kebede (2003) calls the "Semitization thesis." The legacy of this literature strongly asserts that the bedrock of Ethiopian exceptionalism, its religious and cultural accomplishments, is a result of imported ideas from Jewish migration. The historical narrative of Menelik returning to Ethiopia, with not only the Ark of the Covenant but also nobles and priests from Solomon's court, further supports this diffusionist idea. These events all happen at different historical periods and by no means occur in linear sequence. It's a complex history, with significant gaps in what can be known empirically. Kebede argues that the impact of works such as *Ethiopia and the Bible* is that it dismisses the idea that Judaism and Christianity developed and flourished as an indigenous African phenomenon. During the height of European colonialism and the scientific racism that fueled its ideologies—and given Italian defeat at the Battle of Adwa—Ethiopia and its exceptionalism had to be explained away as an anomaly.[4]

The tropes of Ethiopia as the land of a biblically rooted way of life carries over from nineteenth- and twentieth-century Western Christian scholarship to nonfiction titles such as the 1997 bestseller *The Sign and the Seal*. This book presents the story of a journalist's search for the lost Ark of the Covenant and the various theories and claims to its existence. It is an entertaining and gripping journey, styled primarily as a travelogue, with extensive footnotes and bibliographic entries that draw from textual sources dominantly written or interpreted by Europeans. It also offers the typical character outlines of the enterprising pioneer seeking to solve a global mystery—resembling the action movie *Raiders of the Lost Ark* or the mystery thriller *The Da Vinci Code*. The conclusion of the vain search for the Ark in Axum results in a consolation as Hancock, the journalist, attempts to gain details from the monk that guards the entrance of its resting place: How does it look, what does it do, is it real, and can I see it? The response from the monk is flat and direct: "I believe that the Ark is well-described in the Bible. You can read there" (Hancock 1997, 512). On this last question, the dialogue exposes a fundamental friction between empiricism and faith:

> "Tomorrow evening," I continued, "is the beginning of *Timkat*. Will the true Ark be brought out then, for the procession to the Mai Shum,[5] or will a replica be used?"
>
> As Hagos translated my words into Tigrigna, the guardian listened, his face impassive. Finally he replied: "I have already said enough. *Timkat* is a public ceremony. You may attend it and see for yourself. If you have studied as you have claimed, even though it may

only have been for two years, I think that you will be able to know the answer to your question."

And with that he turned away and slipped into the shadows and was gone.

(512–13)

Though I include this passage to emphasize the drama of this mystery of the covenant, the monk's response provides several details worth extracting. The inquisitor affirms his credentials by stating that based on a deep literature review and extensive interviewing, he has investigated this subject for a full two years. This is minute, at best, compared to the decades of ecclesiastical learning that a person trained through the Ethiopian Orthodox traditional Church education system typically receives. Furthermore, not all knowledge is equal in type, certainly not concerning the provenance, identity, and interpretation of a long-debated and even longer-sought-after historical artifact, regarded by believers as sacred and as possessing the presence of God. The monk's suggestion for the eager witness to attend the ceremony and see underscores an Orthodox Christian understanding of spiritual knowledge as revealed truth. The inquisitor, fixated on whether the ceremony will feature replicas or the supreme Ark, sidesteps a higher priority identified by the monk: to privilege the spiritual encounter during Timqet, or during any other moment where the Holy Spirit may be encountered, on its own terms, as a gateway to belief from which knowledge will emerge.

The Ethiopian Orthodox tradition and its reputed significance to religious and African history plays out in a curious fashion during the filming of Henry Louis Gates Jr.'s series *Wonders of the African World* (2003). Over the course of his travels investigating Ethiopia's status as a holy land, he literally bumps into both Minister Louis Farrakhan of the Nation of Islam and the Archbishop of Canterbury of the Church of England (separately). For Farrakhan, like Marcus Garvey, Bishop Henry McNeal Turner, and many other religious nationalists in the African diaspora, the Psalm 68 verse "Ethiopia shall soon stretch her hands unto God" was resonant for its promise of Black liberation and a pathway for Black people to recognize themselves in Scripture (Scott 2004). For the Anglican archbishop, his draw to Ethiopia was to witness Timqet (the feast of Epiphany) in Gondar, one of the most holy celebrations in the Ethiopian Orthodox calendar. This almost theatrically contrived convergence offers a glimpse into the popular Western curiosity to explore the country's Christian antiquity.

However, the claim that the Ark of the Covenant has been resting in Ethiopia since the tenth century BC is a significant focus of attention. The Gates documentary is a useful showcase of the enterprising outsider and the perpetual challenge to Ethiopians' "audacious claim" to be the custodians of the *Tabota Tsion*. The friction between cultural outsider/insider reaches its zenith when the historian gains an audience with Abune Paulos, patriarch of the Ethiopian Orthodox Tewahedo Church (1992–2012), and asks to see the Ark. The patriarch responds by accusing Gates of seeking notoriety, after the latter suggests radiocarbon dating a small specimen of the Ark: "Faith doesn't go with scientific proof. We don't doubt it that it is here in our place. We don't have to prove it to anyone . . . it doesn't bother us. It is here and we believe it." This exchange, as well as Gates's simplistic and culturally insensitive questions to a monk about the physical description of a *tabot*, has been roundly critiqued by Africanist scholars (see *The Black Scholar* 2000) for "pander[ing] to popular Eurocentric viewership, for which grappling with African agency was of little concern in the first place" (Gebrekidan 2015, 21). The Gates episode on Ethiopia contributes one more example of the Western skepticism over the historical claims about the covenant in Axum, claims that require surrendering to spiritual reasoning, the prioritizing of confident faith over material proof representing one fundamental test of a believer.

These inquiries about the Ark and the antiquity of the Ethiopian Church more broadly are informed by an epistemology diametrically opposed to Orthodox approaches to spiritual knowledge, one that can be encapsulated by the Apostle John's provocation "to come and see" (John 1:46), a perennial exercise of belief to overcome doubt. During fieldwork, I would hear occasional comments about foreigners' speculation that the architectural feat of Lalibela, the circuit of churches built out of rock cliffs, had been engineered by the European Knights Templar—this is one of the theories entertained in *The Sign and the Seal*. I also heard from perspectives that regarded Western researchers with caution: Outsiders studying manuscripts or church architecture were understood as extracting and profiting from traditional knowledge preserved by the Ethiopian Orthodox tradition. These are some of the reference points that can be ascribed to why the Church is protective of its representation in media and the academic press. However, what this told me was that Ethiopians followed discourses about Ethiopian Orthodoxy and that it was important for Orthodox Christians to assert and fight for their place of significance. "Today's Ethiopia Is Ethiopia of the Past" (1990), an official Ethiopian Orthodox Tewahedo Church treatise, illustrates this point. The text is a response to the American Bible Society's 1976 translation of the Good News Bible, where certain references to "Cush," traditionally considered as synonymous with "Ethiopia," were replaced with "the Sudan." The treatise argues that this is an intentional mistranslation meant to both "deny the historical and Biblical significance of present day Ethiopia" and "also to deny the Bible itself" (55). The methods by which they challenge the mistranslation is revealing: listing all thirty-three of the Scriptural references to Ethiopia, noting the explicit citing of the country in the works of ancient Greek geographers and historians, documenting evidence of a long history of Ethiopia's foreign relations dating back to the reign of Queen Sheba, and acknowledging the long-established linguistic consistency of "Ethiopia as Cush" in Hebrew, Greek, Latin, and Ge'ez (the Ethiopian liturgical language). The Church's conclusion "that the present-day Ethiopia is the ancient historical and geographical Ethiopia" (50) is meant to resolve the issue. It also reinforces a potent truth for Ethiopian Orthodox Christians: Ethiopia is a land of chosen people and spiritual significance. This fixation on symbols, narratives, and spiritual heritage affirming this truth is internally driven and argued as much as it is romanticized by the outside world.

This brief survey of outsiders being enthralled by Ethiopian Orthodox Christianity establishes how a Western (and Western Christian) gaze has produced an imaginary of a biblically rooted way of life that has remained untarnished and preserved. The assumption embedded in these presentations is that this world is so very different and apart from the post-Enlightenment, secular societies of the authors of these depictions. This is the literary baggage that one has to contend with when approaching Ethiopian studies, with a dose of Edward Said's *Orientalism* (1979) from time to time. What do these investigations of the curious produce? Are they principally projections of Western Christian cultural values? To what extent does Ethiopian Orthodox Christianity as a well-preserved lifeworld present a foil, a "contrasting image, idea, personality, experience" (Said 1979, 2), that permits framing and reifying what is civilized and reformed: the Western modern? I listened to and received examples of Ethiopian exceptionalism and its close ties to Christianity and the covenant claim with this body of narratives sitting in my consciousness. But eventually I noticed that these entanglements were readily being perpetuated by Ethiopian Orthodox

Christians themselves, though on terms of reference situated in their faith tradition's liturgical context.

Regrounding Covenant in Its Liturgical Context

A covenant is a foundational concept for monotheistic faith traditions such as Christianity, Islam, and Judaism because it establishes a relationship of belief in one God and offers an enlightened way of life through a commitment to this relationship eternally. The Last Supper of Jesus Christ with his disciples is the founding event of Christianity and the original Church. The books of Matthew, Mark, Luke, and John (the Gospels) provide descriptions of how this covenant is enacted, and it is imprinted in formalized articulations of belief such as the Nicene Creed and rubrics of prayers verbalized by clergy during the Eucharistic service.[6] This service is an important part of many Christians' devotional life. The Eucharist (Greek for "thanksgiving") is a key element for understanding that covenant is an act of regular commitment and gratitude. It is the focal point of Orthodox Christian liturgy, its raison d'être. By and large, all Orthodox denominations follow a common sequence of prayers and ritual preparations according to an established calendar of observances. The time and place when a Eucharistic service is in motion is what I refer to as the "liturgical context."

In the Orthodox Christian tradition, the Eucharistic service is a call for baptized members of the Church to receive Holy Communion, referred to in Amharic as *qurban*, a sacramental rite that prepares and presents consecrated bread and wine as the body and blood of Christ. For Habtemichael Kidane (2007), the sacrament is about acknowledging the sacrifice (መሥዋዕት) of Jesus on the cross. The sacrament realizes "his permanent presence among those who renew what he did at the Last Supper, who repeat his command (Lk 22:19) and believe that the flesh and the blood are offered on the altar by the same sacrifice that was given up on the cross" (449). In the liturgical context, covenant is a material reality through the act of receiving the sacrament of communion. In Ethiopia, taking *qurban* is not common for the majority of people (see Boylston 2018 for a detailed study of purity/pollution in Ethiopian Orthodox practice and cosmology).

Still, liturgical space and time remain a core element of devotional culture because it is "the supreme act of communal worship" (Abuna Yesehaq, in Daoud 1991, 3). The imprint of liturgical time/space manifests in the habits and behaviors of common believers, such as to perform *mesalem* (ምስለም): nodding, crossing, bowing, or kissing the church gates or walls or pausing for a short while in front of the church. Carroll (2018) identifies an affiliated concept in the Greek Orthodox context, metanoia, "an act of humility and obeisance that is done, particularly during periods of penitence, such as Lent, as a way of showing respect to something that is holy" (36). These honorific presentations are little and big, formal and spontaneous acts of thanksgiving, which the ritual and sensorial context of a liturgy service frames (e.g., prayers that prepare the Eucharistic service begin at 6:30 AM and can be heard over loudspeakers; this typically concludes by noon). As a template of lay engagement, experiencing and participating in the liturgy is a way to maintain the relationship with God, and doing so includes behaviors that prompt the "launching or continuing of a procedure of reciprocal recognition (in the sense of *recognizing one another*) expressed through precious goods and services" (Hénaff 2010, 114–15).

The liturgical context is also shaped by how the Church commemorates the lives and covenants bestowed by Christ to saints, martyrs, and other holy exemplars. In this context, a covenant is an instrument of expanded blessing and grace: Those who pray to the saint will receive their promise of protection and fulfillment. The Covenant of Mercy (Kidane Meheret) is one of the most widely observed and powerful: Those who pray to Kidane Meheret will have their sins forgiven. The celebration of feast days of saints (either their death or birth) involves a special service, a procession of the *tabot* dedicated to them, with readings from their hagiography, if they have one, which includes details of the *kidan* as it was given to them. This is similar to processional rituals of other Orthodox Christian traditions, which involve circling the church three times with flags, banners, candles, incense, and sistrums and other sound instruments, led by an icon, cross, or gilded Gospel book. The Synaxarium, a book and calendar of saints' biographies, reflects how the lives of ordinary people are adopted as moral exemplars. It also establishes a person-centered idea of covenant via saint relationships and the specific intercessions they bring through devotion.

The Ethiopian Orthodox veneration of saints and the liturgical connection to their *tabots* have historically been described by scholars and writers as proof of its Old Testament qualities. From the dimension of ritual praxis, the presentation and preservation of the Torah and the inner sanctum of the temple has similarities to draw from: *Tabots* are stored in the sanctuary, wrapped in gilded cloth, and only specific clergy are permitted to handle it. Ethiopian church architecture is often round in shape, resembling a synagogue. There is limited scholarship on the *tabot*'s development, but what is known is that its prominence in Ethiopian Orthodox liturgical worship can be officially dated to the Ethiopian adoption and adaptation of the Fetha Negest (Law of the Kings), a legal code that shaped church and crown governance in the fifteenth century, by King Za'ra Yacob, who was greatly impacted by reforms to devotional practices, including the observance of Sabbath and other features that inspire comparison to Judaism (Haile 1988). Historical and archaeological analyses evaluate the *tabot*'s importance in local politics and culture and argue that the flourishing of the *tabot* within liturgical rites aligns with features of the feudal society of medieval Ethiopia (Kur and Nosnitsin 2007, Tamrat 1984). Therefore, rather than reinforce a debunked if not scholastically inconclusive thesis of diffusion or syncretism, a more analytically productive question to ask is: What does elevating points of reference to the Old Testament offer for Ethiopian Orthodox Christians?

Thinking about the present day, I would argue that these links to symbols, rites, and habits embedded in the Bible are important features of an Ethiopian Orthodox cultural framework. The ethnographic chapters of this book all engage with these ideas. These are also qualities that can cause friction with Ethiopian Pentecostal Christians, whom I witnessed criticizing the devotional culture involving *tabots* as a form of hollow ritualism. During fieldwork, the contrast between old and new Christians, followers of the Old Testament versus the New Testament, was evident in everyday speech, usually in negative or derogatory terms. Yet, as Alter and Kermode (1987) propose, the notion that the "Old requires completion in the New or is actually superseded by the New" (11) is not how the Bible is approached by all. It bears noting that the theology of Orthodox Christian Churches applies a holistic incorporation of the Scriptures as a body of laws and prophecy unified and preserved by the Hebrew Bible. I would often hear that one of the central innovations of the Ethiopian Church was to holistically join the Scriptures, pointing to the ritual praxis and theological cohesion of the Bluhe Kidan (Old Testament) and Addis Kidan (New Testament).

To further frame the "Old Testament" qualities in their Orthodox Christian liturgical context, it is helpful to remember the concept of "Holy Tradition" or *Haymanot Abew* ("Faith of the Fathers"), as it is referred to in Amharic. The teaching of the Apostolic of Church Fathers is a term that refers to the canonical discourse that includes actions and articulations of the "mysterial character" of Christian knowledge (Lossky 1974, 5), as well as the development of the liturgy, iconography, and other components of worship, all as part of a composite category not separable or secondary to the Scriptures. It's a category that is perfectly ethnographic because it represents all the ways that common believers express their faith, in ways that can look like common patterns or existing templates of how believers have sustained the Church over the centuries.

In this book, I also use the term "spiritual heritage" to refer to how Orthodox Christians articulate their identity as corresponding to an established methodology and body of knowledge of receiving and preserving divine truth. In other Orthodox Christian contexts, such as in southwestern Alaska, the ability of the Church to absorb existing customs into its cosmological and liturgical framework is what renders those Orthodox traditions as coherent to big-system ideas while distinctly grounded in local logics and expressions (Csoba DeHass 2009). Therefore, the spiritual heritage of Orthodox Christians as tethered to the living legacy of Holy Tradition emphasizes two axes of knowledge making. Engagement follows simultaneously vertical directions, knowledge as sourced and forever attributable as divine, unknowable truth, and horizontal directions, establishing Holy Tradition as inclusive to a community of believers who contribute to its perpetuation through faith as it is manifest in their lives.

A Note about Elaboration and Invention

This book is chiefly about the devotional culture of Ethiopian Orthodox Christians and how this vantage point of ethnographic observation and analysis can offer insights for better understanding the elaboration of this faith's tradition. I use the little *t* to refer to its common linguistic use: "an inherited, established, or customary pattern of thought, action, or behavior (such as a religious practice or a social custom)" (Merriam-Webster). Dominant theories on the role of tradition in contemporary social life center on its power to create and maintain identity, belonging, and cultural cohesion. Works from the humanities and social sciences such as *Invention of Tradition* (Hobsbawm and Ranger 1983), *Imagined Communities* (Anderson 1983), and *Nations and Nationalism* (Gellner 1983) have shaped popular understandings of the precarious place of religious life by the end of the twentieth century. As Hobsbawm's introduction presents, "sometimes new traditions could be readily grafted on old ones, sometimes they could be devised by borrowing from the well-supplied warehouse of official ritual, symbolism and moral exhortation" (1983, 6). "Invented traditions," in this view, offer resources for societies to adapt to change while remaining stabilized by its connection to established social norms.

In this chapter, the discussion of Ethiopian exceptionalism and the impact of the Kebre Negest to circulate its covenant story could certainly slot into this interpretive frame of interpretation. However, I have found that these theories are not the best vessels to describe and examine "tradition." To the best of my abilities, I try to make direct nods to a well-established and localized discourse, Holy Tradition, whenever accurate and within my limited range of understanding Orthodox theology and Church teachings. I also aspire to adopt an emic position of Orthodox Christians (which I can only partly share, the anthropologist that I am). Describing tradition as "invented" or "imagined" would immediately be interpreted as misguided and dismissive of the careful development of their theology and canon. Studies of Orthodox Christian societies have addressed how additions to traditions, without which lived religion loses its vital character, are negotiated. Shevzov (2006) details this in her discussion of the Russian social history of the *akafist*, a genre of hymn sung in communal and private prayer. These compositions, specifically ones directed to St. Mary, flourished from the late eighteenth century onward. The number of *akafisty* exceeded the number published by the Orthodox Church, which screened and limited these prayers to avoid superfluous additions. Key here is to establish a pattern of continuity that demonstrates the rich resource base for understanding cultural responses to change over long periods of historical time. Bandak and Boylston (2014), drawing from Ethiopian Orthodox and Syrian Orthodox case studies, argue that "the relationship between the normative, authorizing tradition and the degree of freedom, pluralism and discipline that tradition encompasses" (39) is a fundamental component of Orthodox Christianity and underscores the importance of regulating elaboration in order to maintain tradition.

Conclusion

This chapter offered a survey and analysis of Ethiopia's covenant story, its place liturgically, and its devotional culture. The various dimensions at play motivated me to propose an analytical construct—covenant refractions—

that would showcase the elaboration patterns that it inspired. The following ethnographic chapters reveal a host of meanings and manifestations of covenant and its various affiliated terms. In one aspect, covenant is textual and historical: *Ye Muse Kidan* (the Sinai covenant), *Kidane Meheret* (Covenant of Mercy). It is also liturgical and hence material: the *tabot* upon which the communion hosts are consecrated. The *kidan* of a specific saint also contributes to Orthodox devotional culture through feast-day commemorations and individual prayers, charity, and acts of commitment.

It was also an opportunity to examine several dominant reference points to Ethiopia's covenant story, which has dominantly been presented through the legend of Sheba, Solomon and Menelik, and the Ark's journey to Ethiopia. The Kebre Negest is a text that has effectively codified Ethiopia's narrative of exceptionalism and shaped how Ethiopians interpret their place in biblical history. It has also inspired a host of interlocutors outside Ethiopia. The "outsiders'" understanding of Ethiopian Orthodox Christianity and its covenant story, no matter how off the mark it can be, is deposited back into the exceptionalism narrative. It's both challenged and internalized. I have come to think of the gaze as being directed both out and in.

My goal has been to approach the covenant idea in toto and avoid a hierarchy of classifications. Why? Because this most closely reflects how Ethiopian reference points to covenant operate in popular articulations. I should again underscore that there are those trained to order and analyze according to the theological disciplines of the Ethiopian Orthodox scholarly tradition. I engage with explanations and reflections received from common believers. The material presented here is a rumination on how the covenant idea can extend out of its trappings and its academic engagements and into a realm that is ontologically contemporary and grounded in a worship life.

CHAPTER

2

COVENANT AS A HOLOGRAPHIC IDEA

To better understand Ethiopia's covenant idea as a reservoir of cultural elaboration, we will look at the *tabot* and its centrality in Ethiopian Orthodox devotional culture. The *tabot* is a topic typically off-limits to foreign inquiry. In part, this is because it is treated as the manifestation of divine presence. It remains in the church's sanctuary and only leaves at certain points in the year. It is always covered and enveloped by ornate ceremonial umbrellas, both as a mark of reverence and to protect the people from its power. It must never be seen, it is reasoned, because seeing God directly is too powerful for the human senses. Since *tabots* are highly protected, they have been subject to theft, which is considered by Ethiopian Orthodox Christians to be a deep injury of desecration.

This chapter presents an ethnography of Timqet, the feast day of Epiphany, one of the most spectacular holidays in the Ethiopian Orthodox calendar and the most common occasion that believers come in contact with the *tabot*. Early in my fieldwork, I identified a problem of coherence between this event and its ritual praxis, the two-day procession of *tabots*. I examine the ways that *tabots* travel, through processions of parish churches, and how *tabots* are represented, through hymns that glorify and employ symbols to create spiritual depth. I conclude by proposing how the symbols, rituals, and responses to the Timqet-*tabot* relationship offers an opportunity to observe covenant refractions in a context common and foundational for Ethiopian Orthodox Christians.

The Complicated Definition of *Tabot*

Before detailing its significant role during the feast day of Epiphany, it is necessary to outline the many ways that *tabots* are discussed—and not discussed. On a fundamental level, a *tabot* is understood as the Word of God (*kalkidan*), the Law as it was revealed to Moses at Mount Sinai. It takes its physical form as a modestly sized tablet, approximately fifty centimeters by thirty centimeters, made of wood or stone, inscribed to God under the Trinitarian formula ("In the name of the Father, and of the Son, and of the Holy Spirit"). This item is the altar from which the Eucharist is consecrated. Each *tabot* is dedicated to a particular saint or holy figure. Descriptions from foreign visitors on the *tabot* are often of bemused curiosity. Fortescue (1913) offers one such example: "It is a copy of the ark of the Covenant . . . they pay enormous reverence to the *tabot*, they carry it in processions, bless with it, bow down before it. What then, exactly, is this ark?" The author ruminates on its possible origins, looking toward the Egyptian or Syrian churches for what the item might be modeled after. Unsuccessful in convincing a priest to open it for him, he disappointingly concludes that in the end, "the modern *tabot* contains nothing at all" (314–15). An episode like this repeats the trope of the enterprising foreigner seeking to bring empirical substance to mystical religion.

Ethiopian Orthodox sources seldom discuss the *tabot* in much detail. Asking questions about a *tabot*'s physical characteristics is generally regarded as unseemly. It's also a practical admission of ignorance, as only higher-tiered priests (*qesis*) or advanced deacons would even be able to speak from direct experience. A more admissible line of questioning would be to inquire about its provenance or its history in an open-ended fashion, such as "how did the *tabot* arrive," "how was it found," "how did the *tabot* come to be," or "what *tabots* does your church have." From what I learned about the personification of these items, the words "created" and "made" should be avoided when discussing a *tabot*'s origins.[1] One field contact in the church, Abera, offered to provide a more comprehensive and detailed definition of the *tabot*. He readily offered a direct response about the *tabot*'s materiality, stating that it is made of selected acacia wood (*wanza*) and is consecrated by the archbishop in a rite called *tabot negs* (crowning or enthronement). His description also exposes a common terminological slippage between the *tabot* as an ark (the container of the tablets of the Ten

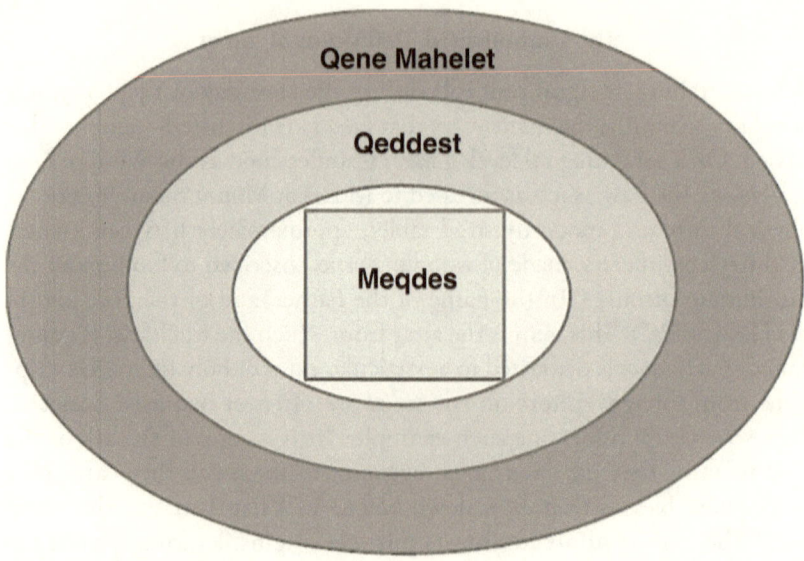

Figure 3. Diagram of the interiors of a typical circular church, defined by three ambulatories: (1) *Qene Mahelet* (lit. chanting of liturgical poetry), where responses to the liturgy are sung by *debteras* (cantors); (2) *Qeddest* (lit. holy), where priests administer to those receiving communion; (3) *Meqdes* or *bete meqdes* (lit. house of prostration), the sanctuary where the *tabot* is kept.

Commandments) and the *tselat* (tablets), an ambiguity left unresolved in the Church discourse or scholarship.[2] He insisted on providing a full written statement on the meaning of the *tabot*, a sample of which follows:

> From the time that Moses received the Ten Commandments from God at Mount Sinai, when he spoke to him in person saying from the wood carved the words Alpha Omega and since that time Moses had praised the name of God in this way. This was the way of worship in that era known as the era of *Abew* [Patriarchs]. Now however and after our Lord Jesus Christ has come to us [born] from Saint Mary, to save the Son of man and he became man. He gave his flesh and blood to us. Our way of worship is known as *Mewatse Hadis* [New Sacrifice] and the era is known as the era of the flesh.
>
> Somewhere between the recitation and writing, the materiality of the object disappeared, and the question of definition became interpreted in

its textual form. I argue that these are indications of a linguistic shrouding of the *tabot*, through the speech that disacknowledges its material characteristics and foregrounds its textual definition as its most important and dominant essence.

In canonical terms, the *tabot* is defined as an edifying property. It is the item that makes a church a church, a veritable cornerstone. I had the opportunity to experience this reality between a church and a nonchurch at St. Gabriel Church in Dessie. Considered the diocese's "star project" when I became acquainted with this parish in 2010, all attention was directed to the large basilica-style church, modeled after the grand Bole Medhane Alem in the capital. However, it lacked a *tabot*. Not knowing how to behave in a church under construction, my behavioral confusion was manifest when I started to cover my head and bent to remove my shoes. I was quickly corrected that I was not entering a church. Apart from the cross at the pitch of the roof, the real church of St. Gabriel was a converted home (see Chapter 4 for a full discussion), with a verandah and windows covered with icon posters, in the style of Greek Orthodox chromolithographs. Its history before consecration in the 1970s had been as a *tej bet* (traditional honey wine bar) and then as an office of the *kebele* (neighborhood association). This contrast between the humble church and the empty cathedral used for pledge drives and diocesan meetings illustrates how this edification appears in practice.

In sum, a *tabot* is material that transcends its materiality. It is also closely connected to the archetype it refers to: the covenant. However, early in the fieldwork, I identified a problem of coherence between Timqet and its ritual praxis, the two-day procession of *tabots*. I summarized this dilemma as "what do *tabots* have to do with *Timqet*?" That is, how do altar slabs dedicated to a vast cosmology of saints and holy figures relate to a liturgical event of Christ's baptism at the River Jordan? I propose that the procession and its expressive medium are less about *meaning* and more about *definition*. Schieffelin (1985) underscores how the analysis of ritual symbols is uncritically assumed to provide meaning. Anthropologists too readily apply importance to symbolic constructs as a model for actors to "make sense" of complicated realities (707), which in turn suggests that transformation is self-evident. He proposes that "symbols are effective less because they communicate meaning (though this is also important) than because, through performance, meanings are formulated in a social rather than cognitive space and the participants are engaged with the symbols in the interactional creation of a performance reality, rather than merely being informed by them as knowers" (707). The standard reply to the question of the meaning of Timqet by laity and clergy is that it commemorates the baptism[3] of Christ as a perpetually transformational event for Christian believers: the granting of grace for all. However, how the feast day is celebrated takes on a form that focuses dominantly on the ritual movements of the *tabots* and their glorification. What was clear to me was that there were symbolic and metaphoric connections being made and that my "incoherence" might offer an opportunity for better articulating Ethiopia's covenant idea by thinking more deeply about the dynamics of veneration.

By focusing attention on the *tabot* as an ephemeral object and subject, I reached certain conclusions about how ritualized actions and traditional forms permit individual believers and Church communities to participate in dynamic and transformational encounters. I refer to Wagner's (2001) work on human patterns of representation, specifically his emphasis on the elaborative mechanisms by which cultural ideas aim to "to get rid of the metaphor," to consider how Timqet is a ritual context for covenant refractions.

> The whole power of a trope of any kind—metaphor, metonym, synecdoche—lies in the identity it states, however it came to be stated. The identity is its own lesson and its own context; to turn it in any way into a relation it is necessary to invoke other identities and misconstrue them in the same way as one intends to do with the original. A metaphor is born of an attempt to get rid of metaphor, and it survives as the boundary condition of our inability to do so.
>
> (20)

As a scriptural truth, covenant takes on several identities, some of which are made explicit in their ritual and textual context. One identifying quality is the participation of Ethiopian Orthodox Christians on *tabot* processions during the feast of Epiphany. The other is the place of *aqwaqwam* rites, a specific genre of liturgical chant, and contemporary devotional songs that are performed to signal praise and honor and to beautify the event. *Aqwaqwam* is the highlight of feast-day liturgy and is performed during Timqet most predominantly. By labeling these as identifiable qualities of covenant (metaphor, symbol, metonymy), I offer content for exploring the liturgical context that magnifies these qualities as points of refraction. Wagner's analytical concept of the hologram complements this book's theory of elaboration. The imagery is itself illustrative[4]—it is a way to conceptually envision how a subject's reprojections through representations dissolve divisions of part-to-whole (Wagner 2001). As we will see, covenant is one of those subjects via the *tabot* and its affiliated identities. The shrouding and sonic beautification of the *tabot* is one reprojection. Another is the liturgical rites and the blessing of the waters that is made possible by the *tabot*'s temporary relocation outside the sanctuary. These qualities do not usurp each other in a hierarchized scale and instead interact with each other to express a unified centrality of the concept as it is lived.

The following ethnographic description of Timqet presents the aesthetic and experiential features of the grand procession. I describe the topography and movement of the processions on Timqet in Dessie, an urban center of approximately a quarter-million people. As an observer, I noticed that the rituals of the feast day serve one way to mark the diocese's jurisdictional bounds, via the passageways to and from the baptismal pool that is the focal point of the celebration. The event is also a moment for the fourteen churches of the district to merge into a singular, idealized body of the Church. While I assert identifying qualities and classificatory boundaries in order to consider the material identities of the *tabot* and its relation to Timqet, these distinctions are not treated as separate entities for Ethiopian Orthodox Christians. As such, I argue that the dissolution of the metaphor achieves a pattern of material shielding and veiling, a guided cultural logic that glorifies and protects a sacred idea and relationship.

Timqet as *Tabot* Action

On the eve (*wazema*) of the feast of Epiphany, the *tabots* of all the churches are released from their sanctuaries. The festivities begin in late afternoon, when individuals and groups of celebrants gather around the outer edges of the church and the church courtyard. The anticipation is prodded on by clapping and singing devotional songs that are specific to the church's saint and *tabot*. These actions of veneration are described colloquially as "assisting the *tabot*" (*tabotun lemerdat*). The *tabot*'s glorification extends into the more ritualized and canonical acts that occur inside the church and provide the material and sensory evidence of the impending release of the *tabot*. A muffled drumming of the *merigeta* (head cantor) is audible from the sanctuary as well as the singing of *mesbak* (psalms). This is the signifying sound for celebrants outside that the prayers required for a *tabot*'s release have been said, after which the singing and clapping crescendos and the

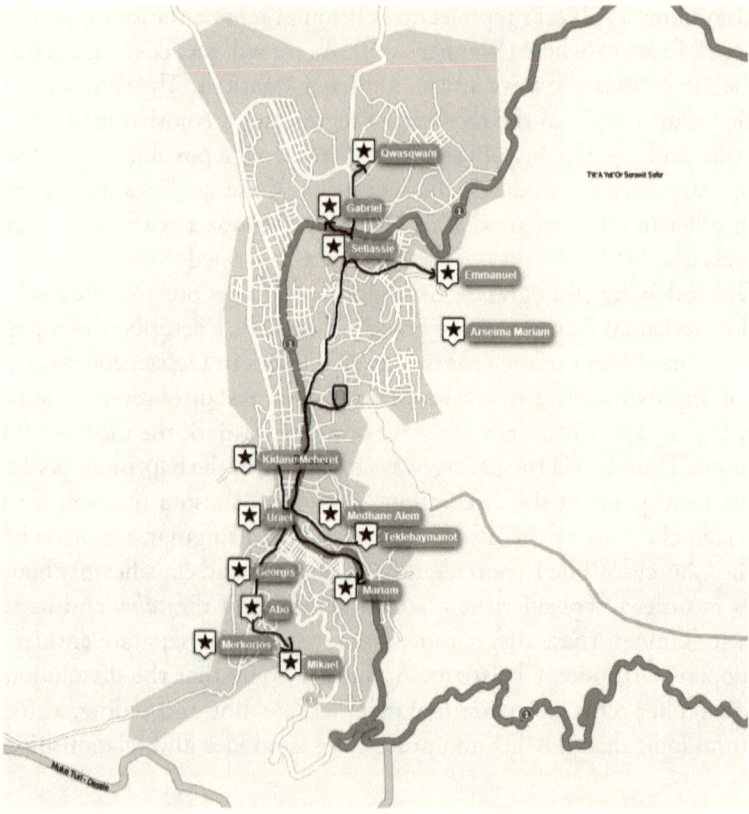

Figure 4. Directions of *tabots*' movements during Epiphany festivities in the city of Dessie (January 19–21, 2011).

ululating starts. It is nearly impossible for most people to get a good view of the *tabot*, whose movement is principally noted by the many brightly colored umbrellas that serve as a canopy for the clergy who carry the sacred object and the "waves" of deep bowing or full prostrations that ripple through the crowd as it passes. On top of their heads, the priests carry the *tabots*, wrapped in brightly embroidered cloths, and large icons of the church's patron saint are positioned at the front of the line. The conclusion of the *wazema* ceremony at the church grounds includes circling around the church three times, after the *tabot* and its supporting clergy and celebrants leave the church and set off onto the asphalt road.

Figure 5. The students of St. Gabriel's Sunday School accompany their *tabot* back to the *bete meqdes*.

Depending on the size of the town or city, the streets become bottlenecked with all the churches' *tabots*. These processions travel to a common destination: a field or location with a large pool of water, referred to as Yordanos (Jordan), the river that was the site of Christ's baptism. This area acts as a temporary staging area for the *tabots*, which are housed in a large tent. These culminating moments are what people mean by "all the *tabots* come out" (*hulum tabot wutal naw*) and establishes this "megachurch" in a football field. The next morning, the liturgical program recommences at 10 AM at Yordanos, with attention heightening at the first occurrence of *aqwaqwam*, a particular mode of liturgical chant and movement.[5] It is a meditative period of nearly forty minutes, between *debteras* (cantors) and Sunday school students who alternate *aqwaqwam*-performing duties. This episode is defined by stillness, composure, discipline, and concentration and is received with awe by celebrants, who cut in with a phrase or two of commentary, typically remarking on the *aqwaqwam* prayer's beauty and mastery.

The energy of the general public in the concluding sequence of the Timqet festivities splinters into a messy order, with the *tabots* now positioned according to the direction of their churches. The front of the line of the *tabots* and motorcade of the archbishop, special invited guests, and other high clergy are flanked by the *tabots*, material indexes of these otherwise indistinguishable items, and by the large icons of the saints of each church's namesake. The processions stop to drop off the *tabots* at their churches and pause extendedly at junctions to sing more praise songs before continuing onto the next church along the route. Along the way, residents stand on their verandahs, as if watching a parade. Once the *tabot* arrives at its church and is deposited in its sanctuary, a short benediction by the head clergy of the parish and/or diocese is offered. The final notes ushering out the holiday of Timqet are singing, drumming, abbreviated *shebsheba* (swaying movements), and clapping by the choir and general public.[6]

Hoben's (1973) understanding of the *tabot* in Ethiopian rural life of the 1960s is that it behaves as a symbol of local identity. In the context of Dessie, despite having over fourteen churches for a city of approximately a quarter-million people, similar essences of the particular and the collective are noticeable. From the time the *tabots* leave the *bete meqdes* to the ceremonial Yordanos and then return back to their homes at the conclusion of the feast day, parish communities ebb and flow both as distinctly individual and as one united body. The demarcations are most evident during the choral performances between the *debterras* and the Sunday school groups. Genres of devotional praise mirror each other, particularly punctuated by the minivans and megaphones that blast often-clashing and cacophonous *mizmur*, maintaining semiautonomy in a sea of masses navigating processions back to their churches. The merging of believers into one worshiping space and the transportation of the *tabots* from their home churches to a football field transform a mundane place into a sacred space, albeit temporarily. Devotional behaviors resemble other important calendrical events such as Christmas Eve and Holy Saturday, when celebrants spend the night in the church compound. *Mahabers* play a role as well, such as distributing tea, bread, a light snack of *kolo*, and fasting food for celebrants. Therefore, *tabots* and the ways they define the personality of parish communities act as a synecdoche for its faithful, a stand-in for the covenant idea as a teleological truth.

Tabots during Timqet not only display their associative and social qualities but also the *tabot*'s material refractions, in particular its ability

Figure 6. The tent and greeting the church.

to move and generate new contexts of identity. Here, I refer to the material ecology of Timqet's symbolic River Jordan in the football field and the Ethiopian Orthodox ritual staging of holy altars in a tent. This location is transfigured during the eve of Timqet and initiates pronounced behaviors such as worshipers directing their bodies to recognize the *tabots* contained there. Worship reflexes like the *mesalem* posture of crossing oneself and greeting a church, as well as aesthetic touches such as cuttings of grass (symbols of blessing) placed on the ground, prompt visitors to kneel and prostrate, some absorbed in extended prayer (Figure 6). Large icons, typically displayed in the *qedest*, the second ring of the church (Figure 3) and in most instances remaining inside, are featured during the processional movements, as well as the periods when the *tabots* are resting in the field or pausing during the *aqwaqwam* ceremonies. During Timqet these media are sign-images for the identity of the specific *tabots*/churches. However, covenant refractions of the *tabot* are not confined to visual media. The aural veneration of the holiday vis-à-vis the *tabots* is evident through the performance of the liturgical prayers and devotional songs by clergy and the Sunday school choirs, respectively. Furthermore, the sonic marking and acknowledgment of sacred presence is an inclusive liturgical event of performers and listeners.

The feedback response of an event that includes multiple senses is further emphasized through how believers document Timqet. It is particularly striking that individuals document, with their phone cameras primarily, an item that is not seen or regarded as material. This is particularly evident during the processions and *aqwaqwam* performances. The presence of foreigners, often directed to prominent places of observation and encouraged to record the festivities, solidifies the aesthetic valuing of Timqet and its ceremonial highlights. Documenting the intangible appears to contradict certain norms about the transmaterial, particularly so with the *tabot*, given the elaborate patterns of linguistic and material shrouding as things whose materiality cannot be acknowledged. This aspect of collective attention, such as "watching" the modes of *aqwaqwam*, interacts with Chau's observations (2008) of Chinese temple festivals and the witnessing of the *honghuo*, a sensory trait translated as "social heat" or "red-hot sociality." Chau emphasizes the ability for modes of collective effervescence in the Durkheimian sense to behave not as events of totalizing, uniform transformation but as instantiating a range of affective reactions: "Many festivalgoers look excited, happy, and engaged, while some others are quite calm; some look awed, even disoriented and confused; many seem not to know where they are or where to go, and are simply being pushed by the momentum of the crowd to wherever there is action; and some look tired or simply exhausted" (499).

What Chau concludes is that "'to watch the *honghuo*' somehow makes people continue to regard themselves as mere spectators while they have actually become full participants" (498). I note that the perspectival opportunities, the sound of heaven (*lisan, dims' genet*), contained within the Timqet processions, particularly when *aqwaqwam* is performed and with the act of *tabots* traveling collectively, indicate that active listening, watching, and following can facilitate participation and authority in this context of ritual performance. In the following section, I present the theological-symbolic and the devotionally affective ways that *aqwaqwam* is experienced. This is done for the sake of analytical productiveness rather than to assert that these two methods of engagement cannot occur simultaneously. By digging further into this meeting point of divine presence, most potent during Timqet and particularly magnified when the *tabots* are honored through hymns, I argue that the feedback of prayer enables the interpretations of the *tabot* as a holographic object, a pragmatic modeling of cultural essences that aim to make understanding and meaning accessible in the face of realities that are "impossible to conceive or represent" (Wagner 2001, 18).

The Material Reality of Immanence

I have presented the events and ceremonial sequence of Timqet as establishing several necessary attributes for defining the *tabot*: It corporatizes a faith community as comprehensively whole and materializes the cosmic habitus of a church. I focus narrowly on the prayer of *aqwaqwam* and the symbolic vectors that emanate from *tabot* ritual praxis to demonstrate how aural veneration frames and contains divine presence as a concentrated devotional encounter. Watching *aqwaqwam* is an opportunity to decode and unpack symbolic references. It is also a sensory experience, a span of twenty minutes that ranges from deep concentration and stillness to exuberant euphoria and giddiness. The devotional feedback of the *tabot* is what defines it as a covenant refraction.

Aqwaqwam, from the Ge'ez *qoma* ("he stood up"),[7] is part of the *zema bet*, the school of liturgical chant or music in the Ethiopian Orthodox Church tradition. This school is defined principally by the work of St. Yared, a sixth-century saint who is credited with writing the hymnography as well as its notation system, tonal modes, and instrumentation. The Psalms take a central position in the hymnography and are determined by the three variations of chant mode as composed in the Book of Psalms.[8] The Ethiopian Orthodox Church is considered remarkable for its integration of drums, sistrum, *masinqo* (one-string violin), flute, *begena* (lyre), and prayer sticks within liturgical prayer. The St. Yared tradition is connected scripturally to the heralding of the Levites, a particular class of clergy (Psaltists), though an indigenous origin story of the saint's inspiration for liturgical music is well codified in the Tradition. Looping back to the covenant in the popular imagination, the stylization of Ethiopian Orthodox chant has been assessed as further proof of the Hebraic flavor of the religion. Ullendorff (1968), the chief author of the diffusionist thesis of imitation, describes the biblical scene of Timqet: "The scene of David and all the house of Israel playing before the Lord on harps and lyres, drums and sistra, dancing with all their might, and bringing up the ark with shouting and the sound of the trumpet is a spectacle that is eminently alive in Ethiopia and can be seen each year at Timqat and on many other occasion" (3).

As a familiar resemblance, liturgical chant is ritually linked to the *tabot*'s Old Testament grounding, as a material artifact of the Ark and the Ten Commandments, but positioned primarily as an example of form replication, at least within literature that engages and romanticizes tropes of Ethiopia's antiquity. However, viewed within the broader tradition of Orthodox Christianity, *aqwaqwam* is an Ethiopian version of liturgical forms and their material-artistic manifestations. Orthodox devotional culture, as a repertoire of practice, includes activities such as icon veneration and akafist prayer. This dimension of worship, its aural expression, confirms an intrinsic characteristic of Orthodox Christianity's "conciliar ideal and constitut[es] a religious territory through sound" (Engelhardt 2010, 108). The collective watching of *aqwaqwam* corresponds to a developed approach within Orthodox Christianity to interpret material-artistic forms as a form of transcendental expression, an achievement of Godly beauty. This achievement is not commonplace but only occasionally present in lived reality. Panovsky's (1991) evaluation of the role of religious art to perform miracles presents a useful argument: "Perspective, in transforming the *ousia* (reality) into the *phainomenon* (appearance), seems to reduce the divine to a mere subject matter for human consciousness; but for the very reason, conversely, it expands human consciousness into a vessel for the divine" (72). Likewise, the experience of watching *aqwaqwam*, an aural signification of the *tabot* during Timqet, possesses similar opportunities of perspective to receive this liturgical movement and sound, understood by Orthodox Christians as inhabiting grace that marks heaven on earth, connoting a union of humanity with its Creator.

My position as a new participant presented an opportunity for informant-led commentary, which was particularly crucial for the *aqwaqwam* hymnal prayers, which contain many little rituals within the larger ceremony. Church students more easily recited the normative interpretation of *aqwaqwam*: that it is a ritual representation of the Passion of Christ. When I asked for a more explicit explanation, I typically received a decoding of the ritual objects themselves, hence an elaboration of meaning via the symbols' metasymbols. I was eagerly told by many that the strappings of the drum are the lashing of Jesus by Roman soldiers; that the rings of the sistrum are five altogether, representing the number of the mysteries (sacraments) of the faith; and that the sound symbolizes the seraphim and cherubim that St. Yared met in heaven. The staff coming down toward the floor is the lashing of Jesus and his removal from the cross, and the contraction (*asragacha*), with the *debteras* (cantors) coming toward one another and then retreating, was the pulling and pushing and physical torments of Christ during the crucifixion. The metaphors embedded into the *aqwaqwam* are a more direct citation of covenant, vis-à-vis the death and resurrection of the Christian messiah. These aspects of Ethiopia's covenant idea, primarily as textual and scriptural, invite characterizations of *aqwaqwam* hymns as mournful. Shelemay and Jefferies's (1994) study of Ethiopian Orthodox chant astutely notes that Western Christian sensibilities to suffering and guilt in foreigner accounts have conflated the mournful responses of the Ethiopian Orthodox celebrants as self-evident demonstrations of human betrayal. My observations of Timqet agree with this assessment. What I found most consistent was the frequency with which believers shared the standardized definitions of *aqwaqwam*'s microsymbols. One clear factor was my foreign status, which skewed this trend, as individuals were likely to feel compelled to provide such explanations to a cultural novice. Furthermore, to decode liturgical information was a reflection of the Church schooling that many Orthodox believers had marginal exposure to. The ability to unpack theological commentary and discourse demonstrated proximity to knowledge about God's energies. Onlookers reveled in revealing these details, signaling that this was a self-generating exercise of affirming theological dexterity and literacy.

The *aqwaqwam* "mise en scène" became more recognizable each time I witnessed it, though rarely did individuals I accompanied articulate why or how these moments were important, just that they were. As I have underscored, engaging in symbolic decoding can be a reflection of education and class. Levine (1967) presents a complementary idiom of *semenaworq* ("wax and gold"), a style of rhetoric in Amharic speech that constructs phrases with hidden meaning, that is, breaking apart the cover (wax) to unearth the gold. His argument extends this innovation to demonstrate the patterned application of ambiguity in humor, insults, gossip, and subverting authority. Beyond a linguistic art, Levine underscores the philosophical import of *semenaworq*, that by "affording exercise in fathoming secrets it 'opens the mind' and thereby enhances the student's ability to approach the divine mysteries" (8). Given the wide social participation of Timqet, it is appropriate to consider the lack of comprehension as part of the general *aqwaqwam* experience. Engagement with realities established by ritual permits evaluating the points of audience convergence as being more than merely the confirmation of doctrinal statements. The ambiguities of uncovering coded knowledge are precisely the conceptual gaps necessary to initiate interpretation and action on the part of laymen (Schieffelin

Figure 7. *Aqwaqwam* ceremony.

1985). With deliberate ambiguity in mind, a more ethnographic presentation with less theological commentary would describe *aqwaqwam* as a dramatic event, one that has a range of tones. The opening of the ceremony is serious in ethos, based on the utter deep fixation by the public, who either look directly at the *aqwaqwam* or stand with their heads bowed. The twenty-four *debteras*, led by the *merigeta* (head cantor), accompany the chant with several key movements, which I was prodded by my fellow onlookers to capture: when the *debteras* shake their sistra back and forth, when the staffs are lifted up and swing down, and when the drum is hit on the beat of each concluding moment. Meanwhile, the *tabots* are stationed to the east, barely paid attention to, and are spatially marked by the red carpet around which another volley of *aqwaqwam* is intoned. *Shebsheba*, a specific mode within the *aqwaqwam* performance when the participants began to move in a circular fashion and sway their bodies, is a distinctively uplifting turn of events. This is a highlight of *aqwaqwam*, when the *debteras* move toward one another, one set moving toward the line, then returning, while the same action is repeated by the other set of participants. The chant verse now has a more melodic structure and grows faster in tempo, punctuated by the pounding drumming, and the public becomes very engaged, turning with dervish-like motions and intensity. Those watching are actively involved in the performance, and their in-the-moment reflections and comments regarding the performers' skill and their assessments regarding their ability to assist are forms of connecting to the presence of the spirit world.

A ritually dense prayer like *aqwaqwam* generates both intellectualized responses as well as affective ones. As Feld (1990) argues in his study of the ecological and ontological holism of Kaluli song, the process of shaping these symbols is a sensorially totalizing experience, a performance that is evaluated as affective based on making the hosts "nostalgic, sentimental and sad" (6) and moved to tears. An Orthodox Christian theoretical frame interprets phenomenology as a matter of perspective that responds to symbolic representation as rooted in the position of the observers, the devotees in this case. Fr. Pavel Florensky (2002 [1920]), an influential Russian Orthodox theologian, elaborates further on this subject as it relates to visual art: "The task of perspective, as with other artistic methods, can only be a certain spiritual excitement, a jolt that rouses one's attention to reality itself. In other words, perspective if it is worth anything, should be a language, a witness to reality" (254). The spiritual excitement during Timqet creates opportunities for believers to witness a meeting point of divine presence on earth, one that links a chain of logic between covenant, feast of Epiphany, arks-tabots, and aural veneration through *aqwaqwam*.

Aqwaqwam as part of the feast day of Timqet plays a featured role in refocusing and transfiguring the *tabots* as a material reality of immanence, grounded in an individual and social experience of veneration and glorification by believers. I also interpret *aqwaqwam* being a part of the genre of elaboration of Ethiopia's covenant idea. The discursive potential of ritual, in and of itself, resembles what Handelman (2004) describes as the vital capacities of rituals to contain inner content that keeps producing. As he posits, "when self-organization becomes highly complex, a ritual has more to live on, or rather, to live through" (14). The material shrouding of the *tabot*, through key modalities of sacred indwelling throughout Timqet and the amplification of glory during the processions, demonstrates how these patterns of veneration further extend the nested references to the covenant by producing, perhaps inadvertently, a holography "of the form of one another's content and the content of one another's form" (Wagner 2001, 46).

Conclusion

Throughout my fieldwork, I was asked if in foreign lands they also have *tabots* in their churches. As time went on, I grasped the depth of this question. The *tabot* is pivotal in Ethiopian Orthodox devotional culture; at moments such as the procession, it concretizes the Church as its body of believers. The *tabot* is also a living artifact of Ethiopian exceptionalism and cements the Church's place as guardians of its national history. When I responded that *tabots* have no direct corresponding place in other Churches, it confirmed a distinctiveness and honor for my fellow inquiring Orthodox. It also initiated an honest appraisal of alternative Christian perspectives on divine presence elsewhere. To ask if others had a *tabot* too was to ask whether other Orthodox Christians were also endowed to commune and possess an intimate relationship with God, the accessible realities of heaven on earth.

This question from the field on the outward gaze centered the *tabot* as metacommunicative of the church and its people and presented an ecclesiological problem: to not have a *tabot* interprets other Christians as lacking. The *tabot* correspondence in Christian scholarship also presented an anthropological dilemma about "traditional religions" such as the Ethiopian Orthodox Tewahedo Church and how to source its vitality given the increasing popularity of Islam and Pentecostalism in the country. Traditionalism is the Church's and its believers' distinctiveness; they lose their defining qualities otherwise. Contemporary studies appear less equipped to discuss this social character of the Church, preferring analytical directions of Christian self-fashioning and individualism (for alternatives, see Harding 2010 and Coleman 2000). The point as it was posed, do they have *tabots* in their churches, implies the potential for a dialogic relation to the sacred within the concept of the covenant, as contained and tied up with the Church and within its social composition. The pressing urgency of eschatological thinking is certainly not absent, as this question is not solely *if* one possesses the *tabot* but *when* it will emerge. *Tabots* are one refraction of Ethiopia's covenant idea, with the liturgical context of Timqet enacting a reunion of humanity and divinity. Rather than an abstract idea of scriptural truth, covenant is configured into locally experienced phenomena and moves in a nonlinear logic that enacts various ways of maintaining sacred bonds in sustaining ways.

CHAPTER

3

THE LITURGY AND STANCES OF GIVING RESPECT

The liturgy service is a central activity for Ethiopian Orthodox Christians and sets the rhythm of their engagement as believers. "Going to church" to worship (*masqedes*) spans a wide cross-section of generations and represents the most doctrinally supported definition of covenant: a sacrament of communion (*qurban*). To take the covenant symbol and metaphor further, considering that the *tabot* of the sanctuary is the altar of the Eucharist, church (*bete kristiyan*) is itself the central axis of the object, the immanent point from which all refractions of the covenant idea emerge. The dominant explanations of the covenant's textual and salvific significance are firmly standardized: The covenant is the offering of the body and blood of Christ to the disciples[1] and ultimately the remission of sins and the promise of entrance into the Kingdom of Heaven to all of humankind. What is less examined in Ethiopian Orthodox scholarship are the actions and behaviors of common believers as they enter church and what these practices produce in their lives. The gravitations to church cannot be sacramentally driven, given that communion taking is relatively rare, given the strict interpretations of pollution and purification that keep it inaccessible. What, then, is liturgical engagement, and how does it contribute to understanding embodied values of church as a social space and temporal condition?

This chapter outlines the various modes of churchgoing as establishing the necessity for Orthodox Christians to proclaim their faith always. More colloquial expressions would describe the call to worship as an ethic of thanksgiving (*temesgen*). I present a set of interactions with liturgical space and time as interlinked and part of a repertoire of devotional actions and motivations. I examine the potency of ritualized behavior of Ethiopian Orthodox Christians beyond its correspondence to symbolic forms in order to indicate the ability of ritualized actions (i.e., prayer as bodily, inhabited, customs of offering condolences) to communicate and demonstrate how honor is conferred individually and communally. This quality of maintaining relations, that is, offering respect through liturgical and nonliturgical contexts, permits envisioning covenant as a way of approaching social ties.

Circumscribing Liturgical Space/Time

A classic action among Orthodox Christians is to carry out *mesalem*: The custom of greeting a church and, by such means, greeting God is a daily act of addressing and acknowledgment. The posture is performed as a brief bow and sign of the cross thrice while en route by foot or car. It is also a short ritual that is conducted while approaching the church gates by kissing and tapping one's forehead three times against the metal surface. A third variation is to perform full prostrations at particular doors of the church, typically ones that correspond to the gender of the believer. These short rituals are accompanied with prayers, both formulized and personalized, that are recited under the breath or against the surface of contact that one is facing, often the floor or wall of the church exterior. Furthermore, *mesalemat* is an act of professing to God at any time of the day, irrespective of whether liturgical service is in motion. This brief ritual is a bodily reflex of prayer, defined in Ethiopian Orthodox canon as "a word by which man communicates with his Creator in Faith, thanking and beseeching Him for the forgiveness of his sin" (Fetha Negest 14).

These acts coordinate with the larger superstructure of formal prayer, *qidase*, or liturgy that is proclaimed inside the *meqdes* (Figure 3). It is in this ritual order that I ground characteristics of the "liturgical" in the Ethiopian Orthodox lifeworld. Liturgical rites are constitutive of several components: cues by a doxology of hymns, through routines of prayer as gathered together as a "collection"[2] of readings and responses to the liturgy, and demonstrations via bodily practice such as prostrations and fasting. Rappaport's (1999) approach to ritual emphasizes these "acts and utterances" as well as their order and sequencing as intrinsic to what formalizes it, making it of a "liturgical" nature. He describes the ability of liturgical orders "not simply to coordinate social life but to provide a

The Liturgy and Stances of Giving Respect   57

Figure 8. *Mesalem* at Medhane Alem Church, Dessie.

well-marked road along which each individual's temporal experience can travel" (177).

Qidase has a particular sensorial quality in locations of dominant Orthodox Christian populations. On a typical morning at 6 AM, the liturgy of the Hours (*sa'atat*)[3] is audible, intoned over a crackling microphone by the voices of two priests and three deacons, the minimum requirement for administering the liturgical service. On the very rare occasion when no feasts or fasts are observed, the liturgy can be amplified, uninterrupted, until the conclusion, shortly before 9 AM. If it is a feast day, an evening vigil is typically publicly broadcast. If it is a major season of fasting, a night service is heard over the airwaves. The sonic presence of the *sa'atat*, omnipresent at certain times of the year, functions as a communing and congregating community of believers. The contemporary experience of the call to prayer is a classic feature of the soundscape in countries with dominant religious representation in the public sphere. This aspect of religiosity in the mainstream communicates a totalizing omnipresence of a sociopolitical body such as the Church, as well as, from certain perspectives, its hegemonic presence in a locale such as Ethiopia. However, it is misleading to accept wholesale that common rituals, such as communal prayer, reflect unified action among its adherents. Bandak's (2012) analysis of the feast of the Holy Cross in Damascus illustrates the complexities surrounding the category of "devotees" and behavior that carries the assumptions of the pious character of individuals. Orthodox Christians' worship cannot be "reduced to any single feature but can instead be seen as a bundling effect, where issues ranging from the existential to the structural are brought together in different kinds of tonalities in which the Christian specificity can be both figure and ground" (542). The reality is that lay engagement as I witnessed it frequently amounts to people darting in and out of the church grounds during *qidase*.

The movement within the church space during *qidase* produces an extremely pluralistic environment, perhaps even looking messy and disorderly to an outsider. The inundation of the liturgical felt clamorous to me and different from my experience of other Orthodox Christian churches. Outside the boundaries of the church grounds, the performative tone of the "Big Fast" was extended into the already highly trafficked airwaves, with liturgical chants composed for Lent being blared from street corners. Compared to Islamic sermons in Cairo (Hirschkind 2006), these types of chants, though employing similar characteristics of modern religiosity, provoked interactions that created a religious aesthetic different in nature from performed rhetoric (i.e., preaching). During Holy Week, *zema* (chant) in the Ge'ez mode, typically reserved for funeral masses and times of great national calamities, was played throughout the day. It extolled the suffering of Christ's crucifixion and corresponded to the overall atmospherics of the liturgical time, such as the liturgical drum not being beaten during most of the duration of Lent. The solemn chants during Holy Week were elaborated to me by Assefa, who held these prayers in special esteem, likening it to "listening with the heart" (*ke lib yemesemat*). One hymn in particular evoked a spiritual connection, as he mimicked the slow and deep-throated cadence of Tezekere, meaning in Ge'ez "remember me in your kingdom." The hymn is broadcast by street vendors who sell CDs of liturgical chants as well as by cafes, tire shops, and garages. Ethiopian Orthodox church parishes now rely heavily on sermons, to create greater public visibility to counter the increased presence of Pentecostal Christians in the public sphere. Liturgical soundscapes are resources that devotees respond to and engage with in ways individualistic and idiosyncratic.

Figure 9. Seklet (Good Friday). A worship space that is mixed by gender and age, clustered according to individual and/or group acquaintance. A typical Sunday service is more stringently gender divided, and religious apparel is less formal.

Furthermore, it is common to have several ongoing liturgies audibly overlapping one another on any given morning. The plurality of sounds thereby acts as a demarcation of the individuality of each church community. Initially, this liturgical multiplicity caused genuine disorientation on my part. Humphrey and Laidlaw's (1994) study of *puja*, a worship ritual held as a commemoration among Jains in western India, similarly grapples with the dilemma of scriptural performances that recite and repeat. During the early months of fieldwork, I asked Selam, a regular parishioner, why it was not confusing to hear the *qidase* chanted at one part while hearing a priest from a neighboring Orthodox church recite the prayers slightly behind or ahead. She did not comprehend my question, along with others who similarly echoed her reaction: "It is all the same Church" (*hulum and naw*). This response aligned with a standardized position of the Church and its believers, that the *sa'atat* is a means to pray in "one voice" and to subscribe full-heartedly to the Christian modus operandi to "pray without ceasing" (1 Thessalonians 5:19).

As it has been presented so far, the liturgical service contains an encompassing quality that effectively influences and can structure devotional acts, gestures, and attachments. The liturgy of the hours as a form of calendrical time can be interpreted as a form of "cultural governance" (Munn 1992, 109). The common anchor of the body and the actions in between ritualized time promote thinking about the liturgy as a refraction of the church and as a spatial and temporal idea. As the following section will argue, participants in the liturgy incorporate various materials as means of access, what Munn offers as a reconstruction of "world space-time": "The body is not only the fundamental means of tacit temporalization (or spatiotemporalization) but also part of the vital means of constant movement back and forth between the self and world time" (122).

Liturgical Materialities

As the ethnographic portrayal of Timqet and the performance of *aqwaqwam* demonstrated, the church arts, particularly liturgical chants, are an essential component of what comprises an individual's worship experience. However, the visual and aural qualities of veneration are not elements exclusively felt or acted upon during liturgy time. A characteristic of Orthodox Christian worship and ritualized prayer is to confer honor to the Holy (Qidus) through a set of media, such as the icon. Its equivalent in Ethiopia, *se'el* (lit. painting) "may properly be termed [as] icons, in the sense that they are portraits of saints imbued with the spiritual presence and force of the saint depicted," from miniatures to murals (Heldman 1994, 21). The craft of icon production and historicity in Ethiopian Orthodox Christianity is less dominant compared to practices in Russia or Greece (e.g., the genre of icon typologies, miracle stories). In Ethiopia, these items are typically commissioned by a benefactor for a private collection or church walls and are not often a personal devotional item. Homes are commonly adorned with more modest chromolithographs, mass printed and laminated reproductions of Greek icons (Simmons 2009). In Ethiopian Orthodox families, leather-bound copies of particular canonical books, scrolls (amulets), and crosses are items passed down as inheritances, rather than the family icon.

Icons and *tabots*, while distinct from each other as liturgical materials, do follow parallel patterns as focal points of veneration, specifically the devotional reflex of prostration. The little ritual of *mesalem* includes prostration as a physical response to greeting the Holy. I emphasize the broadness of this definition because prostrations can be directed to a specific saint or toward the *bete meqdes*. Unlike the Eastern churches that have a central icon to the Theotokos (Mother of God) inside the nave, a station for the icon is typically outside the church, either along the walls covered by the building's roof or in a separate enclosure within the compound near the entrance (Figure 8). Prostrations are more articulated than usual during the season of Lent and in particular during Holy, or Passion, Week, leading to the celebration of Easter. *Segdet* is the utmost demonstration of Christian humility and characterized by certain individuals as protection against evil (i.e., "the shield" against Satan). As the time toward Easter Sunday nears, individual worshippers proceed to prostrate toward the altar to the East. Passing by the busiest streets in the capital, men and women standing by the doorways of the churches will proceed to prostrate, crisscrossing themselves with both hands along their shoulders, tapping their knees, kneeling and then bowing to the floor. To prostrate oneself is fundamentally a responsive action to a liturgical focal point, whether that point is visual or aural.

The engagement with books and reading is also an important component of what I define as liturgical space/time. Books as materials are treated as sacred objects and are elevated with certain ceremonial punctuation. During liturgy, the Bible is presented to the worshippers gathered after the conclusion of the Gospel readings. It is covered in decorative, deep crimson cloth, of the same type that covers the *tabot*, and is kissed by parishioners. The covered Bible makes its way outside the church, and deacons diligently walk with it and a ceremonial umbrella to all reachable attendees. The Book of Psalms holds a particular high place in Orthodox worship, as these hymns were often conceptualized as "lessons." As a general practice, individuals entering the church are advised to read three psalms (*mizmur Dawit*, lit. Songs of David) as indicated by the day. However, people who were not aspiring clergy and did not possess the catechist books such as the Yemezgib Tselot that would inform them of this schedule relied on the chanting of the Psalms during the various offices of the day. During times of the service that are considered canonically to be particularly confessional (i.e., when Eucharist is being prepared), it is common to see people pull out their copies of books such as the Mezgeba Tselot (lit. registry of prayers). One may do this at home, but people generally reserved time during the *qidase* to read from these books.[4] The passages are read in silence or mumbled aloud, individuals often running their fingers along the lines of the page. Certain parts of people's prayer books are written in red, these words being the names of the Holy, relating to a similar practice of bowing and sometimes prostrating every time the name of God is pronounced aloud during liturgy. After every passage is read, individuals cross themselves three times and then bend and remain on the ground in prostration for as long as they need to. This moment, at a semiconclusory segment of prayer during liturgy, provokes a degree of emotional release from individuals, such as light sobbing, wiping away tears as they rise up, which inspired an affective state through the supplicant's interaction with the words and script of *qidase*.[5]

The visceral quality of symbolic memorializing and how it resonates emotionally with people was demonstrated to me by Meseret, who highly valued the ritual on Holy Friday of the "washing of the feet" by the clergy. It is a commemoration of the day when Christ washed the disciples' feet and revealed the mystery of the Holy Eucharist. High priests of churches bring water in a basin to the outer ambulatory of the church, recite the prayer of thanksgiving, and wash the feet of the faithful. Meseret mentioned it to me the day before as a beautiful occasion to be a part of. As she described the dramatized action, her eyes became moist as she beamed with joy. Here, discursive messages of a liturgical rite came alive, demonstrating how common believers relate to the depth of theological ideas, symbols, and metaphors.

Fasting is a commitment to liturgical space/time through the body and spirit. To fast is considered an opportunity to reach a higher state of consciousness of the soul by weakening the flesh. Orthodox Christians adhere to a full-bodied commitment to worship that plays out most intensely during the season of Lent. The established conventions during this season were to have nothing but water pass the lips until 3 PM, when the liturgy is conducted. During this season, all committed "fasters" (*tsominyoch*) would go to attend liturgy. Not only is religious fasting a crucial means to seek the spiritual purity of a polluted body, as it is dogmatically defined, but it also raises a personal consciousness of how the individual carries within them the ability to offer themselves. The vigorous ascription to fasting can be understood as a deliberate act of sacrifice and therefore as part of a typology of covenant as a type of commitment keeping that is ritually marked by a demonstrated offering. Situating this fact within how individuals illustrate their devotion through a range of expressions, we can then consider that the sacrificial offering in this liturgical context is the person as the sacrifice. This relates to the relationship between the sacrificer and the victim and to the substitution of the person through the gift offered.

I personally encountered this regularly by breaking the fast before participating in *qidase*. The night before, when I announced that I would be leaving early for church, the Catholic sisters would insist that I eat before setting out, worried that by delaying breakfast I would feel faint with hunger (which I often did). However, I was aware that I should not, as an Orthodox Christian, eat before the proclamation of the Gospel, even if I was not planning to take communion.[6] To break the fast before going to church to pray served as a strong example of the theological underpinnings of liturgical activities. To commit fully to participate in liturgy is an embodied covenantal action classifiable as an act of sacrifice, and it identifies the donor with the gift, the gift, as understood in Orthodox Christian theology, being grace.

Further engagements with liturgical space/time are evident through the liturgical calendar as it is followed by believers. Ethiopian Orthodox Christian canon recognizes both Saturday and Sunday as honoring *senbet* (Sabbath, the day of rest), though in practice, Sunday is the more stringently observed day. On certain popular feast days, it was not uncommon for some workers to object and refrain from performing specific tasks (e.g., sewing, digging) as acts that "denied God," as I was told was mandated in the Bible. Cultivating the liturgical body often exposes class divisions, as I witnessed with a relative who had an employee wash her clothes on a Sunday, while commenting that it was not she who was breaking God's Law. This anecdote speaks to a broader commentary that I heard voiced by several employers in Addis Ababa about the great difficulty of reconciling cultural habits with labor demands. During Lent, I heard the manager of a top supermarket complain exasperatedly that her employees were half-asleep and moved sluggishly, because of the demand that no substance except water be consumed until mid-afternoon, when the liturgy is conducted. Living up to all the observances of the Ethiopian Orthodox Church involved a field of options that affected both those who subscribed to the regime and those who did not.

Based on this matrix of devotional media and sensory presence, a church cannot be characterized exclusively as a locality but as a behavioral reaction and a temporal condition. This definition relates to what Kapferer

(2004), in the context of Sri Lankan Buddhism, terms as "cosmic habitus" to describe a physical location as having force. "As an aesthetic form itself, it works through participant perception, drawing participants within its space, reorienting and, effectively, re-ontologizing, embodying within participants the Buddha doxa that the cosmic building and the development of the ritual context in which the building is set come to articulate" (42). The *bete kristiyan* behaves as a type of compass of devotional activity making that expands into an array of sensory expressions. Liturgical space/time as it continues outside of the church compound cultivates a spiritual consciousness. Church is both deterritorialized by its media, in particular a liturgical soundscape that shapes individualized programs of worship, as well as territorialized through the ontological presentism of *qidase*. The following section will present several perspectives of individual believers whose behaviors connect and disconnect to liturgical space/time, which I examine to appraise the values and choices of these engagements.

Deterritorializing Church

For Orthodox Christians, the sign of the cross possesses deep content and spiritual force. It is a ritual that is foundational to most of the little rituals within a liturgical routine. It is also what Williams and Boyd (1993) define as the vital movement of the ritual image. Orthodox Christianity is distinctive for its expansive religious media, what I have in places referred to as devotional culture as well as the church arts (e.g., *aqwaqwam* as part of the school of liturgical chant). Thus, aesthetics play a particular role for believers. Williams and Boyd (1993) assert that "art is not a decorative addition to ritual," nor is ritual "a decorative addition to religious belief and practice." These analytical positions are motivated by their aim to study artistic forms as internal to rituals, structured simultaneously by "emotive force" and "theological content" (142). For example, the gesture, as part of a slew of "ritual images" (i.e., bodily, spoken), is complementary to the rites that are encoded by symbolic references. The ritual image is a pertinent key term to associate with practices of veneration, and I refer to one lively conversation with Fisseha and Haile that justifies its place in this discussion. Observing how I crossed myself, the two young men asked why my gesture was different from theirs. I balked. What can be more fundamental and orthodox than the sign of the cross, three fingers that form a point (the Trinity), then the fourth and fifth resting in the palm to signify the dual natures of Christ? Ah, they reasoned victoriously, but by the Ethiopian way, the whole hand is the cross (this would require a diagram to illustrate), and I was not moving my hand down enough, to connote the womb of Mary. As a ritual image, the sign of the cross is neither an illocutionary profession of faith (Austin 1962) nor a decorative flourish. This little ritual is the cohesive component between the communicator and the focal point of addressing the Holy.

The vital movement that links communicator to liturgical space/time is a crucial operative logic for believers dislocated from the Church. Gezachew and his modifications during Lent illustrate this point. A night guard at our home, he conducted his morning prayers on the verandah of the house at 4 AM, when matins (*mahalet*) was chanted by the clergy at the neighborhood church. He held a particular posture of standing up with his palms facing up—because "we hide nothing from God"—when hearing the chants. This portion of the *sa'atat* was primarily hymns that Gezachew articulated; despite being far from the church, he was confident he could follow them without hearing the cantor's voice. Any prayer, especially if corresponding to liturgy, would always be preceded with the prayer of the Cross, which would also signal for him to kneel and prostrate, always facing the East, mirroring the position of the clergy and the consecration of the sacramental hosts. When the twelfth hour arrived, the start of the Eucharistic service, he would read the devotional books, which he explained all had specific purposes (i.e., the books of St. Mathew were to be read accompanying medicine for a set amount of days). He then would read from the Book of Praise of St. Mary according to passages proscribed for the days of the week. This combination of prayer program alongside the chants conducted at the church he described as daily "nourishment," the metaphor of spiritual food often being employed by Orthodox Christians. Gezachew's acts demonstrate that despite his distance from the center of the ritual, the church, he was able to coordinate with liturgical space/time through ritual images such as his prostration and selected readings.

Liturgical space/time also emphasizes gaps and failures as well as adaptation to individual circumstances. Like Gezachew, Senait could not physically attend liturgy, though for different reasons. A resident near the St. Gabriel parish church, she avoided liturgy mostly because of the physical strain it put on her. However, early one evening, Senait announced she wanted to go to church. On this occasion, she insisted that we walk, which was dangerous at this time of night. It took us some time to arrive, given the rough incline of the path, studded with jutting rocks, and because I was supporting most of her weight from her right side, causing us to take breaks every few minutes. Finally, making our way to the main entrance, we presented ourselves to the women's door to the left of the *bete meqdes* and kissed its right, left, and bottom panels, repeating the same to the icons of St. Mary and St. Gabriel along the wall. At church that late evening, I heard the majority of the content of Senait's prayer, pronounced softly but aloud, as she knelt by the mat by the women's door, her upper body faced upright and her hands outreached. She was distinctly intimate and dialogic in her approach, her head tilted and turned to the side as if in deep engagement as she pleaded about her weak body, her deceased mother, and her family, especially her brothers in California, whom she missed. Each of her sentences was punctuated by a mournful meter, a "tick" of the voice that is a colloquialism among Amharic speakers as a demonstration of empathy. She then concluded by leaning face down on the floor and mumbling a few barely audible prayers, what I gathered to be Our Father (*Abatachin Hoy*) and Our Lady (*Emebetachin*).

These modes of deterritorializing and reterritorializing church reflect contemporary pressures of committing to the all-encompassing program of fasting and participating in liturgy. These demands are critiqued as both a preservation of an ideal Orthodox believer as well as evidence of a Church completely out of line with modern life. Gezachew, who also had a day job and could not hear *qidase* in the afternoon, amended this part by saying the prayer of thanksgiving, washing his hands, and then breaking the fast by eating a meal of lentils or boiled vegetables. To return to Gezachew and his prayer program, he regretted that he could not commit all day to concentrated prayer. His adherence to the fast, paired with his structuring of prayer time and space, is an amendment to this "disappointment." Fasting, in addition to being a popularly imagined part of the pathways for gaining "religious merit" (Buitelaar 1993, Mahmood 2004), was an activity that facilitated the "seriousness" of the prayer and meditation by the supplicant. Senait, who was enduring severe health problems and could not fast, felt that her commitment to her faith might not be taken as strongly because she did not completely sacrifice herself. For her, connecting to the liturgical service was missing in her devotional program. Senait commissioned a priest to recite prayers from the Tamera Mariam (Miracles of Mary) and other canonical books at her home during the first week of Lent. The dimension of liturgical prayer is extended to acts of fasting as a corporal manifestation of devotion, aligned with routine of prayers as enunciated at home and at church.

I have included perspectives from individuals who were rather self-conscious about their failure to follow the full program of responding to liturgical space/time. Abiding to the norms of the Lent season, a devotional regime such as fasting magnifies the aspirations of sincerity consistent with Christian subjectification (Cannell 2006). The importance of fasting as a liturgical program inspires individuals to discern gestures of "sincerity" (Cannell 2006). This convention of maintaining "the Great Lent" (*Abiy T'som*), was changing, as Gezachew noted in comparison to his younger coworkers who did not fast (they, he stated, lack "spiritual strength," *mefes tenekare*). He acknowledged, however, that this is the modern age, where he had to work, unlike in the generations before him, when all work virtually ceased during this period. Senait, in her early thirties, had only her mother's generation to compare with and similarly considered the time before her as stronger in faith. These hardships to maintain idealized faithful life reflects what Jackson (2005) prefigures as a deep sense of "I cannot": "To be human is not only to have intentions and purposes, which one strives to consummate, despite limited possibilities, finite abilities and scarce resources; it is to be thwarted, conflicted and thrown by contingency and circumstance . . . though human existence is relational—a mode of being-in-the-world—it is continually at risk" (xvi). Liturgical prayer and its strict adherence socially, I propose, is a mode of renewed commitment to be beholden to a responsibility.

A Refraction of Liturgical Stances

Social obligations built into customs of sitting for *leqso* (mourning house) contain an ethical quality that binds individuals to be obligated to the house of the deceased. This domain demonstrates an underlying ideology of responsibilities, facilitated through gestures of offering oneself that count the person as symbolic. I do not assert that the two domains of church and mourning house are synonymous, that paying a deceased person respect carries the same soteriological foundation of offering oneself to God, as mediated via church. I pose this juxtaposition of stances of respect as cultivated through cultural norms such as *leqso bet* to serve a heuristic purpose, based on an experimental proposal to consider Ethiopia's covenant idea as refracting into social customs. Hence, I pursue these parallels as an opportunity to consider similar intrinsic qualities and definitions of covenant as rooted in prayers of thanksgiving and what I stress as a continuous modes of address, that "the idea of ritual as communication is really people communicating with themselves" (Rappaport, in Humphrey and Laidlaw 1994, 77).

In the urban environs, a funeral is first noted by the call of death, a trumpeter who roams the neighborhood at the crack of dawn. This is an unmistakable sound that cuts through all other peripheral noises and signals the subsequent actions of a mourning community. At the home of the departed, a large military tent is erected, and resources such as seating and food provisions are gathered together by the *iddir*, an association that is specifically dedicated to provide funeral assistance for its fee-paying members. The *mahaber* associated with the family also fills in support roles. A public mourning period at the residence is set in place from the time the death is announced until the three-day commemoration after the burial. This is the timeframe when social pressures are most stressed to attend and "sit" at the funeral house. It is preferable to go inside the house itself, to be observed by the principal mourners.[7] Alternatively, one can sit outside, where close relations typically note who has made the visit and what they have brought, usually food that can be used to support the visitors such as coffee, sugar, biscuits, or grains. Visitors offer words of comfort as well as laments for the tragedy of the loss, focused specifically on the personality and profile of the deceased. Predictably, *leqso bet* is a zone of intense emotions, but in ways markedly contrary to the affective responses to liturgy as detailed in the previous section. As I have noted, the neighborhood is alerted by a trumpet call the morning of the death, and individuals or small groups who approach the *leqso bet* yell and scream and exclaim laments, this activity primarily performed by women. This aspect of the initial mourning can be seen as a substitution for the principal grievers, who usually exhibit subdued behavior throughout the event.

The closer the relation is, the more pressure to participate in this custom, as failure to do so is considered an insult on the "house" of the family. These acknowledgments required public demonstration just as condolences required addressing the mourners personally. To illustrate the rigidity with which this social custom is upheld, I was told of a case of an elderly lady who visited my family's home to communicate her grief over the loss of my grandfather, who died in 1995, for whom she worked as an employee over forty years earlier. After wailing and deep prostrations upon seeing my mother, the visitor explained that she could not properly acknowledge my grandfather's passing until this moment because his house had been confiscated by the government. Only once a close kin relation began to reside in Ethiopia could she complete this gesture of acknowledgment, to the deceased person's remaining family, a representative of their line. The event of death, detached by the distance of time, space, and subject position of the deceased, is refigured by the mourner, who required herself to commit to formal acknowledgment, without which the passing of the honored person hangs in perpetuity.

The demonstrative way that a person pays respect follows a reflex of obligation and reciprocity that is public and an exchange of addresses: Just as the ones "sitting at the mourning house" are representatives of the deceased, the individuals offering condolences are often representatives of their families. This interaction resembles the internal logic of gifting, described by Hénaff (2010) as "becom[ing] a pledge . . . an extension of the very being of the giver who gives himself through it" (134). Furthermore, the offering of oneself as a symbolic stand-in is conducted publicly and openly, as I have emphasized in the *leqso bet* context. Social crises, such as losing a member, is the making of the community itself. Hénaff elaborates further by stating: "A public aspect of ceremonial gift exchange is a relationship: a public act without which there is no community; from the perspective of ceremonial gift exchange, to wish for a gift that remains unknown is to wish for the death of reciprocal recognition" (141).

Social cues for reciprocity during funerals precipitate immense commensality, which in turn produces an ambiguous and flexible zone to relieve personal and family tension. Mourning is treated as a social event and is a domain that includes turning the home inside out in order to fulfill cultural standards of unreserved generosity in the deceased person's honor and thereby representing the respectability of his/her ancestral line. The marked presence of outsiders in the home, what Hénaff (2010) relates to Greek mythology of the presentation of gifts to the stranger (*xenios*, defined as both stranger and host), adds to this occasion's liminal quality to defuse social tension. For example, just as it is a requirement that a person must acknowledge the state of grieving by presenting themselves to closest mourners, no matter in what form the visitors are socially linked to the deceased or their family, the host of the *leqso* must never refuse a person, even if that person is a rival or enemy during ordinary circumstances. The period of *leqso* is a virtual space that carries communal obligations as well as opportunities, such as cases when peace talks are initiated between warring individuals or families. Therefore, recent criticism that the customs of commensality that accompany the mourning period have decreased, such as the full rites of funeral commemoration, reflects not only social pressures to conduct full commitment of honoring the dead but also removes the potential for alleviating strife that persists locally. To respect *leqso bet* customs is an opportunity to strengthen social relations.

I have presented the cultural norms of attending mourning houses as influenced by existing social relations and networks that bind individuals' motivations to carry out these expectations. Within the domains that are spiritually consequential, honoring life and death, the meanings of these little rituals are often overshadowed by explanations as communicated by the Church through its clergy and direct affiliates. To ask why believers come to church is sure to elicit a well-established "creed-like" statement: "Christ shed blood for us" and "died for our sins." Similarly, the significance of *leqso bet* is explained through its symbolic practices. The tradition of feasting inside the mourning house (a minimum of three days) reflects a cosmological outlook that interprets generosity performed in the deceased's name as a blessing that transfers positively to their soul in the next world (du Boulay 2010). The language of consoling the grieving by priests asserts that the expiration from this life is divinely mandated and in God's hands. The point of surrendering to the powerlessness of life is consistently emphasized, as mortality cannot be manipulated by humans. These normative explanations exist simultaneously with the gestures and stances of respect giving, even if the former assumes a more dominant representation in popular rhetoric.

Conclusion

Rituals, gestures, and stances to the canonical rites of the Church are disappearing or have completely disappeared from Euro-American societies, presenting a dilemma for religious institutions that seek to draw in the involvement of their membership. A Jesuit scholar presents this state of affairs when bemoaning how the hourly prayers are no longer audible publicly and with it the community of worship it signifies. For Parsch (1986), the sensation of hearing monasteries at night, sunrise, and sundown resounding with the affirmations of the faithful maintained a temporal consciousness of the life of the Church, Catholic in this instance: "During the nights of Advent . . . the Church prays her true Advent prayer, Matins . . . with a ring of joyful confidence"; and again, "At sunrise the Church call out to us: 'Watch zealously; the Lord our God is near at hand'"; and, "At sundown the Church sings: 'You have appeared, O Christ, the Light of Light'" (Parsch, in Taft 1986, ix).

It is the reverse picture in Ethiopia, where all religious institutions are public and call their believers to worship as part of daily life. Orthodox Christianity, given its historical dominance with the political status quo, populates the social space more than most. The tension between the ideal, faithful community and the distractions of contemporary and worldly concerns (*zemenawi, alemawi*) are vocalized as a common strand of critique. This is a theme common to urban contexts, where orthodox notions of worship confront the "experiences of subjective and cultural fragmentation" (Strhan 2013, 317), with individuals' devotional orientations functioning as pathways for constituting coherence in their lives. It is common to hear that the season of Lent is observed with less rigor than in the past, exemplified through anecdotes of contradiction: A person goes to the cinema and indulges in entertainment but will insist on eating fasting (i.e., vegan) food. Actions that cancel each other out are par for the course. On one occasion, I was subject to intense verbal attack for walking across the church compound during a portion of the Holy Friday liturgical program. A society with a dominant liturgical presence does not produce religious life that is any less complicated than in more secular environments.

Studying ritualized actions such as greeting the Church appears on one level to be symbolic and routinized while also motivating behaviors and values that have extended consequences. How individuals pay respect demonstrates how "the cultural scheme is variously inflected by a dominant site of symbolic production, which supplies the major idiom of other relations and activities" (Sahlins 1976, 211). The liturgy, as a landscape and temporality populated with covenant connections, represents one such idiom. The side-by-side arrangement of interpersonal orientations of coming to church or sitting at a mourning house underscores the various physical means by which one addresses God and, thus, themselves. Ideally, to know how to pray well to God is to know how to offer respect to one another.

CHAPTER

4

Constructing Church Futures

Another dominant way that Ethiopian Orthodox Christians talk about the covenant is through stories of the *tabots* (material arks) and the miracles they produce. With so much attention given to the Ark in Axum, scholarship often overlooks the broader genre of storytelling about *tabots* as a catalyst for social mobilization and a powerful means of resistance. The modern era has at least two rulers with these types of legends attached to their name. The defeat of the Italians at the Battle of Adwa in 1896, a world-historical event for Black liberation ideologies, is often attributed to the *tabot* of St. George that accompanied Emperor Menelik's army. Forty years later, Emperor Haile Sellassie's exile to Bath, England, involved the transport of the *tabot* of Medhane Alem. Its return with the triumph of the Ethiopians against Mussolini's Italy cemented its name, the Exiled One (Sedetinya). Outside of Ethiopia's covenant story, the *tabot* occupies its own domain as a talisman and emblem of the national spirit. *Tabots* are divine will personified, and their biographies contribute to an elaborative discourse that envisions Ethiopia and its people as maintaining a spiritual inheritance.

The following ethnography of *tabot* storytelling recognizes the tropes common to the established genre of Ethiopian antiquity thinking but seeks instead to interrogate contemporary Church ambitions to secure its cultural dominance in the public sphere. In a postrevolutionary era where the Ethiopian Orthodox Tewahedo Church has to fend for itself without the support of kings, queens, and the nobility, I argue that *tabot* stories are co-opted to address the demand to build or upgrade churches and to assert political autonomy and social support. These legends articulate community needs and social tensions under the encompassing logic of divine mandate.

This chapter presents several *tabot* legends interpreted or codified as "historical" by Ethiopian Orthodox Christians in Dessie and Addis Ababa, what I arrange as a genre that positions its discourse and praxis in a dialectic fashion. Hanks (1987) envisions this relationship as "ideological creations [that] become part of practical reality by being realized in action and this entails adapting them to concrete social circumstances. . . . Genres then, as kinds of discourse, derive their thematic organization from the inter-play between systems of social value, linguistic convention, and the world portrayed" (671). I argue that these stories reflect a consistent theme: Ethiopia as a land where the Ark of the Covenant rests and a people who are responsive to divine presence and agency. The way these stories are told also reinforces the linguistic conventions of protecting the sacred image and idea. Talking about *tabots* as extraordinary items that transcend their materiality maintains the fundamental identity of the covenant as a truth that cannot be comprehended and apprehended wholly, hence the instinct to produce refractions.

Most of these popular stories can be characterized as part of the miracle genre. It is through prayer, sustained devotion, and divine will that a material ark is consecrated and can subsequently be housed in a church's sanctuary. Though no doubt the storytellers themselves would describe them otherwise, I consider several key factors that can be considered alternative to this standardized interpretation. I focus on the realities of demographic shifts that have decreased EOTC membership, the national ambition toward socioeconomic development, and the demands of the institutional Church's financial sustainability. I argue that *tabot* legends act as pledges for church expansion and permit parishes and dioceses to stake claims for cultural and political dominance. Parallel to the broader sociopolitical pressures, I conclude by noting that the aspiration for stabilizing the Church institutionally can work in opposition to the indeterminate nature of *tabots* and spiritual landscapes that rely on prophecies, sustained devotion, and waiting.

The Provenance of *Tabots* in Dessie's Postrevolutionary History

When I was introduced to the diocese administration in Dessie, St. Gabriel Church was on the cusp of its inauguration, anticipated by the *tabot* transfer from the old to the newly erected building. New churches are consecrated by their *tabots* through the rites of the *tabot hig* (law of the *tabot*), which renders an altar slab into a *tabot* proper. In the case of St. Gabriel, the inauguration involved efforts by the local diocese to comprehensively construct the church's history. Details were shared during sermons and fundraising initiatives as well as among parishioners who were eager to relay the imminent accomplishment of decades of community campaigning. The history of the *tabot* of St. Gabriel was idiosyncratic and highlighted a particular subjectivity of the covenant as a materializing object. Its origins are sourced from Ras Mekonnen's *s'il bet* (icon or painting studio) in Harrar, a city in eastern Ethiopia; traveled to a church in Addis Abba, where it was then "requested in Dessie"; and housed in the main diocesan church from 1924 to 1976. The struggle to gain cooperation and approval for erecting St. Gabriel Church was the most cited detail of this story, according to personal conversations and the commemorative booklet disseminated by the Dessie diocese during its periodic church financial campaigns. In 1929, Abune Petros, archbishop of Eastern Ethiopia, discovered an ideal location for a church and inquired with the land's owner, Dejazmatch Gugsa, an army commander, to release the hilltop property in exchange for a comparable replacement. After the commander rejected this proposal, the archbishop was reputed to utter these words: "Dear Dejazmatch, at this place, St Gabriel's Church will be built and Christ's Holy Communion will be served. However, neither I nor you will live to see it." The completion of the church, an eighteen-year construction, was fitted around the statement that this vision would occur long after the time the intention was set, expressed through the language of fulfillment. The complications of completing such an ambitious vision for St. Gabriel Church was in this way affirmed by how far into the future Abune Petros saw the realization to transpire. The prophetic words of the archbishop in 1929 fueled contemporary retellings of the significant events and in some ways served to substantiate the fact that permission to transfer the *tabot* was granted only in the 1970s. The trope of hardship and sustained challenge were the values most dominant in the storytelling, though many churches struggle to receive administrative support in a country of twenty thousand churches (Ancel 2011).

In 2011, the deposition of the St. Gabriel *tabot*, and effectively the church's consecration through the rite of *tabot negs* (lit. enthronement), was conducted with much fanfare, and the event served as a presentation of interreligious harmony in Dessie. The role of the elders' council and their lobbying efforts were emphasized as well as this endeavor's being of multiconfessional character. The elders' council was composed of several Muslims, and according to one founding member of this group, there was a vocal coreligionist desire to have the *tabot* of Gabriel, or "Jibril" (Arabic), to be installed, which had so far resided in Sellassie (Trinity) Church since its deposition in 1924. This tradition of religious cooperation had a strong basis historically. St. Gabriel's *tabot* is regarded highly by Muslims, the archangel representing an elevated figure in the Koran, locally reflected by Wolloye Muslims' insistence to support the sponsoring of this particular *tabot*. Their assistance follows a noted trend of benefactorship, such as financially sponsoring priests to serve rural churches or assisting in rebuilding churches.

Despite the history of interreligious cooperation that Wollo is famed for, the dynamics of religious representation was particularly tense during the time of my fieldwork (2010–2012). A year before my arrival in the city, there was a public debacle over the building of Arseima Mariam Church. Local Muslims argued that the designated land was a Muslim gravesite, prompting massive protests. As such, land and its visibility appeared as an antagonistic domain, which I learned as I attempted to take photos of churches and their compounds. On one occasion, visiting another historic church in Dessie, the principal priest-in-residence severely cautioned me against photographing the church compound, despite its establishment since 1908. Revealing the location would greatly increase the possibility of mosques being erected next door; similar territorial arguments over religious space occurred frequently in the capital as well.[1]

Much of the consternation over the confessional competition from mosques and Pentecostal church halls was a reflection of the country's changing demographics and the financial support of religious communities. Pertaining to the regional dynamics in what was often bracketed as highland Christianity and lowland Islam, there was a sharpening confrontation between these two religions, though most individuals articulated this as external interference not representative of local politics. A local tourism official, himself of Orthodox and Muslim heritage, speculated about the competitive spirit between the main confessions and echoed a common thesis that Muslim communities were flourishing because of an injection of funding from Saudi businessmen active in Ethiopia. I heard similar discourse in the form of complaints from locals in the Farensai and

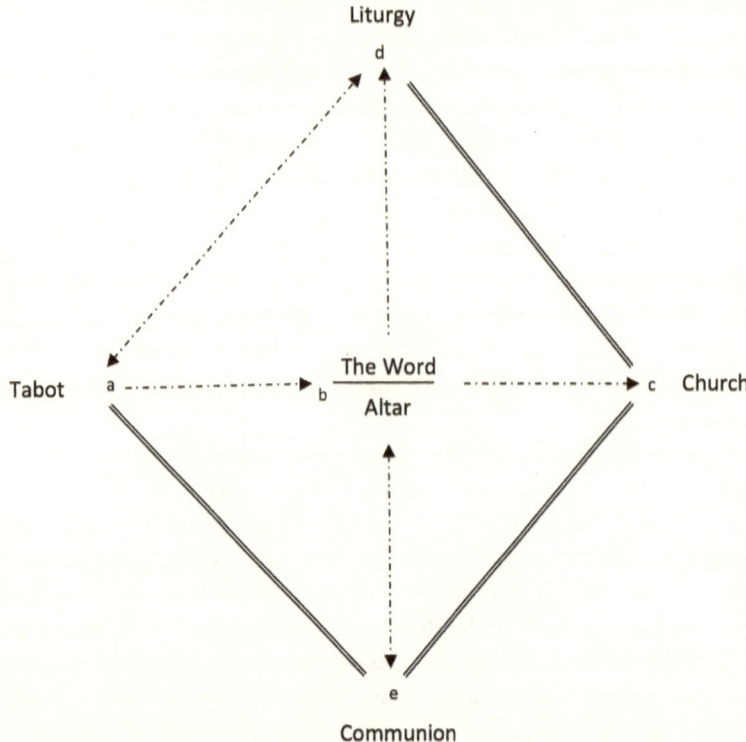

Figure 10. The provenance of *tabots*, according to liturgical processes: (A) *tabot makel* (ark planting), which refers to a saint's manifestation into the earthly properties; (B) *tabot hig* (law of the tabot), a material transfiguration (stone or wood) into an altar; (C) *tabot negs* (crowning the ark), the ceremony making the church consecrated. Between points A and D represents the spiritual immanence as prismatized into liturgical sound (e.g., "hearing the tabot"; see Chapter 2), while the relation between Liturgy (D) and Communion (E) is mediated through worship regimes considering the church as a spiritual locale (see Chapter 3). The double lines between points reflect metaphoric and ritual parallelism (e.g., the *t'sewa* and *tabot* rotation), which will be analyzed in Chapter 5.

Siddist Kilo neighborhoods in Addis Ababa, who reasoned that the proliferation of mosques were being built in areas where few Muslims lived as a sign of political aggression to impose influence for an otherwise marginalized minority typically denied representation in the public sphere. Ethiopian Muslims represent about 33 percent of the country's population, based on the 2007 census, though it is widely believed that this number is strategically underreported (International Religious Freedom Report 2007) to avoid disturbing the national image of a "Christian Ethiopia." In Dessie, Orthodox Christians and Muslims are nearly half and half. Several large-scale protests in 2012 were instrumental in highlighting the political tensions of governmental interference in religious affairs, further illustrated in personal commentaries that religious harmony was only espoused if Islam remained in a second-place position relative to the Orthodox Church.

It is in this social context of the Church no longer financially and politically supported by the crown and an increasingly diverse religioscape that I propose to evaluate the multiplicity of *tabots*. In one sanctuary, more than one *tabot* can exist,[2] and in addition to copies of the main *tabot* (*medenbenya*), there are copies placed there to guard against robberies. Secondary *tabots* called *dabbaloch* (meaning roommate, or lit. "living on top of another") are housed in a sanctuary that presumably will have a church dedicated in their name someday. Visions and petitions from local visionaries and the broader community are typically the circumstances that push *tabots* to "break free" and take up their own home churches. I argue that the multiplicity of *tabots* and the capacity of *tabots* to motivate new church constructions reflect the dialogic dynamics between believers and the divine and assign a responsibility and power to devotees to treat their environs as a context of imminent divine action and thereby a populated Orthodox locale.

The Political Framing of *Tabot* Action

Solomon, from Addis Ababa and a recent resident to Kombolcha (ten kilometers outside of Dessie), shared the story of Kirkos lij (Cyriacus the Child), a *tabot* who garnered much local veneration because of his curative powers. I position his story as a demonstration of the genre of miracle stories that exhibit the subjectivity of *tabots* as personified and wrapped in mystical thinking. About ten to fifteen years ago, the prayers of the people living in the neighboring hills "were answered," as he stated. The area had been plagued with many diseases. He referred to them generically as malaria and HIV, though people also habitually suffer from hepatitis, typhoid, and cholera, to name a few. Certain communities, outside the city limits as he described it, began to appeal to Kirkos lij. This concentration of local devotion urged the priests and locals to appeal to the Kombolcha parish council to have Qedus Kirkos represented, in the form of a *tabot* dedication. The way Solomon phrased it, the consecration of a Kirkos lij *tabot* and its installation inside the Church of St. Gabriel, along with an already existing Kidane Meheret *tabot* inside the sanctuary, was a result of the "*tabot* speaking." While there was no specific vision directed by Kirkos lij toward an action, the collective dedication to him initiated a further installation of his presence locally; that is, he was given a voice through the love of the people. This devotional relationship with Kirkos lij was acknowledged by the local priests once the saint was consecrated as an altar of the sanctuary. The annual feast day of Kirkos lij was especially celebrated every January when the *tabot* comes out, and it was reputed that people have had their ailments cured and illnesses alleviated on these occasions. The exposure to the *tabot* and the respect and honor conferred by celebrants via the appeal to Kirkos lij himself spurred on a particular sort of material healing. Hence, to worship is intrinsic to relationship—Kirkos lij would cease to exist without being acknowledged—thus permitting devotees to be part of the miracle.

At the heart of these *tabot* tales is a fusion between the divine will that initiates sacred presence on earth and the materialization of that presence in the form of a *tabot*. The case of Kirkos lij, narrated in a typically mystifying logic, infringed on the limitations of empirical inquiry, along with similar sensibilities of secrecy concerning the subject of *tabot*s, which I noted previously while documenting the processions (see my Timqet analysis in Chapter 2). In regards to *tabot* action and witnessing, "it" just appeared. There are connections and "leaps of faith" that the listener/believer was meant to make and that I, as the researcher, was not permitted to ask. As a popular genre of storytelling, far more attention is directed to the *tabot*'s genesis than to its materiality, as well as a focus on prayers and miracles that codified these histories. In the case of Kirkos lij, even though Solomon phrased the events as emanating from the devotion of a particular set of individuals, he never ascribed credit of the *tabot* consecration to human will; that is, all energies reflected the subordination of the believers' love and respect to the saint. I consider these narrative techniques as consistent with the linguistic veiling and shrouding of the *tabot*s as transcending their materiality. Through the direct influence and accountability of the devotees was diminished, the significance of witness ("He heard their prayers") accounted for a crucial factor of the dialectical movements contained in these *tabot* legends.

Unlike the standard approach of Ethiopian Orthodox Christians to skirt around the *tabot*'s material origins, Solomon was refreshingly open about this topic and offered his additional interpretations about how churches might emerge. Speaking about Arsema Mariam,[3] a secondary *tabot* of St. Mikael's Church, he volunteered it as an example of a "*tabot* that can go where it likes." He then directly launched into a version of the authoritative doctrine of how churches proliferated in Ethiopia, based on Dersane Uriel (The Homily of St. Uriel). In this popular Ethiopian Orthodox text, St. Uriel is attributed as scattering the blood of Christ over certain points in Ethiopia, notably nine historic Church centers in northern and north-central Ethiopia.[4] According to Solomon, it is St. Uriel who sows the seed of the Holy via this blood; where the blood of Christ dropped, a church will be built. Using the canonical account of how monastic centers in Ethiopia were specifically selected for a sacred pact with God, through the flight of the archangel, Solomon related and extended this action to how a *tabot* may emerge in any given terrain. Citing Church literature also links his interpretation of the *tabot* legend as contained within Holy Tradition. This seemingly abrupt eruption of divine presence was based on his own interpretation of this design of the preordained sacred landscape, from which newly accounted-for *tabots* can be supported. It also reflects what Briggs and Bauman (1992) analyze as ideological strategies of intertextuality that facilitate "negotiations of identity and power—by invoking a particular genre" that enables the authority to "decontextualize discourse that bears these historical and social connections (i.e. utterances) and to re-contextualize it in the current discursive setting" (148).

The Homily of St. Uriel is an insightful document to think with on several levels. Primarily, it provides a Church-authored discourse on how *tabots* emerge. For example, in an episode where the archangel descends over the monastery of Abba Yohanni and instituted a covenant by blood seal, the next paragraph refers directly to the installation of the *tabot* and the various accompanying glory-making actions that are attached (Caquot 1955). This underscores the provenance of *tabots* waiting to be revealed through devotion. Using a comparative case of archaeologies of sacred landscapes, Nixon (2006), studying Sphakia in southwestern Crete, relates a similar phenomenon of "pre-historic histories" in southern Oxfordshire, arguing that landscape "can be thought of as the manifestation of social relationships, relationships which physical effort, as well as rhetoric, can keep socially active," and considers the physical and metaphysical labor of maintaining these structures, which includes "rituals such as the burning of incense, lighting of candles and oil lamps and church services" (105). This pertinent observation finds similar patterns in Ethiopia, a country of an estimated twenty thousand churches, many of which are dormant in the deep interior of the country's rugged terrain and require perpetual engagement from the laity (see Chapters 5 and 6 on the devotional associations and traditions of pilgrimage). Second, the Dersane Uriel maps and frequently references how the natural world now bows forth toward "the Almighty God" and to the exaltation of the *tabot*. Here, the earthly representation of the holy personages reveals a conception of sacred landscape and indicates a theme of "taming the wild" by ordering sacred and profane space, a category of the moral imagination active in Orthodox Christian cosmology (see du Boulay 2010, Stewart 1991).

The Dersane Uriel also contains key political implications as a text codified during the reign of Menelik II (1889–1913). Known as a modernizer, he sanctioned rigorous Orthodox Christian standardization during his era. References in the homily to greater Shoa and Addis Ababa, scarcely a few decades old at the time, act as a way to make these locales part of Ethiopia's ancient history (see the Kebre Negest, which follows a similar pattern of political power as legitimated to time immemorial). This postmedieval rearrangement of divine sanction over imperial domains perhaps buttresses Smith's interpretation of the Ethiopian variation on the covenant idea, which was that the imperial rulers were the purveyors of this claim and mandate. The texts imagine the covenant as attached to monarchs who employ Christian expansion as a way to tamp down pagan beliefs and institute a common code of social definition.

The discourse of covenant as textual and ideological has the capacity to influence the interpretation of *tabot* actions and behaviors yet exists in a political landscape radically altered. After the confiscation of all Church and imperial land holding during the revolution (1974), the patriarchate instituted gradual reforms to gain revenue for supporting local church infrastructures, such as the establishment of the parish council and treasury, effectively handing over responsibilities of stewardship to the laity (Ancel 2005, 2011). Diaspora funding as well as a new class of sponsors and benefactors fueled financial support. Income-generating activities such as ownership of lands and businesses has ensured Church support across its vast network nationally and has provided models of self-sufficiency for communities that lacked strong local leadership or parish involvement. These trends align with Girma's (2012) theoretical approach to the covenant as a resource for social cohesion, wherein he proposes a reinterpretation of covenant as centered on "real people" (nonelites) that use the "metaphysical imperative" of divine election to compose a collective identity that is bonded by a "spiritual order" (144–45). Periodic community initiatives to improve the upkeep of the local church compounds are one example of this pivotal aspect of grassroots focus as a public responsibility.

Tabot Legends and Their Interpretations

As I discussed in Chapter 2, the removal of the *tabot* is enacted by the festal procession as a concretizing and sacramental moment where the people watching are actually participants in creating immanent frames, what Bateson (1972) terms as a type of metacommunication. However, discussing *tabots* outright is a predictably sensitive topic to broach because of perceptions about what sort of information is being desired. Was I asking to know about a *tabot*'s miracles and/or wrath, or did I want to "see it," the classic foreigners' trap? Despite the plausibility of my wanting to hear these wondrous tales, suspicion was a dominant sentiment and part of the secrecy and delicate nature of discovering the historical foundations of a *tabot*'s emergence. Tactically, the provenance of *tabots* is better approached by investigating its liturgical rites (Figure 10) and the genre of popular stories of its miracles. To build a church requires the existence of its *tabot*, either waiting in a sanctuary or existing in the spiritual environs of local landscape, a recursive process of the antimaterial (the otherworldly presence of the Holy) turned into the material (the sanctification of an ark/altar) and then transformed into the immaterial (a veiled, ritual object).

However, to spur the emergence of a *tabot*, devotees are required to wait for signals from God. Miyazaki (2000) analyzes a similar phenomenon, involving Methodists and an Adventist congregation in the Fijian context. He argues that deliberate manipulations of such dialectical relations serve as a strategic ambiguity that perpetuates a productive indeterminacy. Returning to the indeterminacy of *tabots* as denoting a modulated proximity between God and devotees, from a theological perspective, these future realities are defined as a heavenly reunion that assists by articulating their actions as "Christian subjects." This section addresses the ways that *tabots* emerge from devotional attention and witness. Within covenant discourse literature, revelations through signs and miracles are integral for justifying the claim to "a special relationship of intimacy with and faith in God, and hence a special status as servant of the Lord" (Smith 2003, 59).

It is clear that *tabot* legends illustrate an intimate and interactive relationship with believers who possess knowledge of spiritual presence that is closely guarded and socially circulated and shaped. Asking about *tabotat* (the *tabots*) is a very rich arena for observing how people narrate their local histories. Given the circumstances of narrative plurality and protectiveness, teasing out the interpretations of *tabot* legends becomes a polyvocal affair. To sort through the anecdotal evidence of a *tabot*'s subjectivity, I frame the following cases as a "diagnostic event" (Falk Moore 1987), in order to "foreground preoccupations of actors" (i.e., an individual's fate in protracted battles over property) with "background conditions that inform the situation at hand" (i.e., scarcity of land and vulnerability as marginalized property owners), in order to permit arguing against one single operating episteme but instead several that inform social action (731–35). The tensions apparent in parish communities expose similar associated issues of power and authority as parishes strive to fulfill *tabots* to be housed in their own churches.

The Tabot *That Refused*

The drama over the stalling and protest of St. Mikael, in Farensai, a northeastern district of Addis, the capital, crystallized during the Timqet procession in 1995, a case when a *tabot* refused to "come out" (*tabot alwetam*). Addisu, a cab driver and local resident, described a story replete with intrigue, all about local politics, as he summarized. There was bureaucratic obstruction to the community's request that a larger church be built in St. Mikael's name, and this refusal to come out of the *bete mekdes* was a clear response by St. Mikael. "How could a *tabot* refuse to come out?" I inquired. As he described the incident, the priests came to release the *tabot* out of its sanctuary on the eve of Timqet (see Chapter 3), and they were prevented from coming any closer. The member of the clergy that was holding the *tabot* on top of his head became locked in a state of paralysis, unable to speak or move. Describing to a few neighborhood residents about this *tabot* anomaly, they all immediately knew what *tabot* I was talking about, that *Chikun* (the repressed) Mikael in the Ras Kassa area. The reputation it had was that it did not join the rest of the procession of the Farensai neighborhood, which included the Yesus (Genet Le Yesus—Heaven

Figure 11. Constructed façade of St. Michael's Church (Chigun Mikael).

of Christ) and Mariam churches. All of this was discussed in the third person; it was Mikael that refused to join Yesus and Mariam to Jan Meda, where the baptismal pool and Epiphany festivities in Addis primarily take place. By this "threat" of revoking the honor to assist and follow the *tabot* of St. Mikael, the communities of this neighborhood were robbed of the privilege of assisting their Mikael to his sanctuary in the Entoto hills; only a select number of St. Mikael *tabots* have this honor in Addis.

Curious to know more details about this local legend, I visited St. Mikael's Church to learn the version of the incident as narrated by the church representatives. Coincidentally, I bumped into Tsedal, whom I had met and saw frequently as a guest at the Medhane Alem *zikir*, an occasion that involves the *mahaber* (see Chapter 5). In response to the moniker *Chikun*, she seemed to skate over its reputation as being "repressed."[5] She was of the opinion that this grew out of partisan perspectives on the debacle of the church's construction; community members were trying to instigate a legend (*afe tarik*) to support their cause ("*Sow sime awetalet*"—The people named him/it). Based on how intensely the story was told, and especially the *tabot*'s nickname, I had assumed that St. Mikael's *tabot* was not "living" in his own church; perhaps it was one of those *tabots* "in waiting," I thought. To my surprise, not only was there a compound dedicated solely to St. Mikael, but there was a massive basilica-style church supplanted on top of what I learned was the original church. I was aware the matter had been resolved, as Mikael had joined the *tabot* procession at Jan Meda the year after the incident of refusal. The characterization of the *tabot* as "repressed," slightly odd given that a separate church had already been established, was a reflection of the local critique of the events that had tampered with a public pledge of sponsorship in Mikael's name. A local entrepreneur committed a substantial sum of money to erect a larger church for St. Mikael and galvanized broader financial support for an expanded church. According to Addisu, Mikael stalled as a reaction to Yesus Church's plans to thwart this development. In his interpretation, the *tabot* responded to the unjust denial of this honor, showcasing *tabots* as agentive and meta-communicative of the will of believers and divinity.

As it was summarized by locals, this series of developments denoted an active agreement between the people and St. Mikael, sidelined by jealousy, rivalry, and political squabbling. Tsedal suggested two reasons behind Yesus Church's antagonistic reaction. By leading their own procession, proceeding to the baptismal pool at Jan Meda independently and not joining with the other churches in front of Yesus Church, St. Mikael's was exerting independence from the local parish network. She was sympathetic to the viewpoint that the shift in dynamics might be interpreted as contrary to the entire spirit of how Timqet was celebrated, as a communal event of churches coming together as one. From the perspective of St. Mikael Church, to initiate its own path of procession was fitting of its elevated status as a *deber*[6] church of Farensai. This neighborhood's fear of change, Tsedal reasoned, explains why Yesus Church tried to obstruct this project of expansion. She hypothesized that the independence of St. Mikael's Church would diminish the authority of the Yesus Church parish council. The representatives from St. Mikael's insisted that there is no lingering animosity, that all churches are united again, and that any internal conflict is an exaggeration fueled by the local propensity for gossip. Despite the harmonious conclusion, many continued to call it *Chikun* Mikael, the repressed Mikael. Righteousness and vindication, by way of retaining the name, signal that there is a certain sentimental attachment to struggle in fulfilling devotional promises among Ethiopian Orthodox Christians. In addition to maintaining a relationship of honor, there is also a suggestion of the *tabot*'s wrath. This story illustrates the affective power of refusing to be revealed as a community threat.

Listening to the Tabot

Tabot legends illustrate the personality and agency of saints and holy figures and their responsiveness to local social conditions and dilemmas. Conversely, these narrative retellings underscore the difficulty of believers to respond appropriately or adequately to the *tabot*'s will. In the case of St. Mikael's, construction had been going on, yet this length of time, over ten years, was not considered interminable. The construction workers shot back to my question about its completion, "How are we to know? It's based on God's will!" In the case of St. Gabriel's in Dessie, the determinism of parish community in their desire to complete the church was also positioned in similar uncertain terms, as I was told by the head monks there to pray to Kidane Meheret ("Covenant of Mercy") if I wanted such a definitive answer. These are the delineations and the limits to the bond between God and people, as Miyazaki (2000) argues in his "abeyance of agency" from issues regarding the reception of responses and their interpretations by participants in preaching programs and gift-giving rituals in Fiji. Statements that do not satisfy are framed as limits on the human "capacity to make sense of events or even the capacity to act" (32), suggesting that this strategy speaks to a method of anticipating a more satisfying end. This case study approaches the idealization of the covenant from a perspective of when this *tabot*-devotee relationship is in tension and highlights the crucial links of veneration and sustained devotion.

Knowing these particular qualities of *tabot* behavior, we can analytically approach the popular legend of Medhane Alem in Dessie, whose legend is well circulated locally. It covers the misfortunes and miraculous events that transpired when Medhane Alem was listened to and respected. Asking how the *tabot* came to this particular church, the monk I spoke to asserted it was special because it came from Jerusalem. The two young Church officials were more eager to talk about the circumstances and events of how this *tabot* insisted on being built in another location. The plan was to build in the southern part of town, near where St. George is situated today. Construction started, and workers noticed that each morning the lumber

Figure 12. The view of the *tabots* via their ritual praxis on Timqet (Jan Meda, Addis Ababa).

assigned for the building had been mysteriously moved to the hilltop of the present-day Medhane Alem Church. The material kept being found away from its designated location, followed by inauspicious occurrences such as workers being injured and unusually long delays in construction. Finally, Negus Mikael, the king of Wollo province in the late nineteenth to early twentieth century, decided that these were signs that Medhane Alem was fated to be built at this other location. His realization was also mythologized by his bold act of inserting a nail into the foundation of the church, this action itself entering into the local canon of legends. The accounts of this story persistently stressed the speed of construction, three months and fourteen days exactly, and the care with which the construction took place. It was soon realized that the workers progressed faster when they stayed within the church grounds. Therefore, the king ordered that certain purity standards were to be enacted: Workers, including the iconographer, were to be kept inside the church, remaining clean and undefiled from the outside world. This legend represents a formula that is modeled in similar miraculous events of a church's histories, grounded by a series of ecstatic events, with a fair degree of embellishment, which illustrates the elaborative tendencies within the genre of *tabot* legends.

We have discussed that "*tabot* planting" has its political implications, as do *tabot* emergences driven by miraculous incidents. These *tabot* legends resemble myth narratives, which follow a similar cosmological order. In a similar story of an embodied spiritual presence of a saint in rural Greece (Stewart 1991), Panagia Protothronos was reputed to repeatedly leave the church, and this "transcendent intervention" by the icon signaled a change in the building's location (Stewart 1991). Here, the construction of a church and the village's broader identity is "ordained by higher powers, a fact that is symbolized in their church, the product of divinely directed communal effort" (87). Thinking again of Falk Moore's proposal (1987) to evaluate several operating epistemes that inform social action, the social drivers that contribute to *tabot* agency are pivotal and provide pathways for interpreting the covenant idea as a socially active resource. In the case of Solomon, he tangentially analyzed correspondences to the problem of health epidemics locally, with the devotion to a particular saint and the miraculous events attributed to the *tabot* of Kirkos lij. As a young and aspiring local preacher who tended to view social life with more criticism, he judged that there was a systemic moral malaise by the younger generations. In the case of *Chikun* Mikael, there were similar alignments with this analytic interpretation. The breach of *tabot* refusal was framed as a reflection of the tense state of local diocesan politics. In the case of the moving lumber of Medhane Alem, the event was supernatural in character and demonstrated a certain incomprehensibility of divine force. It corresponded with a particular pattern of myths of church foundations, but its orchestration around the social particularities of early-twentieth-century Dessie was more ambiguous.[7]

Churches-in-Progress and Development Aspirations

Since *tabots* and thus churches are intrinsically connected and are instrumental for the future of the diocese, figures such as Abba Mefekeria Seb in Dessie are lauded by residents. A well-known monk and often treated as a local celebrity, his admirers estimate he is responsible for helping initiate over fifty church projects all over Wollo, as well as serving as an avid campaigner for planting acres of indigenous trees. He narrated to me the history of St. Mikael's *tabot*, which serves as an example of the narrative importance of prophecy, spiritualized landscapes, political impetus, and indeterminacy in the genre of *tabot* legends.

Discussing the revitalization of churches in the outer edges of Dessie's zone, Abba Mefekeria Seb phrased many of these foundation stories as scenarios in the exercise of steadfast conviction. I had been prompted by one of his admirers to ask about how the church of St. Mikael was envisioned, with Abba Mefekeria Seb as the primary driver. Abba Hadis, a local priest fifty years ago, saw a hillside location known as Gerar Amba and suggested that St. Mikael should be moved there from the lowland swamp where the saint was stationed at the time. Abba Mefekeria Seb saw the place and was enthralled, convinced that this was the providential location. News about this intention began to circulate locally, and about forty people pledged to give one thousand birr each to construct a church. Abba Mefekeria Seb stated rather pointedly that the bishop at the time, Abba Samuel, and the clergy saw the advantage of having a church of St. Mikael be in a more visible and accessible location to enable more frequent visitation and patronage.[8] After giving his permission to break ground, the church council faced interference by a pair of influential individuals who were strongly against the move. In one heated exchange, Abba Mefekeria Seb proclaimed to the detractors, "When you die, St. Mikael will receive it/you," a quintessential "wax and gold" (*semenaworq*) statement, dually predicting the man's encounter with St. Mikael from his earthly departure and St. Mikael's rightful glory on earth by assuming a place in his sanctuary. Soon after, the high rains caused flooding, and graves on the lowland where the original church was located started to wash away. The people in the area took this as a sign that unless St. Michael was moved, similar destructive actions would continue. The residents of this outlying community asked Abba Mefekeria to intercede on their behalf and take this problem to the city administration. The significance of his words to the administrators was etched into the dramatic memory of Abba Mefekeria as he stated his actions. Refusing to be seated for the meeting, he recalled proclaiming: "I cannot sit while St. Mikael is standing. His *tabot* is buried in the swamp. We need his miracle and we must free him." Shortly thereafter, the administrator approved the move in 1986, during the Derg period.[9] The prophetic part of this narrative was that the main instigator of the resistance died on Tselot Hamus (Holy Thursday), and this was interpreted as an ordaining moment for the foundational story of the church.

This story was chronicled with a mythical aura, but it also showcased a dynamic relationship to St. Mikael, as the actions of the community were not reliant upon divine intercession or in carving out a space for divine presence in the labor of realizing a church (e.g., Medhane Alem). As Abba Mefekeria Seb characterized, twenty years of consistent praying was what actualized the *tabot*, a devotional commitment to acknowledge always. The flooding was interpreted as an impetus for carrying out the plan. The promise of St. Mikael's potential miracle positioned the saint as the central character of the story, though the responsibility was squarely on his devotees. The underlying call in these *tabot* legends is a continuous ethic of promise making and a responsibility of fulfillment, showcasing how the covenant idea refracts into moral imagination.

Church sites proliferating faster than the churches can be built,[10] with their *tabots* waiting in sanctuaries, reflects the current political climate of religious institutions investing in their future. Leaders are given this responsibility to "plant churches," indicating that while there may not be supernatural visions or major enigmatic episodes, modern-day visionaries, both mundane and spiritual, are afforded a role that facilitates these church constructions, which require miracle narratives. In the cases presented, it was the determination of archbishops and their moral imperative that provided the sanctioning voice for establishing houses of worship. It is tempting to look solely at individuals as anticipating *tabot* emergence. Instead, I have offered indications that this legitimation of *tabot* presence is contingent on a human partnership communally structured and maintained. This chapter has argued that covenant is part of a contemporary ethical approach of responsibility to churches, the community's spiritual health and protection. I consider how individuals envision a sacred landscape populated by divine presence that is unrealized (i.e., not made concrete via miracles or *tabot* consecrations) and how these engagements further contribute to Ethiopian Orthodox devotional culture.

The placement of the preaching programs at the front of these churches-in-progress, primarily for fundraising purposes, functioned as a signifier of the responsibility to fulfill this promise. This patterning of adjusted orientation to church space is thematically consistent with how Dessie St. Gabriel positioned its inauguration in 2011. Even when there were large donations to initiate building projects, most churches had to produce the lion's share of funds, and thus constructions stall for many years. This interplay between the demands to complete a promise and the enthusiasm to render that promise fulfilled was on display nearly every Sunday and feast day of St. Gabriel, every 26th of the month. I was asked what I thought of the spirit with which parishioners gave to the church, initiated one morning by a speech of a preacher to fast and do without breakfast and instead give to the church. In addition to the shock of suggesting that those in attendance should deprive themselves more than they already do (standard practice is to break the fast after liturgy), I was moved by the severity of the response to the call, including people removing jewelry from their hands and necks as donations. The staging of these calls at the front of the church, a shell of concrete and iron, relates to what Felman (2003) describes as the promise of consciousness, as postulating "a noninterruption, continuity between intention and act" (34). The condition of incompleteness plays a significant performative role in these fundraising activities, as a display of the community's desire to be defined as spiritually strong and as a means of locking in commitment, via public pledging, to achieve this ambition.

It is not surprising to have an imaginary church, given all that has been stated about the indeterminacy of the yet-to-be-realized but preordained *tabots*. Churches are fundamentally always in flux, given the nature of the *tabot* and its manifestation out of prayer and divine will. In the case of St. Gabriel in Dessie, I was told it had in its sanctuary Lideta (the Birth of Mary) and Kidane Meheret (the covenant of Mary) in addition to the saint of its namesake. As the pattern goes, a time will come when these individual *tabots* will have homes pledged for them.

The idea of the pledge as a technique of pooling local support is a crucial element to consider as the tempo of socioeconomic development in Ethiopia proceeds at an accelerated pace. The fundraising for the Renaissance Dam, a massive construction project to harness energy from the Blue Nile, represents an instance when the citizenry is called upon, a coordinated effort that collects from nearly all corners of society: at secondary schools, through deductions from civil servants' salaries, and "persuasive" appeals for business owners to purchase bonds to name a few methods. While these calls for pledges are highly emotionalized, vocalized as a citizen's duty, the results of these activities as I witnessed it in 2011 was that this mobilization was not voluntary but coerced and hedged all aspirations of a better Ethiopia into the future. To position the opportunity for social improvement as existing in the future speaks to a theme similar to other African locales. Other indicators of "progress" in the form of roads, clinics, schools, and farms inject an element of courting the highest bidder for local investment initiatives. Sadly, this "gold rush" mentality tips the scales toward foreign business, demonstrated most detrimentally over the past few years via mass-scale dispossession of populations whose main source of livelihood is to live off the land.

There is a tension between citizens asked by their states to sacrifice for the sake of development but who currently receive few assurances that their lives are improving or more secure than yesterday. I refer to the issue of land tenure as a potent example of this assessment, one that resembles the strategy of "co-opting" as proposed by Nielsen (2014). The pattern of building houses in Maputo, consisting of constructions without foundations for Mozambican urban dwellers, Nielson posits, is a method to establish their survival by reframing their participation in a system that fundamentally does not serve them, such as in this context, where land tenureship is nationalized and class contingent. He proposes "approaching time as duration" in order to "understand how social transformations might occur in non-linear and non-progressive ways." The collapsing of futures in his assessment is an "internal doubling so that the future exists both as failure on a linear scale while also serving to open up the present in potentially productive ways" (178). In the case of Ethiopian Orthodox parishes, the indeterminacy of *tabots*-in-waiting stands for a future full of expectation yet resistant to linear resolution. To wait for a *tabot*'s home, directed by the agency of its saint, serves an analytical, rather than a literal, point, as an orienting idiom for valuing and exercising patience, perseverance, and sustained devotion. I would venture to say that "waiting indefinitely" carries over to other conditions of dispossession and provides an interpretive guiding light for absorbing these existential dilemmas of waiting.

Conclusion

This chapter centered on the legends that chronicle how saints manifest into *tabots* based on mutual interaction of promising between the devotees and the devoted. Miracles and their circulation as part of local communities' heritage and political claims have been approached as a contestation of institutional power, such as the seers of Catholic Spain in the early twentieth century whose visions and calls to action were treated as a threat to the larger Church (Christian 1996). In the context of Ethiopia's diversifying demography, *tabot* legends slot into a scene of increased religious competition for cultural and political presence. These stories, sourced from a collective of believers to a charismatic monk, demonstrates that engagement with the *tabot* as a form of local history and legend is an activity that is constantly disentangled and set into motion. Employing the refractions of covenant, investigated in the preceding chapters through *tabot* veneration, liturgical stances, and narrative ideas of divine presence and cooperation in Ethiopia, we can begin to identify the covenant refractions that might inform Ethiopian Orthodox Christians' methodology of elaboration.

Furthermore, legitimizing extraordinary events as attributable to the *tabot* hinges on unrevealed knowledge that in some cases manipulates existing tensions and antagonisms in parish politics. The biographies of *tabots*, examined here as a sociotheological genre of ritual and discourse and a merging of refractions of the covenant idea, is a byproduct of the instabilities of social knowledge that requires a constant "emptying out" or externalization (Jimenez 2011, 193). I attribute these linguistic and material patterns of displaying and guardedness to a central paradox of the covenant as a socially authored idea: The *tabot* is an item shrouded in order to maintain its sanctity, yet its importance as the consecrating property of a church requires its revelation by believers in order to emerge. As Ethiopians lose out on opportunities for personal inheritance because of politically volatile land claims reforms, communal ownership has become more pronounced and signals how religious authorities act as alternatives to the government's total ownership over all land. As the next chapter will detail, to navigate this field requires the manipulation of social and economic influence from an active network of interpersonal bonds as harnessed through lay and mutual-aid associations.

CHAPTER

5

Mahaber and the Blessing

This chapter addresses the prolific presence of *mahabers* in Ethiopian society. A category of social life that is modeled on a fellowship of believers and spiritual kin, these are associations run administratively, with membership dues, codes of conduct, and a collegiality among its participants in the tradition of a mutual-aid society. It is also a part of life that blends religious and secular affairs, as *mahabers* can refer to an association of engineers or local businessmen, a parish collective, or an elders council. I share an anecdotal illustration of a person "*mahaber*-less" to demonstrate this point. A radio program narrated a cautionary tale of a recent undergraduate whose life spiraled out of control when he missed his appointment for a civil service exam. Depressed by his diminished prospects—an entry-level post in a government office is highly desired—he turned to bad company and *ch'at* (a popular narcotic), alcohol, and cigarettes. "If only elders could intercede on his behalf," the narrator sympathetically speculated. The young man was depicted as a victim at the mercy of the broader neglect of the community at large. In this light, we can approach *mahabers* as more than mutual-aid organizations or societies of prestige. They function as social structures that equitably facilitate resources in a cooperative and egalitarian mode, what Mauss (1990 [1950]) would label a "total services" system of the elementary kind (7–8).

I focus on the symbolic and ceremonial attributes of *mahabers* in order to outline the active methodology of elaboration through parallelism and mirroring with covenant refractions in liturgical, textual, and historical contexts. I approach the idioms, references, and thematic resemblances as part of a broader social valuing of ritualized relationships that facilitate a spirit of expansive reciprocity and cooperative community relations (Chapter 3). This is in striking contrast to another Orthodox Christian context, Greece, where ideologies of kinship are purposefully narrow in order to guard against competition for the scarcity of resources. For du Boulay (2010), the antagonistic social climate boils down to "harshness of environment," interpreted as the difficulties of survival in the rural terrain, which limits cooperation and where exchange with the wider community is characterized as "a disinterested and symbolic act" (186). I would argue that similar socioeconomic tensions exist in urban Ethiopia. As the story about the delinquent youth showcases, this is a harsh world of very limited opportunities. Access to networks that guarantee employment, bureaucratic favors, or simply a modicum of administrative cooperation can make a serious difference. Such travails are especially reflected upon by *mahaber* members, and this condition is a real driver for the popularity of *mahabers*. Du Boulay (2010) acknowledges that the obligations to "give freely" are opportunities to transcend the fragmentation of society, if only momentarily (187). I suggest that similar patterns of ritual relationships operate, but with greater longevity and sustained cooperation in Ethiopia. I propose that particular forms of Orthodox Christian lay associations contain within their templates an element of charismatic order, a "spiritual giftedness" of being part of a collective. Within the Orthodox Christian cultural tradition, these associations are organized under divinely inspired foundations, such as sacramental ceremonies or tribute societies arranged around a patron saint. These formulate as "ritualized" relationships that are bestowed with a sacred order that people gravitate toward, contribute to, and rely upon, as an intrinsic part of social life.

Establishing Spiritual Kindred

I focus on religious associations as my principal case studies because they enable a more direct comparison of generic forms of covenant and its refractions. In the following case study of the revived honorary feast (*zikir*), we can observe how customs of remembrance and charity represent a continuation of personal traditions that have been adapted in response to the Derg era (1974–1991), a period of near-abolishment of any religious assembly. Because *mahaber* meetings straddled a gray area between secular and religious activities, they were not banned. Despite heavy intimidation by the socialist government against public worship, the Church did not encounter mass institutional devastation and continued to operate, compared to, for example, the Soviet Union and the Russian Orthodox Church. Efforts to break apart religious allegiances were most transparently signaled when *kebele* meetings (the local municipality) were scheduled on Sunday mornings, a time when liturgy would be conducted and *senbete* (parish-affiliated *mahabers*) would gather. As the Church had its financial support undercut, religiously geared assemblies persisted in the domestic realm, such as feasts in the home.

Pitt-Rivers (2011 [1992]) broaches the topic of the "legitimizing concepts" of the rituals of exchange and employs the theological term of "grace" to denote an uncalculated, uncontainable, and a genuinely "free gift." However, by suggesting that people can only return blessings and not generate grace (446), the question of authority reappears. *Mahaber* participants would wholeheartedly agree that the objective of these meetings is to give thanks and be humble in the eyes of God. Any blessing is a residual of this pure intent, yet it is this "charismatic" energy that is the force that continues this tradition. These groups and the various reasons for why they convene are engaged in more than literal reciprocity. The present analysis proposes a conception of charisma of a different sort, drawing from Weber's "routinization of charisma" (1964), a framework that accounts for the formalized or rationalized identity of charismatic power. *Mahabers* are a traditional authority rooted in a sacred order. This order is guided by several patterns delineated within the EOTC domain, such as memorials and allegories of Christian living, as well as local ideologies of offerings and blessing. It's the collective that is charismatic and its charter that permits their formation and importance in society.

On one occasion when Yared, a friend, concluded his family's turn as *mahaber* host, he made a deliberate visit to deliver "*ts'ebel tsadik*" (lit. pious holy [water], meaning an item that is blessed), a modest portion of flat bread (*injera*), to our household. Yared considered it part of his duty as a host of this gathering and insisted we partake of the blessing that his family had participated in. Considering the pathways involved in this ritualized setting, to whom can this blessing be sourced and attributed? On the one hand, it is typical for a priest or two to preside and offer benedictions over the meal and over those gathered, matching ideas of the charisma of office that envisions its transferability via acquired skills, such as the "laying of hands" by a priest (Weber 1964, 366). This disassociating process of charisma signals its possibilities as a more movable category, one contingent on the circumstances of time and context. Items are blessed every day for a wide variety of reasons, yet there are circumstances that are considered more auspicious and sacred than others. A major underlying component of these *mahaber* contexts is the amalgam of giving and receiving that produces a spiritually gifted quality to time and space, one that members of sanctioned collectives such as *mahabers* are particularly skilled at initiating and facilitating.

The *mahabers* effectively establish relations of spiritual kindred, bonds that extend into contexts outside celebration events, beyond the "virtual space" where a mutual devotion is expressed between patron saints and their devotees (see liturgical stances in Chapter 3 as an affiliated activity). These customs of reciprocity confer blessings on the givers and receivers and create authority for lay members to mobilize charitable works. This associative form of devotional culture of Ethiopian Orthodox Christians both cites and refers to a common collection of symbols and idioms within the refractions of the covenant idea. As a domain of ideological elaboration, it reproduces the image of a "chosen people" beholden to sustained devotion through the various forms of *mahaber* making.

A Family's Sacred History

In Greece, ritual kinship within the Orthodox Christian traditions exists in the form of godparenthood and wedding sponsorship, though against the backdrop of an aggressively competitive ethos in the rural political ecology, as described by Campbell (1964). Wedding sponsors in Sarakatsani society are a variation of intercommunity networking, ideally constructed with an outside circle of recognized contacts. The utility of such traditions of spiritual kinship is that they are the most effective; the ritual sanction "locks" the relationship (223). Du Boulay (2010) delves into the mechanisms of this bond more precisely, identifying oil as the legitimating bond and as "an organic force capable of transcending individuals and binding them into a wider communion" (220). Throughout all these presentations of ritualized relationships, normative kinship, via blood, is accepted as a transitory movement, one that will eventually drop out of memory, save for the fidelity to opportunities of renewal, as intrinsic of the living generations who breathe life into the past (200).

This last depiction is crucial for understanding spiritual kinship in Ethiopian Orthodox Christianity. The obligations of giving extend beyond the living, and this is where another integral component of the Orthodox Christian domain appears: the rituals of memorializing. Spiritual kinship is tied to the related ideology for establishing a version of charismatic authority through the spiritual potency of "remembrance." *Mahaber* members' responsibilities are often inherited, thereby effectively dictating that a guardian of this family tradition remain loyal to the spirit of the gathering as it was established before their time. I start with one particular case because it demonstrates the interconnected relationship between honoring the patron saint and reliving the family name, with particular emphasis on the integral role of the expansive household.

Herani was known locally for holding a monthly *zikir* with various food offerings for Medhane Alem (lit. Savior of the World) in Addis Ababa, an occasion when she would serve a meal for invited guests and her neighborhood church community of Genete Le Yesus (Heaven of Jesus Church). Her involvement in this custom only began after the insistence of a family contact, a *bahetawi* (hermit) named Abba Gabre-Meskel. It all started from a reoccurring dream the hermit had about how Medhane Alem *zikir* cannot be stopped and that Herani will take on this custom. Abba Gabre-Meskel served Herani's grand-uncle, a decorated nobleman, who had continued this family tradition from his father, who started this sometime in the 1890s. Herani presented photographs from the 1950s and 1960s of past *zikir* gatherings, the scenes showing groups of middle-aged men huddled around tables full of food and drink. The men were her grand-uncle's relatives and acquaintances who had grown up together, and at that time many were colleagues in government ministries. After the revolution in 1974, this practice altered. Herani's grand-uncle was captured by the Derg government and imprisoned, along with many other members of her family, including Herani. The family became effectively scattered, some escaping abroad while others lived incognito around the capital. The family home was left in the care of *Weizero* (Mrs.) Bezunesh, Herani's grandmother, who carried on hosting the *zikir* continuously until her death several years ago, at which point Abba Gabre-Meskel began to see visions of Medhane Alem's message, prodding Herani to restart the custom.

A culture of commemoration that is activated by memorials, feast days, and anniversary events formulates the means by which parish communities are bestowed the responsibility to behave as *bale habtoch* (benefactors). As the previous chapter discussed, the role of the benefactor has been reconfigured as the result of the political changes of the past several decades. During the Derg period, the Church implemented major reforms that affected its financial and bureaucratic structure. Additionally, the impact of Ethiopians' migrating abroad produced a base of wealthy supporters that wield considerable influence locally as members of the Ethiopian "diaspora."

In many ways, the task of reviving this *zikir* involved piecing together a household from the rubble. The family had irrevocably been disbanded, with only a few of the contemporary generations living in Ethiopia. One could see this from the elongated showcase of photographs of children and grandchildren living in the West—and who likely had never entered this house—on display in the master bedroom, which had remained undisturbed since her grandmother's death. Before her commitment to hold monthly gatherings, the house was empty, and this feeling of abandonment lingered in the background. The rooms were closed off and did not appear to get much light; curtains were partly drawn, gathering dust and stale air. Likewise, the kitchen was furnished with sparse equipment, signs that it was a house unused. The only permanent member of staff was the guard who watched over a compound of overgrown grass. Herani's decision to hold the *zikir* here and not at her own residence seemed fitting to her. It was her grandfather who had held these meals in honor of Medhane Alem, and so, she explained, it made sense to hold it at his house.

Given the emphasis on how much these traditions are a fulfillment of past work, the patronage of a previous generation, it is fair to ask if this activity is a version of a well-developed custom of memorial rites rather than an example of the charismatic gravity of *mahabers*. There are conclusive ways in which *zikirs* are not a memorial tradition, principally given that no service of the dead is read. *Fitat* is generally carried out on the fortieth day after the death, then on the first year anniversary, and then the seventh year. Moreover, *zikirs* are conventionally a continuation of an established custom of a deceased host, though arguably in the case of Medhane Alem *zikir*, it represents an indirect route to Herani's great-grandfather's memory. I integrate this memorial association as part of the system of "charismatic collectives" because it aptly underscores the social dynamics that are core to the *mahaber* form. In particular, creating the imaginary of the household, perhaps more intensified by the absence of a fully functioning house in Herani's case, represents the construction of the conditions necessary to enact a collective charismatic moment in time and space.

The people in attendance were arranged in a circular fashion, around the circumference of the rectangular salon. As host of the *zikir*, Herani's position on the sofa indicated the head of the room, as well as the fact that a hermit, Abba Gabre-Meskel, the most honored guest, was seated to her side. I surmised that he held a distinguished position because she was fussing over him and kept plying him with various items of food, finally negotiating a satisfactory meal of boiled banana and honey. Several guests were carrying items such as bread and *kolo* (roasted barley grains) inside the house. The invited guests were lined up against the wall in somewhat descending order from the hermit. They, in themselves, were a motley crew. Several priests and deacons were scattered around the room, engaged in dogmatic arguments such as whether the Tsige tsom (fast of the Flight of the Holy Family) was to be strictly observed by all Christians. Herani was rather quiet and not at all engaged with the squabbling; she was more preoccupied with serving all the guests, busy running around with the staff brought in for that day. That component of familiar household dynamics, light fighting and fussing, was revealing, given that those gathered were a group of people who otherwise had no occasion to convene. This was an attempt at replicating a family, so essential in a *mahaber* gathering.

Near the end of the salon were seated a rotating group of several women and occasionally an elderly man, mostly parishioners from Yesus Church. They were referred to by the guests I was sitting with as the alms seekers, or *yene beeteoch*, translating as "ones like me," a colloquial expression used to connote sympathy and elicit actions for giving and taking care of others in need. Based on how they were dressed and how undernourished they looked, the two ladies I was sitting next to, Herani's cousins, speculated that this food was likely the only good meal they would receive for the day. There was most definitely a marked class distinction for this group of people, most evident in the very low bows they gave to Herani upon receiving their plates of food. The food was modest, only two to three dishes: potatoes, meat and/or vegetable stew, sometimes cracked wheat, and always homemade bread and *t'ela* (homebrew). This part of the room circulated the most, and each time I sat at these meetings, I would see several new people who would come, receive the meal, and leave with gracious thanks.

The act of giving thanks and receiving blessings was a major component of the *mahaber* event as well. Abba Gabre-Meskel was given the role of offering the opening prayers, the Lord's Prayer, ending with "Igze'o, Maherene Kristos" (lit. "Lord have mercy"), and Be'ente Mariam Maherene Kristos (lit. "for the sake of Mary, have compassion upon us, O Christ

Lord"). Then a senior priest got up and prayed for the souls of the family's deceased. Herani facilitated this part of the ritual by preparing a sheet that listed all her family members who had passed away. It was laminated and adorned with religious symbols (an icon of Medhane Alem) and passed to the clergy present, who offered the prayer. Afterward, the commemorative sheet was returned to the wall to await the following month. A brief teaching lesson was dispensed and concluded by proclaiming how good it was that this *zikir* was being held for so many years and the *bereket* it gave to Herani and those who participated. The ceremonial part of the event ended there. Abba Gabre-Meskel was given the role of providing the official blessing, though there were many variations of this same speech act. After *zikir* feasting, the clergy and others who were present upon their departure often declare a long line of blessings to the host.

Kefu ayenkash	May evil times or intentions be unable to hurt you
Medhanyalem Ayasatash	May Medhane Alem [name of commemorated saint] prevent you from being without
Yih bereket bet yehun	May it be the house of plenty
Zerish yebarek	May your "seed" (descendants) be blessed
Yetefetefyistesh	May you receive multitudes
Yakberelegn	Be honored
Edmey, tenayestelegn	May you be given long life and health
Yedegochu, yeabatochesh ennatochesh amlakyete bekesh	May the God of your kind forefathers and foremothers protect you
Amet amet yaderselegn	May you reach from year to year

The religious rhetorics of "blessing" is high art in Ethiopia, akin to indigenous traditions of oration and poetry, a vast topic independently (see Levine 1965). These actions are a form of giving thanks and the return of grace (Pitt-Rivers 2011, 424), verbalized through intercessory words such as wishes for bounty, the avoidance of evil, protection over ancestors, and the "house's" honor (e.g., "May such kindness and generosity demonstrated by 'my lord' or 'my lady' [*yene geta, yene immebet*] be repaid"). One interpretation is that these pronouncements are a form of prayer, prayers that take on an adjusted and stronger weight when done on behalf of someone else. This public exhibition of giving thanks also connotes an allegiance between the two parties, in a pattern similar to domains of local politics, such as maneuvering administrative channels (e.g., in the courts, police, land administration). Established scholarship on dynamics of stratified power relations in Ethiopia, particularly Amhara-Tigrean, would posit that the rhetoric of blessing is a transparent vassal-lord structuring that has been in operation for centuries. Related to the case of offering protection, being someone's *dembeniya* ("regular," colloquially understood as a "man on the inside") or knowing a *mahaber lij* (a member of an association) serves as a secular variant of the blessing. While a more explicit quid pro quo is involved, such as a monetary kickback, referred to as *shai/bunna* (tea/coffee money), this still reflects an active code of cooperation and an agreement to watch out for one another.

Another perspective concerning the departing blessings would be to recognize the ritual efficacy of sacred speech. Acknowledging that religious language is the mediator between the other worlds (Keane 1994, 66), the ability of *mahaber* recipients to speak these words signals an authorship of a divine source as transmitted through lay individuals. The blessing is a response to a gift, yet what is offered in correlation is not an "equal trade" answer and response reflex of the ritual exchange. It is an exhibition of the recipient's own ability to engage in the spiritual action of a personally voiced benediction, spurred on by the constructed context of the *mahaber* event.

At the core of *zikir* is a reprise of memorial and saint devotion customs. A family's devotion to a patron saint, this idea of bonding between the sacred and the human, is a link that is seen as unbreakable. It is about honoring a family's sacred history and special relationship to the saint in the absence of an actual household present. I sensed a conflation of Medhane Alem and Herani's family name—I could never reach a clear demarcation of whom we were celebrating. Were we honoring Ras Kassa's devotion to Medhane Alem or offering thanks to Medhane Alem via Ras Kassa's family's commitment to the saint, or both at the same time? I found this detail to be marginally important. For example, two sisters who took their mother's *mahaber* seat did not reflect the specific connection between the feast commemoration of the *mahaber*, Ba'ata ("the entrance of Mary into the Temple"), or why their mother had chosen to be a founding member of this collective. Also, the wealth factor should be noted, since it is unusual for a family to be able to afford to pay and commit to hosting the monthly meal singlehandedly; it is more common to do *zikir* yearly.

The Traveling Household

Herani's *zikir* emphasizes how ideas of family and ancestral ties are influential reference points for establishing and maintaining relationships of ritualized giving. Aligned with these ideas is the encompassing nature of the household, as exemplified in Herani's reviving of her family's custom, which entailed opening up the house to the community as a pivotal step in this process. The home prototypically presents a space where individuals frame their connections and expectations, conjuring up the presence of the divine in parallel with family life. Orsi's study of popular devotion (1985) among Italian Catholics of East Harlem serves as one illustration of how their relations to their patron saints are structured around the home. "They brought the holy into their homes, filling their rooms with the familiar figures of saints and the Madonna. They performed careful rituals of rispetto towards these figures and included them in the life and decisions of the domus. In this way, the divine was further involved in mutual responsibilities with the people. This was not a contract or patron-client relationship; rather, it was a domus-centered bond" (225). Once again, the home is presented as an essential locality for performing rituals of respect, honor, and intercession. As the principal inheritor and guardian of the *zikir* tradition, Herani conducts the gathering in an otherwise empty house, this setting being fundamental to the "inertia" of her *mahaber* event.

The home as a ritual stage is clear in the case of the *ts'ewa mahaber*, another association whose ceremonial qualities have metaphoric resonances with feast-day processions and the Eucharistic rite. Near late afternoon, at the conclusion of the *mahaber* event, small groups of women dressed in white shawls drove along the road carrying several items universally associated with this association; the *mesob*, the receptacle for the bread; the *ts'ewa*, a goblet-like cup typically made of clay; and a framed picture of the saint whom the *ts'ewa* honors, covered by church ceremonial umbrellas. The *ts'ewa* and *mesob* are draped in thin cotton or a knit decorative cover and are carried by the next host of the *mahaber* and any assisting members. A similar dynamic of religious associations, with the members as principal actors in the spectacle of religious drama, has been discussed by Driessen (1984) as one of the main characteristics of confraternities in Andalusia. The procession as a demonstration of divine glory and majesty is religiously marked behavior, a manifestation of holy presence as inhabited in these coded representations of the body and blood of Christ. Alongside the communal acknowledgment of this powerful Christian truth, this transferring of the *ts'ewa* is treated with great care, as if handling a delicate object. On one occasion, I assisted in the transfer of the *ts'ewa* in the front seat of my car. Various arrangements were made to make sure the substance would not spill. "Oh, it's such a blessing for you," the *mahaber* members commented as I played a part in the *ts'ewa*'s journey to the next household.

The *ts'ewa mahaber* and its devotional culture most exemplify the charismatic essence of ritualized spiritual kinship, which is additionally noteworthy because it is cultivated in the home by laypeople. The *ts'ewa mahaber* is typically composed of twelve members. Apart from the symbolic significance of Christ's twelve disciples, there are practical reasons, such as the feasibility of each *mahaber* member being able to afford to host one gathering each year. Membership is fairly stable, and expulsion from the *mahaber* is rare. *Mahaber* seats are typically inherited, to ensure the members are from similar age sets. Each *mahaber* unit is of a fairly comparable economic status, though of the four *mahabers* I attended, I noted that they more represented the middle to lower class, as compared to the upper class, who I found less amenable to *ts'ewa* traditionalism (e.g., no street procession, as it might be considered a tradition of the countryside).

Each house is considered a unit, which can include a wife and children or, conversely, a husband and children. Male spouse participation is more unusual. Apart from helping prepare, such as purchasing livestock, he vanishes on the *mahaber* saint day. Assefa made a light insinuation about his wife, Mulu, spending too much time and money on her turn to host the Mariam *mahaber* in October and not enough energy on his children. There is a moderate degree of advance preparation, fussing over the home brew (*t'ela*), which sits in a corner of the room, where it mellows for approximately two to three weeks. This item is a chance to show off for the wives or patriarch of the house the expertise and high quality of household, good *t'ela* being a particular source of pride. As principal managers of the home, women are most involved in *ts'ewa* preparations, even if it is not their *mahaber*. It is principally a family event, and it's common to find children helping, and the credit and honor is understood by the household designation (i.e., by full family name or lineage).

Having described some generic characteristics of the *ts'ewa mahaber*, it is appropriate to discuss how this type of association enacts ritual relationships via sacramental-type means. Colloquially, the expression "to drink *mahaber*" (*mehaber metetat*) refers to the communion chalice (*ts'ewa*) that members

Figure 13. *Ts'ewa* in rotation.

partake of when participating in a *mahaber* gathering. The *ts'ewa* is a clay container in which *t'ela* is poured and served during the *mahaber* meal, typically lunch. What makes it sacrament-like, apart from the obvious mirroring of a communion chalice, is the holy water that is mixed with the *t'ela*, and at some point the cloths that cover it, in similar manner to the *tabot* in church, is removed so that the *t'ela* can be consumed by the *mahaber* members only. Guests can drink the *t'ela* but not from the chalice. The *ts'ewa* can never be empty and is constantly being replenished with more *t'ela*. At the end of the *mahaber* gathering, the transfer of the *ts'ewa* is made to the new house, at which point the new honoree and their family consume the *t'ela*.

The bread is similarly considered a sacramental item and is performed distinctively by the *mahaber* collective. The host takes the large loaf, places it on the *mesob* (straw-woven bread basket), and traces the outline with a knife. This round portion is reserved for members, and the broken pieces are distributed among the guests present. The bread, like the *t'ela*, is created with intentionality, for Mariam, for Medhane Alem, etc., and is turned upside down.[1] The sign of the cross is made with the knife before cutting. In the tradition of the French Basque country in the 1970s, bread giving was an obligation of the female head of household, and every two and a half years they were to bake bread and distribute it to their neighbors during a special mass they sponsored.[2] The custom is interpreted as agape symbolism; the rituals of commensality imitates the era of the disciples, when informal gatherings occupied the space when churches had not yet been established (Ott 1980, 50). The culture of offering in Ethiopia is expansive, and a fair amount of literature on commensality exists, especially as exhibited in the custom of the coffee ceremony as a style of blessing in Wollo (Ficquet 2002). However, since the social environment concerns Orthodox Christians, the idea of "folk communion" is a relevant frame to apply. Tax Freeman (1987), who alludes to this term briefly, primarily as it regards gifts of bread, turns her attention more to the structures of turn taking and rotative systems in Iberia. Such traditions are summarized by concluding that ritualized sharing is an institutional means of managing resources in an egalitarian-idealized society. Rotative logic to *ts'ewa mahabers* is applicable, particularly in regard to specific codes to sharing. When being invited to *mahaber* meetings, I had been told not to offer to bring any additions to the lunch meal, since it was the host who was solely responsible for providing the food. If one wanted to supply food or contribute, then one should host one's own gathering or be responsible for the whole meal in its entirety. It is not a potluck, which goes against the entire logic of the hosting tradition as it is performed in Ethiopia. It is the proprietary role of the inviter to assume total responsibility and credit for the hosting occasion.

The *ts'ewa mahaber*'s strong potency is its sacramental bonding, and the ceremonialism of the departing "hosts" is one manifestation of this aspect. After the Sellassie *mahaber* spent a few hours chatting, a few members expressed the need to start to head home. Eteye Ma'za and members present stood up and walked over to the table where the *ts'ewa mahaber* items were placed, separate from the dining table that had the food we were eating. The members closed down the ceremony by huddling around the *ts'ewa* and sipping, leaving a little in the container to be added by the next host. Dividing the dry food, like bread and cracked barley for each member to take and share with their household, they carefully bundled up their items. Eteye Ma'za carried the portrait of Sellassie (Holy Trinity) while leaving the candle burning inside the house. All the women began to ululate while walking through the corridor onto the front porch, and then Eteye Ma'za handed the icon to the next host. *"Be Alem gebto be alem enquan wetalesh"* ("may He [*ts'ewa*] go in and leave with fortune"), she proclaimed. The phrase that is uttered when it arrives at the new home is "*be Alem gebto be alem yewetalesh*" ("may no misfortune befall your house while the *ts'ewa* is in your house").

Ritual treatments of sacredly potent items, through the handling of powerful items such as *ts'ewa*, are segments of the *mahaber* custom that emphasize the vitality of charismatic force, particularly in the transfer of household to household. Ululation is an expression of glory, an automatic reaction to any "essence" of the holy, and an acknowledgment of the presence of the Holy Spirit, similar to how decorative umbrellas flank the *tabot* when it comes outside of the sanctuary (see Chapter 2). Asking individuals about the original nature of the *tabots* of every church, some will admit they are replicas, but many will react defensively, as the question is an attempt at imputing doubt about the tenets of the faith. The general response about *tabots* is "we don't care if the rest of the world doesn't believe us. We know it to be true, so that is all that matters." It would discredit its essence by qualifying it as a "representation," as all *tabots*, incalculable in number (though the most holy is in Axum), are categorically all the same; there are none of greater or lesser value. A similar articulation exists regarding the *ts'ewa*, as its domestic genesis was never noted. Though I heard no one refer to it as *qurban* (communion), *mahaber* members' expression of reverence bears little mark of its supposed representational status; it is the real deal, a blessed entity.

Regarding the ritual treatment of the lay performance, it is suitable to discuss confraternities and their ceremonial mirroring. Molonie (2004) describes the complex performance of Corpus Christi in Camuñas (Spain), which is an extension of liturgical rite yet assumes a carnivalesque nature and domain that serves as a stage to feature certain historical conditions of local political repression. The lay participants are actors in a "play," enacted during a specific time (Holy Week) and space (church interiors), similar to how nonclergy occupy performative spaces during Timqet (Chapter 2). The nature of inhabiting charismatic roles assumes an alternative quality in *mahabers*. Certainly, there is the symbolic resonance of the Christian community in its humblest sense. However, the center of gravity of the ritual, though far less accentuated and cathartic than the one performed in Camuñas, is in one's living room and directed by *mahaber* members. I argue that the ritual authority is of a particularly dynamic nature in the *ts'ewa mahaber*'s case. *Mahabers* are the drivers of this ritual

Figure 14. Baking bread.

and in fact inhabit positions as facilitators of charismatic processes within ritual action rather than assuming roles of representation. Priests, apart from providing formal prayers and offering spiritual guidance, are virtually in secondary roles, as this is acknowledged as not their domain.

The charismatic authority of *ts'ewa* autonomous from rituals initiated by the official Church can be further emphasized based on one account about the healing power of *ts'ewa*. A friend, Yerusalem, told me of the recent events of the *mahaber* of her mother, who had passed away recently. The empty *mahaber* seat was expected by Yerusalem to go to her aunt, the mother's sister. Incidentally, on the forty-day memorial of her death, Yerusalem's sister's fourteen-year-old son fell very ill. As the Gabriel *mahaber* meeting was soon approaching, it was decided by his mother that she would make a *s'let* (vow) to Gabriel that his life be spared. On the day of the *ts'ewa mahaber*, the teenager was brought to the *ts'ewa*, and it was placed on his head. After pronouncing the vow, she and he both drank from the chalice. For a few moments, the teenager stopped breathing, and all the *mahaber* members thought he had died, until he revived. Based on these series of events, it was arranged that until adulthood, he would serve as a special member of the *mahaber*, under his mother's place. It was considered a special arrangement, since it was exclusively a female *mahaber*, thus cementing the hypothesis of how these associations have a charismatic quality on their own, so much so that they overrode the conventions of the membership.

Mahabers also are effective at providing emotional support. Much attention is focused on the economic pooling or prestige of these associations, but this is not the only aspect I encountered, particularly for the female *ts'ewa* meetings I attended.[3] Partly aided by their small size, *ts'ewa* meetings can fit into people's living rooms. Members in attendance are relaxed with one another, joking, teasing, representing an otherwise social scene. A *mahaber* member, referred to as *mahaber lij* (kid), shares their vulnerabilities and worries. The issue of money appears often, but *mahabers* do not lend large amounts. With the Abune Aregawi *mahaber*, they have a fund of a couple hundred birr, a small amount, according to Galila, one of its members. It's not enough to permanently solve problems, though it is sufficient for medical emergencies. In one case, one member's husband had progressively failing eyes and collected money from several *mahabers* they were affiliated with. Galila described *mahaber* dynamics as one family—"We love each other . . . it is a place to feel safe and to share with each other," echoing one description of *mahabers* as "learning to care for each other" (Habte

Mariam Workeneh, in Demeke 2011, 285). One Sellassie *mahaber* member was very direct about needing money, suggesting she had no means to travel back home to her house. She was admonished by fellow members for complaining and not being grateful for what she had, for example, her own home. She insisted she was not exaggerating, but she was made to feel embarrassed by the others. It is evident that virtues such as being patient and waiting your turn are enforced via outlets such as the *mahaber*. Disappointment with family was also a topic scattered around these afternoon discussions. No resolutions were reached, but these were opportunities to have a forum to be heard and air one's grievances.

Senbete and Parish Development

Family histories are memorialized through the *mahaber* and expand to a broader concept of the household. I introduce a third form of *mahaber*, the *senbete*, as a variation on the themes so far. These gatherings are engaged in pure charity, with no exchange or return expectation, yet connote a spiritually endowed nature to the participant. Typically, at the conclusion of the Eucharist service,[4] a collection of parishioners gather at a building behind their church or slightly outside the compound, to host a meal. The building is a rectangular house constructed in the traditional method, with mud walls and dirt floor, though nowadays thatched roofs are being replaced with tin. These spaces are funded and maintained by the *senbete*, and outside of meeting times, the large room is used to house traveling clergy, such as iterant monks and deacons, or to conduct meetings for parish affairs. Unlike trends of other *mahaber* types, the *senbete* is the most consistently divided equally along gender lines, nearly half men and women, and their class was middle to low income. One way to judge their economic status was by the amount of monetary contributions, an average of seven to ten birr a month, while some *senbete*s have membership dues of twenty birr a month. A couple of members out of the total *senbete* volunteer to bring food items such as specially prepared home brew, large round loaves of bread, and *kolo* (cracked wheat grain), to be served to the members present. Using figures from Farensai Abo Church in Addis Ababa, membership in a *senbete* is high, nearing one hundred people. The individuals typically represent the community living in the same neighborhood, but not everyone attends every meeting; usually there is a little more than half present. *Senbete* membership tended to be an older age set, those in their mid-fifties and upward composing of the majority of the association. Younger members, from the mid-twenties to mid-forties, who represented on average 10 percent of membership, were more likely to participate in *senbete*, as its membership rules were more open and not contingent on inheritance like *ts'ewa* or *zikir*.

To provide an illustration of a typical *senbete* gathering, I include a visit to Ti'ta Mikael, a village church outside Dessie. After Sunday service, I was called over to share a meal with Qes Melke, his wife, and any remaining parishioners, which numbered about a dozen. The meal was for the *senbete* members, he explained, while motioning to the one-room house near the entrance of the church compound. The female *senbete* members were arranging the food on the injera trays, while Qes Melke was having an impromptu meeting with several members inside one of the church's office rooms. I was the only guest; this was a small *senbete*, suiting the size of the church congregation, an average of thirty to fifty people on an average Sunday service. However, it was St. Mikael's feast day, and while there was a meal to break the fast every Sunday, this preparation included sega wa't (beef stew) to fit the special occasion. After a prayer of thanksgiving by the priest, all began to eat, with the biggest portion of meat with marrow passed to me. Despite politely declining to eat such a heavy meal at 8:30 AM, Qes Melke insisted: "It's *bereket* from St. Michael, how can you refuse?" The conversation revolved around how we could make the church beautiful for Mikael on his annual feast day the following month, the repainting of the tin roof being the highest aim. One *senbete* member, a deacon who served the church, committed to two cans of paint. It was a small *senbete* and always more difficult to fundraise for, Qes Melke noted to me. He was a very skilled fundraiser and made sure I left with blessed bread and the name of the color of paint they needed, in case I should feel inspired to help Mikael. At first glance, it appeared like a normal gathering of individuals, not an allegorical relation to sacrament taking or sacred continuance of saint devotion. Nevertheless, the *senbete* assumed a role of guardian of the lay Christian and his or her "incorporation" into a religious community.

Senbete is the most direct correspondence with religious confraternities as defined in the Catholic tradition, as a religious community that serves as an extension of the parish council and acts as the Church's grassroots support system. Similarly, one of the principal purposes of the *senbete* is to feed the poor, and the meals they serve are generally modest in order to serve the largest number of people possible. *Senbetes* also constitute a melding of various influences. To return the charismatic authority of collectives, it is worth investigating further the embedded aura of justice and council that *senbete* tradition contains. This is important because it represents one major characteristic of what *mahabers* engender to the broader community. In Ullendorff's (1968) analysis of the etymology of the *senbete*,[5] he mines the biblical references to reflect on the "Old Testament character" of Ethiopian Orthodox worship. These are many, though his discussion of the conciliar nature of the "community of believers," depicted as "elders under a tree resolving a dispute" (Deuteronomy 25:7–9), resembled a typical scene at a church, any time of the week, but particularly on Sunday at these *senbete* gatherings. The church is referred to culturally as a neutral ground of dispute settlement. Often times, "peace talks" are staged in a church compound, and elders (*shemageles*) are pivotal players in these "peace talks." On one occasion, a *shemagele* meeting was called to "reason with" a woman who refused to follow a court request to provide evidence of property ownership. This was an interfamily conflict, so it was in the interest of the family name to have this issue resolved peacefully and outside the public domain of the legal system. At Giorgis Church, coincidently across the street from a major court in Addis Ababa, a gathering of two family elders and several other affiliated family contacts who were *senbete* members at Abo Church were present. The situation was laid out, and the chair of the meeting offered his assessment, making sure each side was equally appeased. In the end, it was decided among the *shemageles* that the woman needed to meet several conditions (namely, cooperate with the neighborhood administration) within a "compassionate" timeframe. This was not agreed to, and no resolution was reached. However, in the opinion of several of the *shemageles* involved, the incident was not a failure, because those involved had followed the proper cultural procedures.

The frequency of appealing to *mahabers*, particularly to its senior members, also signaled the limitations of families' ability to solve their problems internally. Mequanent (1998), studying the patterns of *mahaber* formation in their religious and secular settings,[6] presents several examples of how rural farmers appeal to *mahabers*. Two instances illustrate these dilemmas of interfamily strife and the necessity to have public, unbiased recourse and a means of retribution. In one example, Mequanent describes an incident where an old man asks a *mahaber* (which type remains unspecified) to send an investigator to find out if his children are stealing coffee from his field, including forcing the accused, his sons, to take an oath on the Bible if they deny it (506–7). Another case cited involves circumstances where a *mahaber* chairman, termed as the judge (*dagne*) or "Muse" (Moses), was asked to intercede in a theft of a father's farming equipment from his son. The authority of *mahabers* maintained an elevated position in society, even when family relations have broken down.

The charismatic collective as I have argued via several *mahaber* forms rests in their ritualization, that is, their ability to achieve a spiritually gifted status through the manipulation of time and space via ritual and ideal types such as sacral "role-playing." With *senbete*, this formula becomes conflated with other cultural frames. *Mahaber* activities, especially as they grow out of professional work environments, present a dynamic fusion between the traditionalist templates of lay activities and a desire to engage in community making, such as Ato Tesfai's *mahaber*. Every 27th of the month, this collective of army veterans meets at Medhane Alem Church and brings prepared meals in a round-robin fashion, never meeting at home for their *mahaber* purposes. Ato Tesfai's turn was on Patriots Day, a national holiday as well as coinciding with the feast day of Medhane Alem, which he viewed as auspicious: Medhane Alem is the guardian of soldiers. The main objective of the *mahaber* was to distribute food under the name of Medhane Alem *mahaber* of Army veterans, much like the aims of the *senbete*, though the membership of this association was specific and not defined by parish. Ato Tesfai counted the value of his association as a way to maintain relationships among old friends and coworkers who have since taken different professions and do not otherwise see one another regularly.

The flexibility with which these institutions were inaugurated, as well as people's engagement with several associations at a time, was a dominant pattern among Ethiopian Orthodox Christians, most of whom were employed in urban centers. These religious associations maintained member bodies that are penetrable, as new participants can be endorsed through a guarantor recommendation system via existing members. The link between work culture and association engagement is one pivotal component of how *mahaber*s exist as such a wide-ranging activity and entity. Unlike *ts'ewa mahaber*s, these *mahaber*s that grew out of the workplace were not gender specific. Marta, an employee at a private enterprise, was approached by her coworker, Azede, about a cause she was interested in supporting: funding a monastery near Wenchi Kirkos in her home country. They spread the word among several friends at work and helped sell tickets at their respective parish churches, and on the significant feast day, many of the partici-

Figure 15. *Senbete* proceedings.

pants went on pilgrimage there. The pooling of resources together and the cooperation for an event and cause serve as one foundational step for *mahaber* formation. Azede and a few supporters formed a Kirkos *mahaber* as a result—they only meet yearly because membership has not reached a high number—though Marta decided not to join, since she could not commit to one more *mahaber* obligation.

Anticlericalism and Orthodox Autonomy

The ways *mahaber*s stray from classic confraternities as they are understood in the Catholic tradition is illuminating for several key reasons. A broad definition of confraternity is a religious community, principally male, organized under the protection of a patron saint. It participates on the feast day of their namesake and occupies a place alongside administrative councils in its local political economy. In large part, the prestige and charismatic authority of these associations are key aspects of their appeal and membership participation, and these characteristics are generated from the pseudoclerical ceremonialism that surrounds these associations. Terpstra's introduction to the collection of historical confraternity studies, *The Politics* *of Ritual Kinship* (2000), marks significant trends of these associations. In addition to serving as a window into alternative lay devotion culture, confraternities were the precursors of modern institution making, specifically in the context of Renaissance Europe. Emerging with a vengeance during the Counter-Reformation, these brotherhoods, with a wide variety of types, had a reformist zeal that marked a shift from their more egalitarian origins toward a more aristocratic character (Terpstra 2000, 7–8). These brotherhoods experienced a revival in the nineteenth century, when the liberalization of governments forced the Catholic Church to assume a diminished and divested position, though the popularity of confraternities had largely diminished in lay Christian traditions.

Among contemporary studies of religious brotherhoods or communities, the theme of anticlericalism reoccurs, as participants in these associations are understood as attempting to negotiate a place, individually through the collective, into the new social order, particularly in colonial contexts. Antagonism with clergy was prevalent with the Tlingit brotherhoods of southeastern Alaska, who reappropriated the confraternity in order to preserve aspects of local memorial customs and moiety identity (Kan 1985). Tlingit communities were attracted to Orthodox brotherhoods, according to Kan (1985), because this custom allowed "accepting it [Christianity] on their own terms," noting aspects such as prestige rules, mortuary importance, purity, and pollution ascriptions as valued within the cultural logic (215). The idea of blessing (*laxeitl*) was similarly operable in ceremonial participation and their parish responsibilities (e.g., to hold candles during the reading of the Gospels during service). Similarly, disputes over orthodox practice and the Church institution's exercise of power were evident in Catholic Europe over the course of the twentieth century in France (Badone 1989) and Spain (Behar 1986), land ownership and management being a large point of contention. Driessen (1984) summarizes the divisiveness of these dynamics as it appeared in an Andalusian town in the 1970s: "One of the very values embodied in the *confradias* is independence *cum* local patriotism, which openly conflicts with bureaucratic authority and interference from outside in the *pueblo*'s affairs" (79). So while religious communities were originally intended as a cultural practice to supply parish support, they were conversely being used as a weapon and means to redress dilemmas unresolved by broader Church-lay relations.

These examples of strong parish infrastructure among Church communities reflect the local historical developments of the symbiotic relations between Church and state, further entrenched in Eastern Christian territories where the emperor was head of the Church. Several of these issues hold in Ethiopia, a major one being the feudal land system (Crummey 1972), a political-economic order that established gradational relationships between serf and lord. This legacy of a dominant political economy has influenced scholarship on saint veneration that aligned with the dynamics of vassal/land to patron/clientage (Eisenstadt and Roniger 1984). Given recent reconfigurations of parishes, the power dynamics of authority have been modified to include more active parties. The lay collectives analyzed as honorific associations offer an opportunity to view the personal dynamics between clergy and *mahaber* members. As such, members of the Church would be more resistant to espouse a categorical distrust of the Church, as illustrated with the conservative Catholic communities of Europe. In some cases, priests and deacons can themselves be inducted into *mahabers* as members. What this says about clerical and secular roles as they play out in the local scene is that liturgical roles in secular and religious domains are not strictly divided. This aspect, of priests as participants, actually permits considering how their inclusion creates a middle area for lay as vested with authority. This contrasts with clerical formalism in the liturgical context, examined by Carroll's (2018) ethnographic research on the materialities of the Orthodox liturgical lifeworld in a London parish church community. This study features the methods and trajectories by which Orthodox Christians are transformed through sacramental engagements, such as the priest who assumes the office he holds through the vestments and community he serves or the initiate who through baptism becomes a person who "participates in the Priesthood of Christ, not through his sacred functions but by virtue of his sanctified being" (Evdokimov 2001, 85). It is this vacillation between social stratification in this world and equality in the next that composes a key quality for how Orthodox Christians understand the transformative potential contained and facilitated via the Church as "one Body in Christ."

The domain of commensality provides another means to observe the tensions of hierarchy and communitarianism in Ethiopian Orthodox Christianity, investigated by Boylston (2012) in the town of Zege (west-central Ethiopia). This study critically examines the paradigm of "individualism" as contingent on the mediation of substance exchange, which includes an expansive set of activities, ranging from hosting a *zikir*, partaking of *qurban*, and encountering *buda* (evil spirits). By identifying a fundamental premise, that "social unequals should nonetheless be equal in the eyes of

God, from whom they borrow their worldly power" (212–13), Boylston communicates the paradoxical essence of encounters on an inter-relational and super-relational level, emphasizing that "you can share substance with God, but not while sharing substance with other people. But perfect consubstantiality with God is unsustainable, while consubstantiality with people is unavoidable. This is a paradox and a tension that animates Orthodox religious practice" (212).

This discussion has positioned as its central axis the domain of the collective and the leadership roles it confers. I have explored this objective formally by studying the typologies of *mahabers* as they exist in an urban environment. The decision to devise an analysis of archetypal forms of lay associations possesses the potential to consider certain universal principles that govern this domain of devotional activity. Furthermore, to study *mahabers'* organizational features enables examining how Ethiopians adapt to another collective institution that has gained local prominence, the NGO (nongovernmental organization). The context of Dessie was a particularly saturated area given the legacy of the famines that positioned it as a humanitarian aid and health station in the 1980s (i.e., most of the major hospitals and higher clinics of the North and South Wollo zones are based there). But it is nevertheless accurate to state the prevalence of this sector in Ethiopia more broadly, given government ambitions toward achieving large-scale socioeconomic development. During my time in the field, I often wondered about this NGOification, which influenced "grassroots" politics, its cachet contained and disseminated via buzzwords like "empowerment" and along with other appeals to "social capital," a reflection of the deeply entrenched discourse propagated by institutions such as the World Bank in developing countries (Mosse 2006). I noted how these themes interacted with *mahabers* and found certain correspondences, such as *kebeles* that partnered with female *mahabers* and agribusiness collectives. These features of bureaucracy as they developed locally reflect greater political pressure for groups to achieve visibility and legitimacy in the public sphere. This climate of group rights at the microlevel corresponds to critique of the term "community," which is particularly vibrant in the US political lexicon. For Joseph (2002), examining the trends in American identity politics, "community" has devolved into a rather noxious term and reflects how "capitalism and, more generally, modernity depend on and generate the discourse of community to legitimate social hierarchies" while nevertheless arguing that "communal subjectivity is constituted not by identity but rather through practices of production and consumption" (iix). These comments are instructive and should be kept at the forefront of this discussion, given how religious *mahabers* are adapting to altered conditions, such as the Church's vision of increasing the size of dioceses and parishes that rely more heavily on collective mobilizations of human and monetary resources.

In closing, I refer to a uniquely Orthodox Christian interpretation of the religious collective, inspired by Berdyaev's perspective on Russian spirituality and the uninstitutional nature of the Church. His interpretation of the religious collective bears relevant correspondences to the manner in which *mahabers* relate to the established authority of the Church.

> Individualism is foreign to Orthodoxy, to it belongs a particular collectivism. A religious person and a religious collective are not incompatible with each other, as external friend to friend. The religious person is found within the religious collective and the religious collective is found within the religious person. Thus the religious collective does not become an external authority for the religious person, burdening the person externally with teaching and the law of life.
>
> (Berdyaev 1952)

Focusing on this understanding of the embeddedness of the idealized Church, it is the religious collectives that seek and are truly able to achieve this "mystical transfiguration," through multiple intersecting contexts such as *tabot* praxis on Timqet, behavioral stances during liturgical space/time, and through the genre of *tabot* legends. This conception of religious authority, or lack thereof, can be located in the ritual patterns and arenas where charismatic energies, the spiritual qualities of time and space, are decentralized and assume a position of autonomy (i.e., "the Church is not outside of religious persons"). Conversely, this interpretation of nonauthority, articulated by Berdyaev as not an expression of "individualism," is not employed at the expense of cooperation and resolution with the broader community and Christian fellowship. All the social benefits of *mahabers*, the prestige, support, and blessings, are all byproducts, since at the core it is almost as though there is no self without the group. Discussing the necessity of sharing with strangers and on a monthly basis, Eteye Meseret, a *senbete* member, gave a reply that encapsulated the integrated nature of humanity: "The pieces without the entire bread are meaningless. They don't amount to anything."

Conclusion

In Ethiopian life, there are few purely secular domains. This reality influences the decision to not present *mahabers* as exclusively religious. However, the *mahaber* has an affiliated Ethiopian Orthodox framework that draws from the Church's engagement with what I refer to as covenant refractions. I emphasize its cultural sourcing in light of Ethiopia's postmonarchial, postrevolutionary history and my resistance to refer to it as postsocialist. The strong influence of Chinese business investment and that form of socioeconomic development should inspire analyses that consider Ethiopian government regimes, including the current party of the Ethiopian People's Revolutionary Democratic Front, in power since 1991, as more hybridized and receptive to alternative political systems. However, it is clear that the Derg (1974–1991) and its specific interpretation of Marxism-Leninism affected religious life. Yeshi, a friend who lived in Addis in the 1980s and herself was conscripted in the *zemecha* (the educational campaigns), noted how *kebele* meetings were forced to meet on Sunday mornings. Churches were open, though "bled from the inside": People were informed on if they were seen going to church and charged with "counterrevolutionary activities" for meeting in private spaces. Scheduling meetings at that time would assure people did not go to church and that no gatherings such as *senbete* could occur. The association was co-opted but not banished: Ethiopian Orthodox devotional culture was too much of a social asset to do away with.

Mahabers are also a strategy for creating kin networks as a resource in an environment with diminished protections for citizens. To have a *mahaber lij* present at the courts, *kebele*, business administration, or elite school or university program is a boon and often functions as a ticket into a world of finite opportunities. Therefore, the *mahaber* recreates the value of a select community guided by common mandate (i.e., to their patron saint, to their defined charitable cause) and demonstrates the associative qualities of Ethiopia's covenant idea.

CHAPTER

6

Movements of Sacred Promise

The devotional seriousness of pilgrimage has been classically illustrated by outward manifestations of sin that are severe in their embodiment. Kulubi Gabriel is often cited by Orthodox Christians to exemplify the phenomenon of penance in Ethiopia (Pankhurst 1994, Gascon and Hirsch 1992). These contexts were dramatic and evocative in the popular consciousness, in particular the image of pilgrims who carry large boulders on their backs, akin to the spiritual and physical submission exhibited by supplicants to St. Mary at Tinos (Dubisch 1995), who likewise communicate their suffering by how they are received by a holy place. In this sense, adapting to the role of pilgrim proved to be more difficult than I anticipated. Since few tourists went on pilgrimages in Ethiopia, apart from partaking in important events such as the feasts of the Cross (Meskel), Epiphany (Timqet), and Christmas (Genna), my participation as a pilgrim generally mystified people. Despite my common membership as an Orthodox Christian yet as a marked outsider, I overlooked that the motives and circumstances of my pilgrimage, or *menfesawi guzo* (spiritual journey), were not well defined. I had not made a personal promise. This was poignantly reflected in a colloquial speech—"How did you arrive? How did Gishen receive you?" What I learned from the various pilgrims was that their arrival at a sacred place and the impetus for their commitment gradually became cemented into a personal tradition. I propose that pilgrimages possess the potential of becoming what Robbins (2010b) calls "traditions of innovation" or, put more intrinsically, domains that permit inserting "something new in something old."

This final ethnographic chapter explores the pilgrimage to Gishen Mariam as a context that inspires personal commemorative events, such as memorials or vows, to be transformed into "traditions" that sustainably influence broader communal commitments. A cross-shaped mountain located approximately seventy kilometers away from Dessie, the four churches of Gishen draw heavy flows of believers every September. It is most well known for hosting the relic of the cross of Christ's crucifixion. As a result, a pattern of storytelling about Gishen as holy place features dominantly in pilgrims' experience. The analytical frame of the genre is reincorporated as a way to illuminate this work's central objective: to demonstrate how the methodology of elaboration by Ethiopian Orthodox Christians communicates central values of preserving and protecting sacred ideas and relationships. I explore this argument through the praxis and discourse of Gishen Mariam in order to examine how protecting the relic, or as one pilgrim phrased it, as "serving the Cross," cultivated a sense of moral duty. I position this impetus for personal and collective devotional action alongside the frequency of the vow (*s'let*). The following extended vignette of two pilgrims' movements sets the stage to demonstrate how this branch of devotional culture represents a core essence of vitality of Ethiopian Orthodox Christians.

We had descended Gishen Debre Kirbe, a flat-topped mountain seventy kilometers from Dessie, after the conclusion of the feast of the Falling Asleep (*Erafta*) on Tirr 21 (January 29), which commemorates the departure of St. Mary's soul to heaven. *Qidase* was proclaimed by early morning and built upon with the additional rites of glory and exaltation to St. Mary. The believers moved to an outdoor stage to witness the presentation of the *tabot* and preaching by a few notable clergy. After being released shortly after one in the afternoon, Haile and Fisseha, English teachers by profession and geology students at Wollo University, and I made our way down the mountain. They were eager to get back to the city; they both had term papers to write before having to return from school leave on Monday. We said our goodbyes to the members of St. Gabriel's *mahaber*, who maintained a lodging house near the church grounds and provided the meal and refreshments after the service. Most were busy lounging around drinking *t'ela* (Ethiopian beer) or napping after the long hours at service, which concluded by breaking the fast, which could have been nearly twelve hours long, if you count those who had arrived for vespers the night before. As we made our way down the mountain, Asfaw, one of the leading members of the St. Gabriel Sunday School group, had yelled out to me, "We're family now, the house of Abraham" (*ahun beteseb nin, bet Abraham*). We collected our *gabis*, backpacks, and containers of holy water and set off.

After coming down the first set of high steps, the energy of the environs calmed. The populated paths were deserted, the vendors that sold commemorative T-shirts a day earlier were nowhere to be found, and booths that had blared CDs of devotional songs for sale were inaudible. It was quiet except for a few people huddled around a small *madbet* (kitchen). Haile and Fisseha quickly figured out that the group was a memorial for a middle-aged man's father. His family lived in Gishen, and it had been a year since his father's passing. Following Orthodox Christian tradition, a memorial meal should be prepared one year after the time of death. It was a common practice to share the food by giving out the blessed bread and the *te'la* brewed for this occasion. The host graciously and joyfully extended a bread basket and insisted I partake. Haile and Fisseha hesitated to linger but suggested I taste some of the *te'la* offered, one of them remarking, "You can't refuse such a blessing." We took a seat on the side of the road, sipped quickly from bull-horn cups, and quickly thanked our host.

On the climb down of the second set of steps, we encountered an old man who carried bundles of indiscernible items, likely his bedding and most of his essential belongings. He was a monk, I was told. "Look at the oversized cross around his neck and cross staff made of reinforced steel." His monastic robe was gray with dirt and age. Also, more noticeably, he had nobody around him; he was unaccompanied by family or friends. This unremarkable fact, a monastic's solitude, was discernible and stark in relation to most of the others we met, who traveled collectively. Physically, the *abba* appeared tired, but his energy seemed determined and purposeful, as if resolutely heading to his next task. It was a few weeks before Lent, and it was his aim to spend that time, fifty-five days of fasting and deep prayer, at Debre Libanos Monastery, approximately three hundred kilometers to the south. After much protesting, the monk allowed Haile and Fisseha to carry his things the rest of the way down to the base of Gishen. "Where is he going? How will he get there? How will he manage?" I asked. Reaching the bottom of the mountain, the young men started to ask him about how he planned to get home. "By transport? Mule?" "I'll walk," he said reluctantly, which prompted the men to conclude the monk had no money to catch a bus. Haile gently slid a few ten-birr notes into the monk's hand, gripping his hand as to not allow him to refuse the offer. After a lot of tugging back and forth with the money, Haile suggested the monk bless us for a safe return as a fair exchange. In a hushed and mumbled voice, he recited the Lord's Prayer and Our Lady, followed by his own benediction, wishing us a safe journey. Then he walked away.

The early departers were milling around the buses, some of whose drivers were missing, others waiting to be unblocked from bad parking. Settling on the next bus pulling out, our original crew reassembled and departed. The company I was with, Haile and Fiseha's acquaintances from the Dessie Gabriel parish, were genuinely tired, yet the mood had a palpable sense of calm. There was no reading from prayer books or counting of rosary beads (*mekuteria*), as there had been on the journey *to* Gishen; the tension of anticipation seemed to have dissipated. People started getting phone calls again as we began to approach more network towers: husbands and wives on the other end of the line asking when they would be returning and if they could pick up fruits along the road, as they would be cheaper than goods in the city. After fewer than twenty minutes on the road, we stalled in the intense midday sun: A bus had tumbled on its side and blocked the road. Everyone from the caravan of buses ambled down to see the commotion. No one had perished or was injured, and all the passengers had found spaces on other buses. Several young onlookers started taking photos of the accident on their mobiles. "Look at how close to the edge it is, how it barely missed the cliff," Fisseha exclaimed. Middle-aged women looked on curiously, audibly lamenting. Fisseha prompted me: "Don't you want to take pictures?"—a facetious comment on my copious documentation, which they had witnessed over the past two days. In this instance, I was horrified and a bit stern in my response. "No, I don't see why I should take pictures of an accident. People could have died." What I did not say was how I believed this action glorified tragedy and was a flippant reaction to the fragility of life. He looked at me blankly, not comprehending my indignation. "But it's a miracle [*tamerat*]. They didn't die. This is proof of God's power and love. That's what we are celebrating, what people want to be grateful and thankful for."

After the shock of the incident died down and the requisite amount of time was spent theorizing about how best to extricate the vehicle from obstructing the road, people began to grumble about not moving, and the traffic began to catch up with us. Inside the bus, we remained quiet for a while longer, until it was noticeably silent. Abera, a childhood friend of Haile and Fisseha, exclaimed, "How can we sit like this after reaching such a holy place?" He was almost rebuking our complacency at how quickly we had forgotten the gift of our safe passage. "Let's sing [lit. praise]. Where's the *mizmur* tape?" he called out. The driver's assistant shuffled around for recordings of *mizmur* and but came up empty handed. "What shall we sing?" he threw back at us. There a few grunts from my companions, who laughed off his proposition. Mildly irritated by his friends' lack of support, Abera started off on his own, with a few people joining him at the choruses. A few ladies several rows up began to rhythmically clap in sync with the melody and threw out the missing words when Abera stumbled over forgotten lyrics. Then I noticed Haile and Fisseha next to me mouthed the lines of the songs, their voices louder and more assertive. Before long, the bus had become a raucous choir from this impromptu volley of exuberance. The singing became a seamless performance, principally from this collective of twenty-something men, with one person starting a new tune the moment another had finished. Despite the newfound energy, about an hour or so in, the young men started forgetting the words past the first stanza. The women who fed them lines earlier had apparently transmitted the lyrics down from a young boy seated in the front of the bus. The mystery chorister was revealed and made to take stage in the center aisle, fully reciting six, seven, eight stanzas without pausing. "What about 'Emmanuel'? Do you know how 'Hello to You, My Lord' starts?" Abera and his friends yelled out. Each time, for nearly three hours, the kid provided the lyrics, to the astonishment of his elders. My traveling companions were highly impressed by the ten-year-old boy's fine memory, rewarded him with compliments and cash tips, and beamed with delight at how much "ease and joy" (*q'lal ena desta*) flowed through him.

We neared the outskirts of Dessie as the sun was setting. The kid started to sweetly sing the lyrics to the popular "Our Virgin Mother, Come." Tired from clapping and singing for so long, the men near me participated with little energy, but with each passing stanza they became more enthusiastic, eventually bellowing the lyrics.

The kid: *Bechighnet kefu angete yasdefale*
cheineqatene ababeso lekefu yesetale
anchi neye kegone kaleshe aleshenafem
lazihe alem monynete ejene aleseteme

> Loneliness is harsh (lit. evil)
> Makes one bow one's head in suffering
> If you are beside me, I will not be defeated
> I will not fall prey to the foolish ways of this world.

Start of clapping and ululating:

Everyone: *Denegel enate neye dereshelenyi*
wagane yalegnem ena yamiyatsnanagni
kategebe hunyina ayezosh bayenyi

> Our Virgin Mother, come, arrive for me
> I do not have kin that will comfort me
> Be near me and strengthen me.

A purely metaphor-focused analysis would render Fisseha's and Haile's actions as an accurate plotting of the covenant refractions as I have presented this idea in this book. The fellowship of the *mahaber*, glossed as *bete Abraham*, was an important reference to the potent allegory of chosen people. The roadside *zikir* demonstrated the seal of covenant, an act of remembrance that produced a blessing that dispersed to any and all passing through this event—a materiality of grace enacted via social merging. The emotionalized insistence to be properly grateful initiated a spontaneous performance, idiosyncratic to each praise maker, to give thanks (*temesgen*). I caution against interpreting these thematic reoccurrences of Ethiopia's covenant idea in praxis as predetermining devotional action. To note the pervasiveness of paradigmatic thinking is to recognize how imbricated theological ideas are in cultural outlooks, a result of processual interactions between discourse and praxis (Hanks 1987). My analytical pursuit is to further extend the framework of covenant refractions and examine how it can be considered a historical feature of the ingenuity of Tradition to function as a resourceful strategy for adapting to contemporary cultural change.

The Holographic Relic

Every year on the twenty-first of Meskerem (September), around a quarter of a million people climb the mountain of Amba Gishen and celebrate the arrival of the piece of the True Cross in 1446. Located seventy kilometers away from Dessie, pilgrims from all over the country congregate to celebrate this event on the feast day of St. Mary at the church of her namesake. The Cross's arrival in Ethiopia is a story well elaborated by Orthodox Christians, whether they make the pilgrimage or not. It is a story that connects several historical epochs and commemorative occasions. The basic timeline of this history is as follows: In the fourth century in Constantinople, Queen Eleni, the mother of Emperor Constantine, vowed to find the cross of the Crucifixion. After half a year of excavation, it was found and eventually divided into four pieces, bestowed to the churches in Alexandria, Antioch, Constantinople, and Jerusalem, with the right arm given to the Church of Alexandria. In the fifteenth century, as a reward for Ethio-Egyptian military cooperation, the relic of the True Cross was transferred to Ethiopia, where it has remained since.

The legends of Gishen are creatively articulated by a variety of sources and perspectives, transforming the holy place into a domain that inspires pilgrims to attach symbolic connections to amplify its spiritual significance. I propose that there is a common methodology for how believers elaborate upon Gishen as a place, legend, and relationship that is found in the ways that the Ethiopian story of the covenant is described. Symbolic layers added by Ethiopian Orthodox Christians act as a way to fortify the potency of the ark or relics and indicate how the covenant refractions enter new contexts and circumstances.

In order to understand the layered aspects of Gishen as a pilgrimage site, I look at the celebration as it is ritually and temporally positioned in the liturgical program that starts with the feast of Meskel (the Exaltation of the Cross). This is a feast and bonfire ceremony that celebrates the discovery, or "exaltation," of the True Cross by Queen Eleni in the fourth century. Not only is the universal Christian community recalling a pivotal event in Church history, but pilgrims to Gishen are stepping into their journey, four days later, on the heels of this massive, wide-scale celebration, and their participation serves as an endpoint in this scripturally inspired narrative. Taken linearly, the connection between Meskel to Gishen is the excavation of the relic in the fourth century and then the deposition of that relic at Gishen in the fifteenth century by King Zara Yacob on the 21st of Meskerem, St. Mary's feast. As a temporal sequence, these commemorative movements retain a tight continuity. However, several aspects indicate the recurring theme of the textual convergences as a method of spiritual importance and reification.

Figure 16. Church of Egzeiabher Ab' (God the Father).

Two details drew my attention to the curious temporal registers, which behaved contrary to chronological logic. The place of Gishen is considered holy because it possessed the True Cross. However, the church where this item is held is not regarded as a shrine to be approached, nor does the namesake of the church, Egzeiabher Ab' (God the Father), celebrated the 29th of every month, elicit any special attention (see Figure 16).

Instead, the focus is on the date of deposition, St. Mary's day (the 21st of every month in the Ethiopian calendar), and the alignment with her defines movements to Gishen so much so that the location is abbreviated as Gishen Mariam and not by any of the other three churches there. The legend of Gishen as it was historicized in the popular imagination required viewing historical events as converging. This issue became most obvious when I noted the confusion regarding who or what we were commemorating: Queen Eleni's assistance to uncover the True Cross; the help of another historic Eleni (a sister of King Zara Yacob), which was instrumental in securing a place for the relic at Gishen; or St. Mary herself. Or perhaps all three simultaneously?

Figure 17. The exhibition of Negest Eleni during Meskel, September 2011.

Pilgrimage to Gishen Mariam falls in the month of Meskerem, a time of renewal marked by the end of the rains and with several holidays commemorating a seasonal shift. Erecting bonfires is an act that characterizes this time of year and corresponds to the memorialized act of Queen Eleni's discovery. Memhir Eshetu, a deacon well educated in Church history, proceeded to tell me this story, which had tropic similarities to another nationally revered item, the ark in Axum (*Tabota Tsion*). Casting the dramatis personae as if he were himself an intimate eyewitness, Memher Eshetu stated that Queen Eleni was the principal figure who succeeded, following the advice of a holy man, in finding the True Cross, which had been buried under a garbage heap for three hundred years. The pageantry of the cross during the Meskel celebrations on the 17th of Meskerem included a serialized play of this history, the Ethiopian Orthodox Tewahedo Church's equivalent to the Stations of the Cross, common in Catholic devotional culture, with Negest Eleni (Queen Eleni) paraded out in a pickup truck (Figure 17).

The culmination of this celebration is the bonfire (*demera*) that reenacts how Queen Eleni was instructed to erect a large fire that would produce drifting smoke leading to the location of the hidden Cross. This narrative as performed demonstrates the interlinked aspects of the Gishen legend: The Archbishop of Wollo and the diocese urged attendees to continue the commemoration four days later, thereby presenting the pilgrimage to Gishen as a sequel to Meskel.

When piecing together all the details of the legend of Gishen Mariam, I was told by Memhir Eshetu, a deacon and theology student, to collect all the histories of Gishen, as all the legends are facts (*hulum tewufit ynetinyaw*). I was struck by the self-consciousness behind the multiplicity of historiography, in response to my question about which Eleni was responsible for the Cross's entrance into Ethiopia. In Memhir Eshetu's narration, Ethiopian Orthodox tradition fast-forwards to the fifteenth century, when the Cross reaches its present location (seventy kilometers north of Dessie), via subsequent stopovers along the terrain, to churches in Addis and Debre Berhan (ninety kilometers north), an intertextual reference to another legend of miraculous endowment of Dersane Urael, the Homily of St. Urael (see Chapter 4). The identity of the central character of the narrative, Queen Eleni, became ambiguous as I probed Memhir Eshetu further. Thinking perhaps he had misunderstood me or I him, I asked directly: Who was the main proponent for having the relic deposited at Gishen, Queen Eleni of the fourth century or Queen Eleni of the fifteenth? His reply, that I was asking about one and the same person, I found perplexing, but this matched other observations I had encountered about the malleability of historical time for Ethiopians. This literary manipulation relates to what Bakhtin (1981) has theorized about the novelistic genre and the interaction between the languages of the narrator and author, which he labels as a "dialogic tension" (314). As I stress here, the chronicling of Gishen is a multiauthorial venture, but one that unites under linguistic conventions influenced by "verbal-ideological history," which "is not a unity of a single, closed language system, but is rather a highly specific unity of several 'languages' that have established contact and mutual recognition with each other" (295). Narrators of Gishen are actively engaging with a genre of storytelling that permits their interpretations of miraculous provenance.

Memhir Eshetu's statement that all the legends are facts was hardly considered by him to be a radical comment on Ethiopian historiography but rather pointed to the proclivity for creative retelling and layering of the past.

The conflation of the refracted subject of the holiday and the manner in which history overlaps substantiate the potency of significance and illustrate a patterning of historiography that departs from the Western-guided orientation of linear time. Stewart (2012) examines the tendency for post-Enlightenment thought to produce a historical thinking that clings to chronology as a guarantee to manageably record and keep the past. As I evaluated in Chapter 5 in the case of Herani's *zikir*, an issue of who was being memorialized was investigated, and this was likewise an issue of merging together several generations of ancestors and their devotions to Medhane Alem ("Savoir of the World," i.e., Jesus Christ). The objective of honor in commemorations thus operated as a link in a chain, as the established relationship between the bearers of tradition, past and present (from grandfather to granddaughter), and their historical connection to the saint moved interconnectedly. The past was a resource to bring into the present by creating new order in the sequence of people's lives.

The foundation story of Gishen was repeated in various ways, in preaching programs, on historical DVDs, in pamphlets, and most frequently by the pilgrims themselves. Darge, a Gondare driver from Addis, knew the sole monk in charge of entering and guarding the lower chambers of Egzeiabher Ab Church. There were three vaults of passages before reaching the guarded item, the right arm of the True Cross. Abba Hawas, referred to by the title *senter ayetam* (lit. "he will not be in need of a splinter"), could access the second layer but never entered the third. Darge had had the unusual opportunity to speak to this monk during a previous trip to Gishen, casually among several other visitors to the church compound. Darge learned this information secondhand through clergy who spoke of corpses of holy men and deserving souls transported by eagles ("symbolizing angels," as he decoded to me), interned on the grounds of Gishen. Another legend that circulated concerned the late Patriarch Paulos, who was reputed to have tried to enter the church's chambers, resulting in a fire erupting at the entrance to the third level. Those who could come into contact with relics were restricted, even for monarchs, as illustrated in the legend of Emperor Menelik's incident, who fell ill as a result of attempting to approach numerous relics, such as soil from Jerusalem, brought during the same expedition in the fifteenth century, housed in the stores of the church. "*Egzeiabher alasfekedum*," Memhir Eshetu stated to me. That it has to be God's permission was a sentiment that extended to contemporary pilgrims' journeys to Gishen.

Pilgrims often marveled at the unique physical terrain: Gishen is a cross-shaped mountain, and this fact was spoken about nearly as frequently as the place's possession of the relic. At Gishen, a common activity was to trace the contours of the mountain and visit all four churches during the course of the pilgrimage (see Figure 18). Anthropological studies of pilgrimages, such as Bowman's (1991), emphasize the interplay of intersubjective narratives of experience, political histories of the holy site, and the construction of discourses by several interpretive communities. In the case of Orthodox communities, both in Jerusalem and in Gishen, more than the attachments to articulated sacredness of the place, via icons or holy water for instance, it is the fact of being in Jerusalem during the holy feast days that "significant realism of the holy places comes in play" (111). The crucial nexus that differentiates the various contestations of the Holy Land are how pilgrims direct their "meditations of their imaginations" (114). For Ethiopian Orthodox pilgrims to Gishen, there is a literalism to holy places—pilgrims sleep in churches, drink holy tea, and tread sacred soil to be further exposed to God—that is materially mediated. Laity are not mining for meaning or content but instead searching for channels toward spiritual transfiguration.

At Gishen, Memhir Aklilu informed me that "everything here is holy, even that cup of tea you're drinking." Others made similar statements, such as that the earth and the air here contained pure and special properties. Regarding the holy water, consumed with immense vigor, liter after liter, like "taking medicine," as several pilgrims put it, pilgrims on the edges of the mountain pointed down toward the direction of a tunnel that connects the Gishen mountain to Jerusalem and from where the water is sourced. This element in the Gishen corpus of tales serves as one example of the inventive conceptions of the place based on pilgrims' interactions with its popular imaginings. This part of the legend, of how the Cross had gone underground in multiple cases of gold and wood and chained at the bottom of the Church of Egzeiabher Ab', was retold with particular animation. In the tale of what Memhir Eshetu labeled the "Cross's journey" to Ethiopia, each stop along the way to the cross-shaped mountain was bathed in sound and radiant light, until it reached its resting place. The relic's great power, radiating all over Ethiopia and curing all ailments and afflictions, was deemed too intense for human eyes and has since its deposition been buried three vaults deep. The sacredness of the place then has been buried, hidden, mystified, made uncontainable in a single location, and spread to

Figure 18. At one of the arms of Amba Gishen, with Abera, Fisseha, and Haile (l–r) for the Feast of the Dormition, January 30, 2011.

all corners of the Cross' terrain. The mountain *is* the relic itself and indicates how a material center, a notion of a contained shrine and locatable sacrality, takes on new forms.

The Cross has a further textual hagiography, the Chronicles of the Cross, called the Meshafe Tefut.[1] This book was considered one of the treasures of Gishen and was cited often as the source of all these miraculous stories. This book was afforded its own mini-procession during the pilgrimage event, being ushered onto the stage as grandly as the Holy Book. Parts of the legend, such as the trials of the kings and the Cross's journey into Ethiopia, were parsed out in short recited narratives and read at such select times of the year. These readings were considered part of the pilgrims' program, to hear these stories at this holy place, representing a creation of a sacred knowledge being disseminated in a manner reflective of how feast days were structured by the reading of saint hagiographies (*gedl*), which contain testimonies of their *kidan* (see Introduction). What was striking in the case of the Meshafe Tefut was that individuals treated the chronicle as a sacred item. Hence the textual elaboration of a relic developed holographically, much like was theorized for *aqwaqwam* prayers at Timqet. To apprehend a sacred item in material form, additional refractions were necessary to construct its realism for believers.

Most all of these historical testimonies and experiences were retold at second hand: The author was never a direct witness. Given what I have proposed about linguistic veiling as a methodology of elaboration and protection, similar issues were active at Gishen, particularly as they related to gender as a "corrupting component" of sacred space. Unlike Hayk Estephanos (forty kilometers north of Dessie),[2] where only men are allowed, Gishen is not a monastery and so permits women to enter the grounds. Boylston (2012) studied the stratified hierarchies between people and their lived cosmos in Zege (in northwestern Ethiopia) and the materialities that mediate relations between this and the other world. "Pollution" in Ethiopian Orthodox dogma is a condition that perpetually requires what Boylston describes as "limiting social connection and social entanglements so as to facilitate contact and mediation with God" (120). Given the fact that adhering to ritual prohibitions such as abstinence or fasting was not sustainable for everyone, this standard applied primarily for clergy on the spiritual behalf of the wider community. On occasion, individuals feared coming close to the church building because of their own awareness of being unclean. When I visited a church with Mekonen, a graduate student, he pointed out a few people standing next to graves on the outer ring of the church compound, which was, in his opinion, a mark of their conscious, polluted state being communicated (to God, to others, and to themselves). Mekonen then reflected on how he typically felt more confident coming up to the church steps to do *mesalem* or celebrate *qidase* during periods when he is not sexually active. In one encounter, during the *wazema* of the Dormition feast in January, I was questioned on my state of purity by my fellow *mahaber* companion Weizero Wube: "Can you take *qurban*? Are you clean?"

Given its especially hallowed distinction of housing this relic of the Holy Cross, as a woman, I would never be able to visit Egzeiabher Ab' Church, which was explained with recourse to a legend of women turning into stone when attempting to enter. Yemeselech, a young woman from Dessie who took me around the exteriors of the church, was less concerned about our potential to corrupt sacred matter.[3] We passed along a short grove of acacia trees typical of traditional churches and walked to the right, to the women's side. Though I saw no women in the compound, not long after we entered it, a man dressed in a white *gabi*, not strictly lay clothing yet not a mark of any special clerical authority either, sternly raised his voice at her, reminding her that I was not allowed in. She reassured him that we knew and that I was just being shown the outside of the church. Using the occasion to ask how this restriction made her feel, she first set my mind at rest, lightheartedly acknowledging that some people take themselves too seriously. However, she was unquestioning that these customs are there for a reason. As spending time in the church complex was part of the pilgrimage experience, the polluting position of women in Orthodox dogma and devotional culture influenced movements on the mountain. Reflecting on dimensions of Gishen as a place, legend, and relationship to maintain, we can relate Yemeselech's action to how the place's "center" is treated as its most dangerous property.

As I discussed in Chapter 3, the styles of veneration in Ethiopian Orthodox worship are characterized by a particular approach to its devotional culture. I refer again to the terminological issue of the ark (*tabot*) being conflated or flatly mistranslated as "replica" or "relic." In the context of Gishen, the Cross is a relic but is seldom displayed publicly, as compared to Eastern Christian traditions in Greece and Russia, where relics are often interacted with through glass cases. The best way to illustrate how Amharic speakers define a holy object such as the Cross is to note the lack of a qualifier of "relic" (*qers*) or even the partial aspect of the item, since I never heard anyone refer to the relic held at Gishen as "part of the Cross." This terminological ambiguity is similar to how any *tabot* can easily be confused with the *tabot* in Axum. The subterranean position of the relic and the sense of abandonment I experienced when I approached the church compound reemphasized the embodiment of reverence, which is a perpetual calibration of proximity to sacred space/time.

As described by many pilgrims journeying to Gishen, believers arrived in time to hear *wazema* and stayed all through the night until the morning liturgy. Many who have not formulated an explicit devotional program articulated the opportunity of experiencing the liturgy at this special place and time. This resembles what Humphrey and Laidlaw (1994) label as a "prescriptive ontology," that is, ritual actions that are shaped by their established efficacy, which is analyzed through various modes of making *puja*, a daily ritualized form of Hindu worship (103). The practice of sleeping in the church's compound and hearing hymns intoned over the course of the night was popular because of the belief in gaining "grace" by exposure to such concentrated prayer. This quality of liturgical space/time is consistent with the notion of the materiality of prayer, which I investigated as a type of sonic iconography, and physical movements as a type of ritual image (see Chapters 2 and 3). In those case studies of ordinary and extraordinary events during the liturgical year, I showcased how the diversity of actors, such as the confluence of liturgies performed in a given parish, are phenomenologically and conceptually understood as one worshiping body. Amid the intervals of chaos that cluttered a pilgrimage event, participants always pulled together for prayer and celebration. At Gishen, middle-aged to elderly women who had come to receive communion went at the start of evening prayer. At this stage, people began to light candles outside and inside the church, an activity that continued until sunrise. Another group, younger men and women who are religiously conscious, typically secured a spot for themselves to rest and sleep on the church grounds, joined by their friends or other family members around 4 AM. More pilgrims began trickled in from 6 AM on and arrived from all parts of the mountain. The main point of attraction was St. Mary's church, where the archbishop of South Wollo, Abune Atnateos, and other high clergy presided over the service. However, the celebrants hear the service read from the other three churches of Egzeiabher Ab', St. Mikael, and St. Gabriel, as well. The surrealism and holism of uniform ritual performed in a diversity of places in a location as remote as Gishen served as the embodied "center" of the devotional experience for pilgrims. It is surreal given the intersecting echoes of the same encompassing object, the divine liturgy.

The climax of the Gishen pilgrimage, the service of St. Mary on the 21st, was defined by its mythohistorical legacy, and this reality served as the foundation for Gishen's "spiritual magnetism" (Pruess 1992). The ritual commemoration of the relic's arrival assumed a more potent position in participants' engagement than any encountering with the relic itself. This would seem to go against the established anthropological literature on pilgrimage, which identifies the focal point of holy sites to a locatable entity such as a shrine. The relic of the Cross supports what Bajc, Coleman, and Eade (2007) describe as the objectified destination of pilgrimage being movable. The dispersing nature of pilgrims' movements in several essences, either as physical or through the narratives of their experiences, underscores the fractal-like "scales of complexity, as they both mirror the centring at archetypal destinations and express a potential for transformation. They may also begin to form their own patterns of centring" (325–26). The narrative, phenomenological, and devotional encounters of Gishen pilgrims reflect this phenomenon. The subject of celebration is immaterialized, as no one ever witnesses this relic. People only know of its potency though its legends and, more dynamically, through a series of calendar observances that illustrate and embody its encompassment.

Throughout this book, I have endeavored to propose a framework that considers how the devotional culture of Orthodox Christians renders covenant refractions as part of a methodology of elaboration. The narrative elaborations and the liturgical orientations of Gishen pilgrims suggest that its generic resemblances are a method of exemplifying a cultural idea but also an exhaustion of the resources of explanation in indigenous thought (Wagner 2001, 45). The muted fact that the mountain holds a piece of the True Cross perhaps makes more sense if other domains of creative expression are brought into the fray of observation, such as the chronicling of the legend and charitable acts to St. Mary as "gifts to Gishen." These activities are also methods that allow the relic to live as a contemporary phenomenon, one that is discursively consistent, such that devotional activities contribute to a unified objective to honor the role of God in the daily lives of individuals and communities.

To arrange a paradigmatic symmetry between the Cross and the covenant underscores the dialogic nature of protection as a principle of responsibility that cuts both ways, as a blessing and a burden. To illustrate this point, I refer to what Natnael labeled as foreigners' misconceptions about Ethiopian claims to holy relics. This conversation was spurred by an episode when visiting the church exterior of Egzeiabher Ab'. Quiet and nearly abandoned, I spoke of my confusion to Natnael, a supporter of the Church and a native of Dessie, about the muted nature of the relic at Gishen, both materially and liturgically redirected toward honoring St. Mary. "Of course, anyone could just take it [the relic of the Cross]," I was told by Natnael. This represented the crux of what Natnael took as Western ignorance about Ethiopia's claims to Christian heritage. Communicating in English: "I hate when they [foreigners] say we guard the ark." This was a preposterous proposition to him. Ethiopia has been entrusted to protect the Cross and thereby was "protected by it," as Natnael phrased. One not merely guards but serves the Cross. The fact that they, the community of Ethiopian Orthodox Christians, continue to hold this

Figure 19. Billboard of attractions in Amhara region, reflecting a sea change in Gishen's access to the broader public.

providential role is Gishen's reoccurring miracle and the substantive essence behind the historicity of the legend.

For Ethiopian Orthodox Christians, particularly those who advocate for the protection of remote churches and monasteries, the fear of losing Christian heritage often appears in people's statements about how these places cannot be publicized openly (Figure 19). This relates to the approach of preservation, which is exhibited in intense protectionism bordering on paranoia. The fear of losing these treasures is real and provokes cataclysmic reactions. One such example was relayed to me in conversation about the incident when an ancient cross was smuggled out of the country by an art collector, which provoked deep mourning by the townspeople of Lalibela. As I have detailed, techniques of linguistic shrouding and material obscuring are indicators of covenant refractions.[4] One encounter with a monk who quickly surmised that I was a Protestant missionary reflected this tendency to suspect and fear outsiders. "We have to be careful these days," he said, adding, "Ethiopia is slowly slipping out of our fingers," while he turned back to me and inquired about whom I would share my research with and that I should know that in the wrong hands it could bring harm. Unlike Natnael's attitude, which eschewed any pretense that human efforts can block the fate of divine election, that is, the futility of "guarding," the monk espoused the opposite sentiment via his nervousness toward me, insisting on putting up walls to the outside (non-Orthodox) world. What both viewpoints represent is the moral imperative of covenant as protecting and preserving sacred items and relationships, which is characterized as an honor and a responsibility.

Personal journeys to Gishen compose a corpus of popular legends that are circulated among pilgrims. Just as there are established stories of Gishen, tales of brushes with death in contemporary pilgrims' experiences circulated as widely. Here, I recall Haile's pointed remark to me as we walked down from Gishen about being thankful for witnessing God's love, exhibited by the fact that no one had died in that bus accident. This episode relates to what Shenoda (2012) characterizes as being impressed by "gestures which God makes," borrowing Wittgenstein's phrasing of the "conception of the miraculous, one that is largely contextual, one that relied on interpretation and one's willingness . . . to be impressed by such gestures or accounts of them" (481). The following section briefly evaluates the narrative trope of "miracles as a challenge to faith" and as a regenerative domain that adds new content to traditions of pilgrimage.

Miracles as Testing Faith

Gishen as a recurring miracle in the popular imagination is active in several essences. First pilgrimages are an activity of devotional culture that contains "exaggerated risks," where difficulties experienced by individuals effectively confirm the exceptional, such as the merit in arriving at the mountain successfully. In the case of Gishen, given the reckless drivers, blocked roads, close calls, and accidents experienced en route, a pilgrim was sufficiently nervous by the time they arrived at the foot of the mountain. People also openly contemplated worst-case scenarios and recalled anecdotes about how dangerous a pilgrimage had been for their friends and acquaintances. On several occasions I was shown a leaflet marketing the miracles of Gishen that showcased photographs of buses dangling off the side of the mountain. Getting to the destination was a veritable gauntlet, with sheep and donkeys and throngs of people fighting for a meter and a half of passage space. The threat of danger and the encounters of trouble on the road composed part of the spiritual journey and was interpreted as a form of penance. The Turners analyze this part of the "liminoid" experience and reference Catholic folklore on extreme sinners whose moral decay was so great that they were prevented from completing the pilgrimage (Turner and Turner 1978). This aspect was made personal to me on another occasion when I took an unscheduled trip to Lalibela, one of the nation's most holy sites. It was a thoroughly dangerous journey for me, with several near fatal moments. This was explained to me as being caused by my lack of intention and for not having made a commitment that was devotionally sourced.

The theme of cleansing and spiritual renewal as it relates to the sacred geography of Gishen was exemplified by the ritual at the Teleyayen River, which translated as "we are separated." At about the midpoint between Dessie and Gishen, a river crossed the road, making it only traversable during certain times of the year, after the rainy season had concluded. It remained a firm practice that all vehicles stop at this point in order for people to bathe at the river. Some people washed their upper bodies, but most dipped their feet and waded awhile in the waters. It is believed that one must wash away all the sins and evil they carry before approaching a holy site. The liminal atmospherics of the threshold is a mainstay belief in Orthodox Christianity regarding the ambiguous zones between sacred and profane space (Paxson 2006). Therefore, a trip to Gishen was understood as leaving another world behind, and the work of this act was punctuated by such phenomenological orientations.

The sense of the momentousness and merit of arrival intensified as the road became harder and people had to go the rest of the way "by oneself" (*berasachew*), thereby turning the entrance to a holy place into an equalizing experience. A cultural code was enacted during this last leg, the point where I noticed a more pronounced performative dimension to the pilgrim's trail. People began to pause out of exhaustion, exclaiming "*ayzoh, ayzosh, ayzot*" for the elderly, essentially meaning "it's OK. Relax." The significance of this phrase in Amharic vocabulary as a humanizing metonymy was later made apparent by Sister Teshale, from the Kobo Ursaline congregation, who enjoyed reminding me that *ayzoh*, literally "be still" in Amharic, was a phrase from Scripture repeated frequently in the Bible. On the trail, these words were kindly and compassionately uttered, often by men who briskly passed the slower travelers. "You're almost there. *Berchi*" ("hang in there" or "be strong"). However, it was those who were physically struggling and out of breath that were repeating this phrase to their traveling companions. I would often be a target for sympathy. "*Ayzosh, Ayzosh,*" I would hear softly behind me as I felt slight pressure on my back, people leaning on me both to push me up and for their own support. The gates at the top of the mountain made for an impressive image, one often described to me as emblematizing the joy and relief upon arrival. Older men and women uttered "*temesgen, temesgen*" ("thanks be to God") successively and rhythmically upon climbing the stairs. Some paused, raised their hands emphatically, and kissed the ground. Similarly, Stanley's analysis of the Maharashtrian pilgrimage illustrates how the pilgrims' bodily movements are altered as the journey progresses, particularly as the individuals join together to form a mass unit, linked in their shared "performance" (Morinis 1992, 74). Haile and Fisseha instructed our company to ululate as we approached the top, making sure to express the gratitude and joy we felt at beholding such a remarkable site. These stages along the journey were used to mark one's proximity to God. These utterances were a form of embodied action, a corporeal testing being enacted by the pilgrims (Coleman and Eade 2004, 16). In this pilgrims' process of passage, the journey and arrival to the place was sweeter than the reward of remaining at Gishen, the proverbial anticlimax to anticipation.

Just as these stories of fatefully overcoming danger evoked the trope of spiritual challenge, so did ones of tragic occurrences. A heartbreaking story circulated after the Ethiopian New Year 2004 (2011 in the Gregorian calendar), of a wife and husband who had lost their young son in an awful accident: The father, not noticing the child, who had wandered behind his car, ran him over. As devastating as the death was, the added injury was that the mother was en route to Gishen Mariam during this time to conduct her yearly pilgrimage. To engage in a spiritually worthy activity while simultaneously having such a destructive force occur operated as a central paradox for those remarking on this story exemplifying the unknowability of God's intention in everyday life. It also served to stress Gishen as a place to be reckoned with. The popular hagiography of Gishen as authored by Ethiopian Orthodox believers was continuously furnished with new material, which was added into its popular canon. The following section considers how vows catalyze charity at Gishen. I argue that these individual promises to give are a crucial transacting force behind the sustainability of churches and contribute to greater social impacts to continue pilgrimage as a personal or group tradition.

Vows as Tradition Making

Vows (*s'let*), an individualized promise, as contrasted to one applied to a group of people, such as a covenant, resemble more closely an oath as a unidirectional offering. Herzfeld (1990) offers an archetypal definition: "The oath intimates the terrors of divine punishment. . . . A man whose word proves worthless is a mere husk, a body without socially recognized spirituality. It is through the hand," referring to the hand on the icon of the saint, "that a man realises that spirituality" (308). This characterization highlights how vows are agreements enacted by devotees to pledge oneself to God in exchange for a favor conferred. Furthermore, the vow as a form of promise making fosters interventions, both earthly and divine.

Promises as interventions addressed and granted by saints inspire thinking about notions of disassociated will. Mittermaier (2012) discusses dream stories in a Sufi community in Egypt that engage with "idioms of being acted upon," which, in Chakrabarty's words, seek "to account for histories that involve 'gods, spirits and supernatural agents alongside humans'" (in Mittermaier 2012, 256). *S'let* for Ethiopian Orthodox Christians is inspired by addressing everyday dilemmas by channeling them through charity. The first section will examine petitions to Mary as interacting with the dimensions of her covenant (*Kidane Meheret*). I will then consider the motivations for coming to Gishen that evolve from a personal drive to give back to the Church.

S'let *and the Appeal*

Before making my first pilgrimage to Gishen, I had learned of the place from a story about my great-grandmother. Eteye Marta, her close confidant, recounted how in 1934 my grandmother was not only baptized but given to the Church of Mariam at Gishen. I was puzzled by this detail, how could one be "given" to a church? I thought she might have meant St. Mary, but I was mistaken. She was given to the *tabot* (*le tabot new yetesetechew*), the tabot of St. Mary acting as a godparent in place of a person. A baptism by the *tabot* differs in that the child is given to deacons and priests at the altar. They receive her or him with a piece of the *tabot* cover that is used specifically for such baptisms. This custom is commonly understood as a result of a vow, an indication of unusual circumstances that propel the person to make this bonded, formal promise. From then on, a *tabot* child (*ye tabot lij*) is known as the godchild of Gishen Mariam.

S'let to Mary continues to operate strongly for expectant mothers whose previous failed pregnancies caused anxiety and pressure from their families. One such case occurred on a pilgrimage to Moye Mariam in the Northern Shoa region (two hundred kilometers south of Dessie) on the feast commemorating St. Mary's birthday (Lideta). A lady in her early thirties was featured throughout the service. The *tabot* had made its procession around the church, and the offerings were being made to the church, such as grains, legumes, candles, chickens, perfume bottles, small change, and a pair of goats. Some of these items were then immediately auctioned for the benefit of the church. However, one set of items, ceremonial church umbrellas, was exhibited to the small congregation and accompanied by the story of the lady who gave these items to the church. She had been barren for many years, and her inability to conceive had caused her great anguish. She pleaded with Mariam for help, and once her pregnancy was a success she resolved to show her gratitude to a church reputed for its miraculous *tabot*. I was told that had this story not concluded so positively, she would still be bound to fulfill her promise to Mariam, since a prayer was proclaimed in her name, and this promise was unbreakable.

These two cases of vows, both to St. Mary, contained a binding commitment to fulfill a promise and underscore St. Mary's importance as the bearer of appeals. This was stressed by Selam, a pilgrim whom I accompanied to Moye Mariam that turned to me during service and with the deepest sincerity possible insisted to me that I pray to Mary, as "she listens" (*Mariam semalich*). St. Mary is the central figure of intercession; this is further substantiated by the popularity of Kidane Meheret. This covenant refers to the trials of St. Mary, who came to pray at her son's grave at Golgotha ("place of the skull," Mark 15:22) and pleaded with God to allow her to do this peacefully and without persecution. She received protection from the angels and was taken to heaven, at which time the covenant of protection was bestowed to her.

People construct their vows guided by the established Orthodox Christian liturgical orientations to space/time. This is framed by a major feast day, a culmination of a major fast period, or a journey to a place that holds special meaning to the person. To refer back to a direct citation of Kidane Meheret, I present Belainesh's *s'let*, who made a vow to weave a basket for Kidane Meheret. She interpreted a recent dream of hers where St. Mary exclaimed to her, "Have you forgotten me?" This indicated her neglect to pay heed or respect to the protective power of Kidane Meheret. She worked on the basket for many months, intending to present it as a gift to Kidane Meheret on her annual feast day, Yekatit 16 [February] (Figure 20). She also considered it important to give this item to a specific Kidane Meheret church, rather than the one in her neighborhood. Though she stressed that

Figure 20. Belainesh presenting the *mesob* (basket for Kidane Meheret on her feast day, Yekatit 16).

it was a tribute to St. Mary and that any church dedicated to her would do, this particular one was well known for its *tabot* and holy water.

I have remarked that once the vow has been communicated, it is nonnegotiable, regardless whether the result is granted. This contrasts with Orsi's study (1985) of Catholic devotion in Harlem, New York City, where one devotee refused to continue praying to St. George because he stopped listening. On one hand, this rather human frustration reflects an intimacy between saints and devotees but also speaks to the character of relations intrinsic to devotion. I contend that for Ethiopian Orthodox Christians, expectations of outcomes are deliberately left open-ended because the risks of rupturing the links in the relationship are considered detrimental. For individuals like Belainesh, the indispensable use of holy water by Ethiopian Orthodox Christians served as an appropriate parallel, in that the indeterminacy of holy water represents staying committed to the human/divine relationship. Holy water was a solvent for solutions in many daily predicaments. It enabled approaches of formulating know-how that equipped individuals with a deepened sense of awareness of their limitations at achieving control over results, and it established and reinforced proximity to divine power. Holy water at one level is, then, a material intervention, which contains real intercessory power that places responsibility on individuals through an expanding sociality of problem solving. It was a form of robust knowledge, formulated by allowing space for things to go wrong, a failsafe to make sure the condition is not willed to fail. When Belainesh's child got lice, her recourse was to use holy water despite her knowledge and access to clinics and medicine. Her strategy was guided by a logical calculation based on an efficacious deployment of this material in the past. Since holy water solved the problem, or, I should say, improved the condition over time, this made holy water a material whose utility was confirmed by a faith in the authoritative agency of human/divine cooperation. What her actions showed was that devotion to a saint via their curative materials was a condition of working at a relationship.

As the customs of *s'let* and *mahaber* meetings have indicated, devotion is the driving action of all engagement with the Holy. Amit Desai (2010), discussing the nature of *bhakti* (devotion or devotionalism) in Hindu sects, identifies how devotees reapply practical experience into how they evaluate their moral stances in relation to their religious identification. One crucial means of "participating in God" is through understanding suffering as managed through dependency (e.g., total submission). Continued crisis is interpreted as a failure to keep this divine promise and the structural links of devotion that bind it. Correct devotional practices also promote different grades of relationships, as *bhakti* devotees reject and/or modify the nature of their commitment as part of the process of refashioning themselves as stronger members of their *panth* (sect). What this discussion shows is that the efficacy of the relationship to the saint is reflected in continued commitment, which is constantly reappraised. In the following section, I provide examples of how individuals' commitments, through their ability to influence others to make similar promises, as a type of "contagious giving," correspond to these aspirations to strengthen bonds that rely on dialectical and collaborative effort.

Gifting as Mobilizing Orthodox Christians

On pilgrimage, the tradition of almsgiving is an integral part of devotional action. On the road and slopes around the rugged backcountry, deacons and priests with ceremonial umbrellas and a poster-icon (a laminated photo-reproduction) of popular saints such as Mikael, Gabriel, and/or Mariam ask for alms. Ignoring their outreached hands was considered a grave error on the part of traveler. The period that led up to a feast day represented a special time when pilgrims must give and indicated a fellowship for the alms seeker, *yene beete*. The symbolism communicates how the giver is the same as the taker—we are all in need of something that someone will grant us (i.e., I, as the giver, could end up as the seeker). On saint days in parish churches, the same pattern of alms making existed. Priests and deacons supervised the flow of donations to the church and saint via the stations of large framed portraits of the patron saint of the church, with its side lace curtains unveiled in honor of the day. Church umbrellas are turned upside down, and monetary donations are placed in them. Incidentally, the same items are used to cover *tabots* when they leave the *bete meqdes*, hence demonstrating a ritual transfiguration of earthly tokens used for sacred purposes. A long row of alms seekers, who typically call out *"se'le Mariam"* (in the name of Mary), are stationed by the church gates. People then placed their coins for each person in front of a cloth or plastic covering. While the almsgiving was performed seemingly almost as a perfunctory obligation, many include this activity in their *s'let*, as did Belainesh, who gave to the *yene beetoch* at the completion of her vow.

On their spiritual journey to Gishen, Haile and Fisseha approached the wandering ascetics and *kolo tamariwoch* in much the same way. The *kolo tamariwoch* are fixtures on the pilgrimage circuit, the literal translation being "grain students," as they subsist based on donations and goodwill. They are teenage boys from about fourteen to seventeen who are students of the traditional Church schools and survive through the charity of fellow Christians. These students, who can be blind or maimed, travel in groups along the asphalt road and farm trails with knapsacks and their collection of religious books, hoping for a free space on the back of trucks or buses. Several fellow travelers reveled in this classic image of the pilgrimage and imitated these students' focused devotion with their own bag of books that they read along their journey. To assist *kolo tamariwoch* or other disciplined Christians such as monks or nuns (e.g., by offering transport, food, shelter) was often considered a spiritually advantageous action. Helping these individuals on their admirable quest reflected well on the person doing the assisting; it also shares thematic resemblances with the grace of giving and receiving as discussed in Chapter 3.

When embarking on the pilgrimage program, Orthodox Christians often performed *subaye* (spiritual retreat), typically for seven days. This is an intense period of time when individuals disrupt their habitual patterns and often detach themselves from their families, such that spouses may conduct *subaye* separately. This period involves a series of morning prayers, rigorous attendance of services, visiting monasteries, fasting, giving of alms, and confession and consultation with their *nefs abat* (father-confessor). This period of deep prayer is often scheduled during transitional periods and is "broken" by communion on a significant feast day. An example of a person who habitually went on spiritual retreats was Meseret, who had traveled from the capital city and accompanied her *mahaber* annually for the past four years. Each member purchased food stuffs and prepared meals for the poor, many of whom congregated at Gishen, particularly during its feast days in September and January. These *mahaber* participants represented archetypal forms of pilgrimage conducted as a group, with almsgiving as a custom to continue annually.

Pilgrimages are contexts where personal commemorative events, such as memorials or vows, get incorporated into traditions given their ability to sustainably influence broader communal commitments. Like Meseret, Seifu's story was motivated by the search for spiritual support and an opportunity for almsgiving in the form of charity projects. His life was successful as a land developer from Addis Ababa, yet he had "his troubles," as he described. As a diaspora returnee from Sweden, he went through a divorce, which led to an estrangement from his daughter and put his business in jeopardy. Though he did not communicate his actions as a *s'let*, he began to visit Gishen to be closer to God and to be assisted through this difficult time. As he began to make his way out of his troubles, he continued to come, in his case twice a year, in September and January, and he became one of the main financiers of the large iron and cement gate that had been installed at the entrance a few years ago. These contributions he articulated as "gifts to the Church." Several individuals whom I joined in Gishen spoke highly of Seifu. His actions were described by Eyob, a family friend, in terms of his love for Mariam (*mariam wodadje*), a characterization related to what is understood as the model behavior of giving back to the Church, *ye betechristian agelgaye* (lit. server for the Church). Gifts for the Church are synonymous with gifts to the saint, and in Seifu's case they were initiated in gratitude for success and relief from years of bad luck.

In turn, Seifu inspired other relatives to make the pilgrimage, though none of them were part of a formal association. Abebe, a convenience store owner visiting from America, followed Seifu's lead by sponsoring development projects around the Hayk Monastery near Dessie as well as later financing a bell that was a central part of the St. Gabriel Church inauguration in 2011 (see Chapter 4). He described these actions in terms of giving thanks for what he had been given and to be close to God again. For him, it was a return to a time and reality that cannot be accessed from his new home in the United States. Abebe's aunt described the experience as teaching herself and her teenage kids to how to do pilgrimage and as an opportunity for intensive devotion. Being there and communing together are the focus in people's discussions to me about what draws them to embark on these journeys.

On the one hand, what I conclude here is a reprise of a trend of reallocating benefactorship to the laity. Girma's (2002) research on the misappropriation of covenant as a political concept has been delineated previously (see Introduction), and research on the post-Derg bureaucratic reforms to the Church has made clear that patronage rested on the responsibilities of the laity. The current objectives of the Ethiopian Orthodox Church to maintain its public relevance functioned in this domain of political representations and increasing investment from local businessmen and foreign diaspora advocates. Abebe's sentiments for getting a bell from America for the new St. Gabriel Church was phrased as a kind of caretaking: As a successful resident of the city (Dessie *lij*), he felt responsible to give back. The distance from his hometown was narrowed through his acts of continuing to give to Gishen Mariam and the community he continued to contribute to as a participant.

Conclusion

This chapter has considered how covenant refractions are implicated in another form of promise making: the vow. Pilgrims' journeys are directed by a desire to force interventions into the regular patterns of their lives. This intentionality is not exclusively devotionally inspired, given how pilgrimages are events of social catharsis. However, for many individuals who do embark on these activities for spiritual reasons, they often frame their acts around the pronouncement of a vow. Hence, they engage in what Nietzsche has encapsulated as an intrinsic human performance, man as the "promising animal": "To breed an animal with the right to make promises—is not this the paradoxical problem nature has set itself with regard to man? And is it not man's true problem?" (Nietzsche in Felman 2002, 3). As we have seen, certain individuals double down on the promise, as vows often provide the spark that starts a tradition, such as an annual charity commitment. The original intervention and the narrative that chronicles it become part of the elements that keep traditions bound.

I examined the ways individuals articulated the location's importance to the history of the Church, which for many Orthodox Christians, *is* a history of Ethiopia. Here, the resemblances between Gishen's relic and Ethiopia's covenant story are most obvious. In similar fashion, the issue of guarding a secret object falls into the rationalist trap that to see is to believe, rather than the other way around, or, to phrase this truism as Natnael put it, "it is the Cross that protects us, not the other way around." It is the strength of devotion that is tested by the challenge to keep the faith. Pilgrims interpreted their own narratives of perseverance and encounters with fate by relating to testimonies of miracles and tragedies in order to frame their understanding of Gishen as a sacred space.

Finally, I have evaluated the customs, traditions, and stories about Gishen as another specimen for paradigmatic thinking by Ethiopian Orthodox Christians on sacred ideas and relationships. For the entirety of this work, I have proposed an alternative direction for studying covenant as a subject/object that has inspired a corpus of resemblance, thematic connections, and intersections. As an analytical exercise, the ultimate aim has not been to assert that "all roads lead to covenant" but rather that "covenant" has functioned as the Church's most dominant and productive concepts— its most important, they would insist. As an anthropological experiment, the axis of attention has been on the content and forms as they are mobilized, cited, and expressed and on what these engagements accomplish. The results presented here are an infinite sample of the multicentury conversation with Holy Tradition by believers who see revelations of the Holy Spirit as inherited resources to renew a sacred relationship as mediated by the Church.

Conclusion

This book is a study of Ethiopian Orthodox Christians and the specific directions they take toward creating an engaged devotional life. Engagement can look like a lot of things. It can mean participating in the Divine Liturgy every Sunday and on major holidays and festal seasons. To others, it can mean saying a quiet prayer and making the sign of the cross at the sight of a church. Fulfilling a promise to complete a pilgrimage for a major life event or crisis might be another believer's expression of faith. When observed in such a holistic fashion, it becomes clear that there are many ways that Ethiopian Orthodox Christians do their religion.

Their devotional culture offers a rich arena to disrupt common perceptions about the Ethiopian Orthodox Tewahedo Church (EOTC), as well as Orthodox Christianity more broadly. Popular and academic literature focuses on the age of these churches, often framed as the long-lost relatives of Catholic and Protestant Christianity. The binaries of traditional/modern and unreformed/reformed assist in drawing out these contrasts. Orthodox churches are typically presented as highly stratified institutions, with a strong emphasis on mediation led by priests and other vested authority, and traditional gender roles that maintain distinct spheres for men and women. These are the characteristics that are most dominant, with less focus on the common believers, individuals who do not hold a formal or ordained capacity. Who they are and what they do occupy the bottommost space of the organizational pyramid. To make their devotional culture the center of gravity offers a new way of defining the EOTC in contemporary times.

Patterns of church life represent one scale of observation that defines devotional culture. The celebration of feast days in the EOTC calendar offers one template of engagement and showcases a time and place when the lay community is most collectively visible. Mutual-aid societies, generally referred to as *mahabers*, are another pathway for common believers to participate in Christian fellowship outside of liturgy or other activities on the church compound. Visiting and contributing alms to a monastery or to a historically significant church serve as a vital entry point for a wide spectrum of Orthodox Christians. Gestures such as pausing and greeting a neighboring church represent a foundational action for a believer, small yet profound. These directions that individuals pursue in their devotional lives are expansive and require paying attention to the qualities of engagement rather than counting the frequency of participation.

Referring to these habits and tendencies as patterns or types of activities is useful for our analytical purposes, but it also resonates with a certain Orthodox Christian frame of thinking. Lay engagement is described as a series of templates because these activities follow a certain structure that is shared among a community of people and has been repeated by this community of believers since the founding of the Church. All devotional actions that Orthodox Christians do, from the liturgical service to lighting a candle in front of an icon, are understood to be part of a long and uninterrupted continuation of "Church Tradition" or *Haymanot Abew* (Faith of the Fathers), the teachings and actions of the apostles of Christ and spiritual leaders of the early churches. These archetypes of veneration practices are important for remaining connected to this spiritual heritage. As the ethnographic material demonstrates, the forms of devotion culture allow for the content—its internal applications—to shift and change according to the demands of those doing the practice. Elaboration of tradition is actively taking place while still grounded in a centralized framework of church teachings.

Identifying when and where an elaboration of Church Tradition is happening provides an opportunity to present Orthodox Christianity as constitutive of the lives and actions of its faithful. How Ethiopian Orthodox Christians think and talk about the covenant, both as narratives and as materialities of God's promise of protection, offered one dynamic space for arguing this point. The ritual context of Timqet (the feast of Epiphany) and the procession of *tabots* (altar slabs of wood or stone) establish an important frame for encountering celestial time and space. *Tabots*, understood as inhabiting the agency of saints and the holy, are also vessels for articulating local events of miracles and struggle. These examples of the Ethiopian Orthodox liturgical and historical consciousness showcase the active nature of elaboration. This is a departure from scholarly literature that describes *tabots* as replicas of the Ark of the Covenant, which ignores a body of knowledge developed within devotional culture that illustrates how the EOTC conceptualizes this core theological principle.

The multiple, complex ways that the covenant idea shows up as ideas, idioms, customs, symbols, and articulations in the lifeworld of Ethiopian Orthodox believers initiated this book's theoretical premise: that Ethiopia's story of the covenant is a domain of nested reference points that inspires celebrants, through their devotional activities, to expand and elaborate upon a network of meanings, what I refer to as "covenant refractions." These refractions shape how they communicate and express their faith. A dominant point of reference—that the Ark of the Covenant rests in Axum, as willed by God—remains in the foreground of this layered understanding of covenant. But it is only one of many nodes of connection. By referring to these reference points as refractions, the intention is to explore what this linking helps establish. As stated already, replication is one method of staying true to the historical continuity of Church Tradition, the operating logic of Ethiopian Orthodox elaboration. However, these refractions of the covenant idea offer a way to interpret how Ethiopian Orthodox Christians understand intimacy with the holy. The veiling of the *tabot* is more than a metaphor here. It is a filter of establishing and modulating distance and proximity to divine presence in the material world and an awareness by believers of their implication in and responsibility for the sanctity of this reality. The very ambiguity of what a *tabot* is and the ways that this ambiguity is maintained offer an opportunity to explore the contours of an ontological approach that has developed around Ethiopia's covenant.

This book provides a deeper view into what it means to be a lay member. In Ethiopia, it is common to encounter men who hold clerical offices such as priest, deacon, or *memhir* (a specific class of religious teacher). Women's official roles have developed over recent decades and include positions in church administration, Sunday schools, and as *mezmur* performers, a certain genre of church music. The "common believer" refers to Orthodox Christians outside these public capacities. Linguistically, it is a local gloss found in Orthodox societies to denote the ordinary, the mass of people who come to witness the liturgy on Sundays and on important feast days. By lifting this term to greater analytical prominence and value, I am codifying a type of ethnographic standpoint from which many idiosyncratic and individualized perspectives emerged. I believe there is an evocative impact to insist on this category. Here, I am addressing the bias found in societies with dominant Orthodox Christian populations. The person who comes to church is not a noteworthy interlocutor, precisely because there exist established and authorized sources schooled within the theological pedagogy of the Church. What this study demonstrates is that there is a devotional culture of Orthodox Christianity, developed by participants with minimal formalized knowledge, who account for the Church's enduring dynamism. For those unfamiliar or embedded in Orthodox Christian societies, this research details the comings and goings of the faithful, who are often treated as part of the background. Arguably, in settings where religious competition is increasing, to better understand the positions of faith communities and their adherents will be essential for ensuring religious institutions' vitality and relevance.

Likewise, capitalizing "church" helped mark key distinctions about how it operates as a social and temporal space. This contrasts with standard analyses in the social sciences that present the Ethiopian Orthodox Tewahedo Church as an institution governed by a centralized bureaucracy and liturgical framework, that is, its sacraments and calendrical rites. Through ethnographic description and analysis of five types of lay engagement (feast-day commemoration, gestures of paying respect, *tabot* narratives of miracles and resistance, *mahaber* and mutual-aid societies, and pilgrimages and vow making), it is possible to conceive of "church" as operating on parallel register of daily life. Sociological approaches to religion, from Durkheim to Bourdieu, have accounted for the ways that institutions help constitute notions of what it means to be and requires to be part of a communal identity. In the Orthodox Christian frame of reference, the process of "being churched" takes a specific meaning, one tied once more to tradition. "Tradition is possible and operative through the activity of the Holy Spirit within *the life of the Church* [emphasis added]. It is the Holy Spirit that gives the Tradition flexibility to adapt to new cultures and new situations when the previous formulas and expressions might be inadequate. The Holy Spirit allows Tradition to be both dynamic and constant, creative and timeless" (Constantinou 2020, 139). In this cultural milieu, participating in the life of the Church is a spiritual communion of fellow believers that transcends contemporary time and space and permits individuals to tap into a historical legacy of faith. This is crucial context for envisioning believers as guardians of the Church eternally.

While much scholarship exists about the covenant and its particular discourse within Ethiopian Church history and political philosophy, little of it applies a conceptual focus on the liturgical and social dynamics of Ethiopian Orthodox Christians and their Church. This study advocates for widening the lens of analysis to include a body of knowledge that is best accessed through devotional culture: "Ethiopia stretches her hand upon God," the narrative of Sheba and Solomon, and the material presence of the Ark of the Covenant in Axum. These classic understandings of the covenant function as prized narratives for Ethiopian Orthodox Christians and will endure. They are also reflective of a time when Church and crown were bound tightly and when a greater proportion of Ethiopians were Orthodox Christians. The Ethiopian revolution in 1974 that deposed the monarchy and the increasing number of Muslims and Pentecostal Christians have altered the foundations of the classic covenant story as a type of political philosophy.

Facing the reality of a country with a shrinking Orthodox Christian majority is an opportunity to consider the relevancy of Ethiopia's covenant concept going forward. From a demographic point of view, Orthodox Christians make up close to half of the most populated regions: Oromia, Amhara, and Southern Nations, Nationalities, and Peoples' Region. Counted together, this amounts to about 70 percent of the country's total population and indicates that most Ethiopians live in a plural society with no dominant majority. Understanding how to negotiate harmony in a country with many forms of diversity will be the leading issue going forward.

I have considered how Orthodox Christianity as an affinity framework is built around shared religious praxis and ethics, one that operates on a supra-level of more localized bonds such as language, ethnic identity, or regional historical memory. "Devotional culture" served as an organizing term to group together practices that are a part of people's daily lives and routines. However, arguing for an affinity framework as a source of social good in Ethiopia is a hard case to make, given recent evidence to the contrary.

Tigray, Ethiopia's northern regional state bordering Eritrea and a revered religio-cultural zone for Orthodox Christians, has been embroiled in conflict since 2020. The three major players in this conflict by and large represent populations that are dominantly Orthodox Christian. This includes

Eritrea, whose population is 63 percent Christian, most of whom are Orthodox. Unlike other international examples of sectarian conflicts, where religious differences are strategically mobilized to inflict greater brutality, the Orthodox Christians involved in the fighting in Tigray canonically, liturgically, and sacramentally are one and the same. Many revered locations for Orthodox Christians are concentrated here, including the church of Mariam Tsion (Mary of Zion) in Axum, reputed to house the Ark of the Covenant. In online forums, commentary on the conflict has followed partisan lines, with little to no presence of a middle or neutral position. A call for peace and the end of hostilities by the Ethiopian patriarch Abune Matias, who is Tigrean, was presented in media outlets as driven by his presumed ethnic and political sympathies. Silence from other church leaders about the atrocities committed by all participants in the fighting was similarly painted as aligning with the ethnic politics of their local governments.

Fractured relations between the federal government and some regional states, most violently in Oromia and Tigray, are widely understood as a consequence of the nearly three-decade legacy of ethnic federalism. A political system established in 1994 as a way to recognize the ethnic, linguistic, and cultural diversity of Ethiopia and to promote self-rule and local autonomy, it has been operationalized a "divide-and-run" policy of the main party for most of post-Derg Ethiopia, the Ethiopian Peoples' Revolutionary Democratic Front (EPRDF). While the political structure and party system has gone through revisions since Abiy Ahmed became prime minister in 2018, many of the systemic issues remain, such as unequal power sharing, land grabs, and competition over natural resources.

The "national question" and the search for a narrative of coherent Ethiopian unity has been the subject of much scholarship in Ethiopian studies (see Levine's [1974] Greater Ethiopia thesis). This discourse has influenced political analyses in journals, newspapers, and other public media to present Ethiopia's political fragmentation as galvanized by "identity politics" and one that arrives at an inevitable failure. A view from religious studies can offer a more nuanced interpretation of this pressing challenge. Ethiopian Islam and Pentecostal Christianity have adapted to the conditions of cultural diversity and are flourishing in multiethnic regions such as in the Southern Nations, Nationalities, and Peoples' Region and in parts of Amhara. Orthodox Christianity has a historical tradition of cultural adaptation as well (i.e., translations of the divine liturgy into local languages).

Seen through this lens, local cultural values and ethnic and linguistic differences can coexist and even support other layers of identities.

Given Ethiopia's religious demography, a comparative analysis of religious identity will be crucial. Similarly, dialogue between disciplinary perspectives, such as the social sciences, humanities, and discourse generated in seminaries and theological institutes, permits examining the factors that may facilitate coalition building and cooperation. From a faith-based perspective, the dilemma is not about how Ethiopians assert their identities but about how they make community. The ability to share a common bond without dismissing or erasing histories languages and cultural values that are different from their own is rooted in the principle that faith is a form of inclusion, one common to most all religious traditions.

The work ahead will be to bring Ethiopian perspectives, communicated in Amharic, Tigrinya, Oromifa, English, and other languages and formats, into scholarship with one another. Since the COVID-19 pandemic required remote engagement, a platform like YouTube is now a rich field site for Ethiopian Orthodox discourse, activism, and humanitarian assistance. It is also a location where knowledge production in digital spaces can contribute to misinformation, dehumanization, and justification of wanton violence. Investigating the vehicles, formats, and social spaces where these exchanges are taking place will be important for better understanding the expanded role of lay people as receiving and interpreting these narratives. The intensity of changes facing Ethiopians will likely initiate further explorations of the ways that conceptual links, points of reference, and patterns of elaboration can help make sense of the recent past and the present day. Tools for grasping multiple, even contradictory, positions and developing a capacity for dialogue and have one's viewpoint altered will be crucial to the growth of healthy civil discourse.

"Religion" is perhaps the rare domain of deep time that is simultaneously vast and distant and personally immediate. The historical consciousness so active and ingrained for Orthodox Christians of Ethiopian and Eritrean origin can be a vital resource in a time when truth is destabilized and uprooted. Oftentimes, Orthodox Christian identity is presented as a fulfillment of an imperial or ethnonationalist project, particularly from the position of institutions and leadership. The conflict between Russia and Ukraine is a most recent example. As much as it can be co-opted, a bottom-up, local-level application of Orthodox Christianity can also serve as a paradigm of resistance. Scholarship on religion has a unique scope of observation, one that spans a longer history and that might serve as a release valve for our more presentist view of time. In the Horn of Africa, this region's deep history of Orthodox faith as a cultural and ethical orientation of life has the capacity to act as a through line out of this crisis and a pathway to resolution and reconciliation. Endangering this heritage kills the lifeblood of the people, with consequences beyond the duration of any political party or ruling class.

Finally, I hope this book opens up new questions and areas of inquiry about how communities of Orthodox Christianities envision themselves as participants in societies that extend beyond geography, ethnicity, and historical circumstances. This area of inquiry is influenced both by the more fluid movements of individuals to and from the homelands of their Churches and by the increased power they leverage in geopolitical affairs as naturalized citizens in locales like the United States. For Ethiopians abroad, these trends are most apparent with activism spurred by escalating political tensions around governance under the ethnic federalism system, causing regional conflicts with human fatalities on a large scale and immeasurable trauma for generations to come. Who or what is an Ethiopian will continue to be contested. The Orthodox Christian faith tradition might be the last remaining domain of social life and identity formation from which to build common ground and affinity.

Acknowledgments

To trace all the hands that have contributed to this book's completion, I have to go backward and forward.

Ethnographic fieldwork in Dessie and Addis Ababa was pivotal to my personal growth. It was also hard work that required daily discipline and tested my patience. Without the support, encouragement, and trust of my friends and new family, my acceptance and free movement as a researcher would not have been possible: Turuworq, Kejela, Selam, Genet, and the Dejazmatch Belai family. A special note of thanks to the late Lealem and late Salonite Belay for your friendship, which shaped this critical and formative period of my life.

This project received the support and guidance of the Patriarchate's office of the Ethiopian Orthodox Tewahedo Church in Addis Ababa and is indebted specifically to Wolde Senbete, who facilitated introductions to the Dessie diocese in South Wollo and Gishen as well as Memhir Daniel Seife Mikael, a rich academic resource throughout the years. From our initial meetings, Abune Atnateos was very encouraging, as was Abba Tsige Sellassie, who always made it his duty to provide a welcoming atmosphere for my research involvements at Dessie-area churches. A great deal of gratitude is owed to Memhir Belai Worku, who was a strong advocate of my studies and facilitated several important collaborations. In addition to my gratitude to the St. Gabriel Sunday School group, a special note of thanks goes to its chairman, Misganaw Taddese, an exceptionally kind and forthcoming. Qes Melke, Ato Teferi, and Yemera were also crucial points of contact whom I called on consistently over the course of my fieldwork.

I met Abba Mefekeria Seb at the prompting of Berhanu Dilbu, and it was a privilege to get to know both these individuals personally. There are several individuals who are named, using pseudonyms, in pilgrimage and feast day events I attended as a PhD student: Thank you for generously sharing the Church with me as a fellow seeker. In Addis Ababa, the Kechene Medhane Alem clergy and administration, in particular Qes Abey, Ato Basha, and Ato Eshetu, were all a joy to work with and were particularly thoughtful about pointing me to individuals that would enrich my fieldwork activities.

During fieldwork in Dessie, I lived with the sisters of Kidane Meheret Catholic Church: Sister Zewdinesh, Sister Tagesich, Sister Zebib, Sister Miseret, Sister Marina, Sister Kibenesh, and Soeur Tsehaitu. This community was a loving home in a new and unfamiliar place. Their steadfast support was so enduring that I am certain the quality of time I spent in Dessie was greatly influenced by their limitless positivity. To be given a place as an honorary sister at your table is one of the most immense privileges I can mark in my life. This opportunity would not have happened without the lobbying of Weizero Helene, my step-grandmother, who linked me with her parish church in Addis. As such, a special mention is extended to Abba Gebre Mariam Amente (of the Catholic archbishop's office) and Abba Daniel Assefa at Gulele Institute, who both exhibited an earnest desire for this success of this study.

The writing was as challenging as the fieldwork. During my years as a researcher in London, I owe a debt of gratitude to Marta Mulugeta, Andrew Chadwick, and members of the Tsion Mariam Church at Battersea, in particular Qesis Berhanu, Beliyou Mengistu, Edna Berith, and Alessandra Guiffrida. Many friends, colleagues and mentors, including the revolving cohort at University College London's Anthropology department (2009–2014), have had a hand in this work: as supporters, cheerleaders, a listening ear. Special recognition goes to Timothy Carroll, who has served as a consistent source of support and rich dialogue throughout my development as an anthropologist of Orthodox Christianity.

Stepping back further in my scholastic journey, my movement into anthropology was made official by Dr. Patty Gray. Her tutelage as my master's degree advisor, as well as the experience I gained conducting research in Magadan under her guidance, was instrumental for my development as a fieldworker, which continues to be a critical piece of my self-definition.

Jumping to the present moment, producing a manuscript worthy of publishing has been a major undertaking. Getting the manuscript over the finish line is thanks in large part to the active encouragement and regular motivation of Errol Henderson and Kylie Quave. To my family of friends, with a special shout out to Medeia, a huge encourager of my intellectual pursuits. Thank you to the editorial team at Fordham for believing in this project, and thank you to the reviewers, who offered incisive feedback and careful reflection on the manuscript.

And lastly, and most importantly, boundless gratitude goes to my mother. Your wisdom and parental love were the few stable elements in an otherwise rocky post-fieldwork experience. This book would not have been written had you not stepped in, and so this work is dedicated to you.

And to loved ones who got me here who could not witness its full realization: I chose to study pilgrimage at Gishen Mariam because of its connection to my grandmother, Emama Edjigaheu, whose name I carry but have never met. At the time, I could not have known that I would lose my father and brother within the next five years. With the distance of time, this project has transcended its academic objectives to offer a way to hold loved ones closer. I hope my journey makes them happy and proud.

Glossary

Abba—a mark of respect for a monk or priest
aqwaqwam—from the verb "to stand" (*meqwom*), it is the style of prayer specific to the Ethiopian Orthodox tradition
bahetawi—hermit
bereket—a blessing
bete Abraham—"house of Abraham," an expression of united spiritual kinship
bete kristiyan—"house of Christians," church
bete meqdes—the sanctuary, the innermost section of an Orthodox church
debtera—a distinct class of clergy who do not officiate rites but whose extensive training in the Church schools qualifies them as having mastered the performance of liturgical chant and reading incantations
fet'ena—a test, a spiritual struggle to overcome
fitat—a lengthy prayer for the deceased, read at the time of burial, at the forty-day memorial, and at the one-year memorial
gedl—hagiography, the testimony of a saint
haymanot—religion, dogma of the Church
Hig—law
Hudadae—Lent, a fifty-five-day fast preceding Easter
imnet—belief; also, ash distributed from the censers used by clergy after service
kal'kidan—"word of Promise."
kebele—a governmental association that administers at the neighborhood level
kidan—covenant
leqso bet—a recently deceased person's house, where their relations congregate to offer condolences
mad bet—a small, traditional mud house or room where all the cooking takes place

mahaber—"association," a communal unit fashioned for the purposes of a common goal, secular or religious

mahelet—matins

memhir—the title of teacher, referring also to individuals trained in traditional clerical schools and qualified to teach subjects in Church education

menfesawi guzo—"spiritual journey," referring to activities such as fasts and attendance to church services that compose the actions during pilgrimage

menokse—a monk or nun

mequteria—a rosary

mesalem—to bow down, prostrate and cross oneself when approaching a holy place, a specific way of greeting a church with reverence

mesged—prostration in response to specific liturgical moments and locations

mesgid—mosque

meskel—cross

mesob—a large woven basket that serves as a dining table during a communal meal

mist'ir—sacrament (lit. "mystery")

mizmur—spiritual songs or hymns, derived primarily from Psalms (Mizmur Dawit) as part of St. Yared's hymnography

net'ela—a thin white cotton cloth; essential church attire

qetema—grass reeds distributed during Easter

qidase—the Divine Liturgy

qirs—a relic, treasure

qolo temariwoch—students of traditional Church education, denoted as the poorest of the poor because they subsist on grains (*kolo*)

qurban—communion

sa'atat—the liturgy of the Hours

sebket—preaching conducted following the liturgy and/or vigil service

Segdet—prostration, specifically referring to the activity that is performed on Holy Week

senbete—an honorary association that supports the parish church and administers monthly meals for the public from the church compound

shai/buna—literally translating as tea/coffee, used to refer to the monetary compensation given to one for his cooperation; an oblique term for a small bribe

s'le—"in the name of"; a call often heard among alms seekers who will evoke a particular saint (i.e., "s'le Qedus Mikael"—in the name of St. Michael) to elicit donations from church attendants

s'let—vow

subaye—spiritual retreat, typically seven days before a major feast day

tabot—the ark housed in the sanctuary. Each Orthodox church contains several *tabots* (pl. *tabotat*). The rite of *tabot hig* (law of the *tabot*) transforms a stone or wood into an altar. *Tabot negs* (crowning the ark) is the ceremony making the church consecrated, and *tabot tekele* (ark planting) is the term referring to a saint's manifestation into the earthly properties, as an ark (see Chapter 4).

tamerat—miracle

t'ela—an alcoholic drink brewed at home from barley and hops. It is a common food that is blessed and given during monthly or annual celebrations of feast days, sacramental rites (i.e., marriage, christening) and memorials.

Timqet—"baptism," a feast day celebrated on January 23

ts'ebel ts'adik—lit. pious holy [water], meaning an item (e.g., bread) that is blessed by a priest and given to anyone who has participated in that ceremony. These items are also given away to the poor, usually on a celebrated feast day.

tselat—tablet

tselot—prayer

ts'ewa—chalice; also the name of a type of Orthodox Christian confraternity

ts'om—a fast

wazema—vigil service, conducted on the eve of most important church holidays

yene beete—meaning "one like me," an expression both used to refer to an alms seeker and to denote all of humanity, who are essentially impoverished

yenefs abbat—literally translated as "father of the soul"; spiritual father, typically a priest who guides and counsels a follower of the Church

zikir—a ceremony involving at least one clergy whereby an offering is made for a particular saint

Notes

Introduction

1. See Ancel and Ficquet (2015) for a detailed history of this separation, whereby the Patriarchate of Alexandria granted ecclesiastical self-governance ("autocephaly") and recognized an Ethiopian Orthodox "abune," or patriarch, as the head of the Church and not subordinate to the Egyptian Church.

2. "Coptic" as a label for Ethiopian Orthodox Christianity is more common for believers in the diaspora. For instance, during the periodic disputes between the Ethiopian Orthodox diocese in London over their alliance or resistance to the Ethiopian Orthodox Patriarchate in Addis Ababa, certain believers would find solace by attending a Coptic liturgy, which is canonically in their right.

3. In statistical reporting, the category of "Christian" can occasionally remove the important internal distinctions between Orthodox Christian and Protestant or Evangelical Christian, with a very small percentage of Ethiopian Catholics. Observing the trends over the past decades, the number of Orthodox Christians has decreased, and the composition of the country's Christians is now more diverse.

4. This designation means that clergy cannot celebrate the Eucharist in Eastern Orthodox churches, and vice versa, and that those baptized cannot take sacraments from non-Oriental churches.

5. "We have seen that if collective life awakens religious thought on reaching a certain degree of intensity, it is because it brings about a state of effervescence which changes the conditions of psychic activity. Vital energies are over-excited, passions more active, sensations stronger; there are even some which are produced only at this moment. A man does not recognize himself; he feels

himself transformed and consequently he transforms the environment which surrounds him" (Durkheim 1965, 469).

6. There is a linguistic differentiation between the covenant of Moses and all other *tabots*. However, I seldom heard a sharp distinction in speech or the qualifier of "replica" used in Amharic, indicating that these colloquialisms effectively diminish supremacy of *tabots* as being greater or less than.

7. I do not provide linguistic equivalents of "veneration" in Amharic or other dominant Orthodox Christian lingua franca such as Greek or Russian, primarily because several affiliated subterms fall under this category, hence its more useful application as an English discursive term. The linguistic parallel to "worship" is important to underscore. The latter was used as an epithet to separate Catholics and Orthodox from other Christians (see the Second Council of Nicaea, AD 787), giving this word have more purchase for Western audiences.

8. Confraternities are a corresponding form, popular in the Middle Ages in Europe and particularly well established in research on the proliferation of guilds in Catholic Italy and Spain. Unlike these contexts that show a parish church having about one confraternity attached to it and usually given a ceremonial role in an annual feast day, *mahabers* function independently from the administration of the Ethiopian Orthodox Church.

9. A fourth-century theologian from Cappadocia and regarded as one of the Church Fathers.

10. This book alternates between this term and "Ethiopian Orthodox Christians." The label "believer" has been well problematized in anthropology (see Ruel 1982) and admittedly difficult to circumscribe. However, since it is part of the lexicon of dominant Orthodox Christian societies, I use the term as an ethnographic idiom.

1. Ethiopia's Story of the Covenant

1. The literal translation of Tabota Tsion is "tablet of Zion," calling into question what is housed in Axum, the container of the covenant (the *tabot*) or the actual tablets (*tselat*) received by Moses. Further discussion of this ambiguity is discussed in Chapter 2.

2. Liberia, the other uncolonized country, occupies a unique category separate from Ethiopia. Its founding is closely tied to the United States and its program after the Civil War to "repatriate" formerly enslaved Africans.

3. The Ethiopian patriarch Abune Paulos (1992–2012) is often quoted as stating that Judaism and Christianity have continuously existed in Ethiopia for more than three thousand years, which used to emphasize the deep roots of monotheism.

4. Kebede (2003) argues that the reality of an advanced civilization on the African continent disrupted the "Eurocentric paradigm" of supremacy and required a resolution: to emphasize that civilizational advances were an outcome of Semitic settlers from South Arabia. Emphasis on the mixed racial features of Ethiopia, found in sources like *Ethiopia and the Bible*, is another response to Ethiopia as the African anomaly.

5. Mai Shum is the lake that is used in Epiphany celebrations as a symbolic River Jordan.

6. See Matthew 26:26–28: "And as they were eating, Jesus took bread, blessed and broke it, and gave it to the disciples and said, 'Take, eat; this is My body.' Then He took the cup, and gave thanks, and gave it to them, saying, 'Drink from it, all of you. For this is My blood of the new covenant, which is shed for many for the remission of sins.'"

እርሳትውም ሲበሉ የሱስ እንጀራ ያዘ ባረከውም ቆረሰውም ለደቀ መዛሙርቱም ሰጠ አለም ንሡ ብሉ። ይህ ሥጋይዬ ነው። ደዋም ተቀበለ አመሰገነም እንደሁ ሲልም ሰጣትው። ከዚህ ጠጡ ሁላችሁ። ይህ ደሜ ነውና ለደስ ሥርዓት ስለ ብዙ የሚፈስ ኃጢአት ለመስተሰረይ።

2. Covenant as a Holographic Idea

1. Getachew Haile (1988), in his historical study of one *tabot*'s history in the Amhara region (Atronesa Mariam), speaks of its attributes as synonymous with the saint: "Since the tabot personifies the saint, 'it' takes the gender of the saint. Mary the tabot is a she and, being Mary, she performs miracles. . . . In fact, people often seem to forget that the object is a tabot, or a slate and its container. It becomes Mary or Gabriel, etc, endowed with a supernatural power to heal or kill. It is terrifying to see a tabot. It is like coming face to face with a deity; at the occasion one prostrates oneself to the ground in awe, dread and respect" (14). I found similar phenomena, one example being when onlookers remarked on the approach of the Epiphany processions, articulated as certain saints approaching.

2. For a perspective from liturgical architecture, see Fritsch and Gervers (2007).

3. The Baptism of Christ by John the Baptist or John the Forerunner (Metmekiya Yohannes in Amharic) is another key summary of this holiday in popular culture. He is a mirror figure to Christ (Hart 1994, du Boulay 2010) as well as the last prophet of the Old Testament. During this feast season, his figure is featured prominently in music videos that recreate the baptismal event.

4. Wagner (2001) provides a definition in more instrumental terms: "A projective hologram—what 'holography' means to most people—presents a mental image of its subject. The holographic plate, which registers the interference pattern of two beams of coherent (parallel and unidirectional,

nonradiating) light reflected from a single source, makes parallactic displacement an integral function of viewing that source. Seeing 'around' it is part of seeing it. Every point on the object is registered at once on every point of the plate, and the imaginary quality of three-dimensional space is represented as a personal focal point existing outside of the observer" (19).

5. It is often problematic to term these church traditions of music and dance as "performance," which equates it too readily with a form of entertainment. All expression, according to the liturgy of the Church, is to "dramatically present to participants . . . and beckon us to the wedding feast of the Lamb of God in His coming Kingdom, unto the ages of ages" (Dauod 1959). The expression of *aqwaqwam* (movement of the prayer staffs) and *shibshiba* (bodily movement corresponding to the musical mode) are skills mastered over the course of many years and a form of liturgical worship particularly mastered by *debteras*.

6. The *tabot* of St. Mikael on the feast of Timqet is not deposited back in its home church until the following day. The commemoration of Kana ze Galila, when Jesus performed his first miracle at Cana by turning water into wine, falls on St. Mikael's Day (every 12th of the month in the Ethiopian calendar), thereby initiating an additional day of procession.

7. According to Damon (2006), it can also be translated as "the (good) way of standing."

8. This classification of *araya*, *ge'ez*, and *ezel* is frequently cited by Sunday school students and *memhirs*. The principal significance of these distinctions is the times of the liturgical year it is performed: *araya* (fast beat for celebration), *ezel* (slow beat, with fewer instruments, during fast seasons and funerals), and *ge'ez*, for ordinary liturgical time (neither great feast nor fast).

3. The Liturgy and Stances of Giving Respect

1. As paraphrased from the Anaphora of the Apostles from *The Liturgy of the Ethiopian Orthodox Church* (2010). Other variations in liturgy include specific statements of "the blood of the New Testament" in the Anaphora of St. Cyril (356) and in the Anaphora of St. John Chrysostom, the "blood which is indeed the drink of life" (334).

2. Individuals devise their own program of readings and personal rituals based on the time in the liturgical calendar and their own appeals toward alleviating trouble. Such strategies will be discussed further in Chapter 6.

3. The Liturgy of the Hours (Horologion) is performed seven times a day, the chief being the 3rd, the 6th, and the 9th hours. At monasteries, the Divine Liturgy is heard every day, and certain exceptional churches also hold this service daily.

4. Bibles generally are not read at church by lay people during service. Consistently, *memhirs* told me that all prayer is Scripture derived and that the *qidase* is all from the Bible. One could interpret this reiteration as in some part a response to Pentecostal critiques of the "hollow traditionalism" of the Ethiopian Orthodox Tewahedo Church, that its worship has become too detached from "the Word." Concurrently, these books are regarded by certain Orthodox Christians themselves as the remnants of more "folk" followers (*balageroch*) of the church. Several Wolloye talked about how they read the Bible and not the hagiographies like their parents and grandparents.

5. The intensity of prayer is historicized with the popular retelling of two saint stories: St. Tekle Haymanot, who prayed so fervently that his leg fell off, and St. Yared, who upon singing hymns to the royal court was stabbed in the foot by the king but continued singing.

6. The nuns and the children who made up the congregation at Kidane Meheret Catholic Church did not eat before their liturgy services; these primarily occurred on Sunday mornings, and therefore it was not habitual for them to consume breakfast before 9 or 10 AM. According to the liturgy of the Ethiopian Orthodox Church, as stated in the Anaphora of the Apostles, "after partaking of the Holy Communion a man shall not wash his hands or feet, shall not take off his clothes or bow down or kneel, shall not spit, or let blood, or cut his nails or cut his hair, or go on a journey, or sue in the court or go to a bathing place, or eat too much or drink too much, or lie with a woman. None of these or the like should be done after receiving Holy Communion" (Doaud 2010, 137).

7. Similar rules of conduct were followed after the death of Meles Zenawi, prime minister of Ethiopia, in 2012. Tents were installed in the compounds of *kebeles* (local municipalities), where mourners signed a registry and followed grieving customs.

4. Constructing Church Futures

1. The classic example of the shifting nature of Muslim-Christian politics was highlighted by the recounting of recent attempts to build a mosque in Axum. Even liberal opinions were vocal about the impossibility of such a proposition, stating that it has always been a holy Christian city and that this fact should remain unchallenged.

2. I heard that churches have on average three to five *tabots* at a time. The principal *tabot* of the church's namesake is the article that permits the rites of the Eucharist to be sanctified. However, I have heard of instances where more than two Eucharist services can occur at once in a single church building. This is predicated by having another tablet house (*tabot menber*) inside the chambers of the sanctuary (Fritsch 2001).

3. Arsema Mariam is particularly revered in South Wollo. *Tabots* are historically personality driven, as explicated by Getachew (1988). Battles between Christians were staged by their respective patron saints. He also suggests how tabots and place names merge in identity grounded in the context of medieval Ethiopia (fourteenth through sixteenth centuries).

4. There are variations about the provenance of this story and its sources, exclusively from the Book of Enoch. Two variations exist: that St. Uriel, along with all the other archangels, at the time of Christ's death, collected his blood in a chalice, and another is that St. Uriel dipped his wings in the blood. The archangels are also known to be the guardians of the *tabot* of all churches (Wondmagegnehu and Motovu 1970).

5. The tag of "repressed" is a trope within *tabot* legends. For example, the "exiled" Medhane Alem (Sedetinya) is a well-known church in Addis Ababa, whose *tabot* also has a similar history of indeterminacy.

6. The classification of churches consists of *gedam* (monastery), *deber* (large parish church), and *geter* (ordinary or village church).

7. As a newly incorporated king into the consolidated empire in the late 1800s and a convert to Christianity from Islam, Negus Mikael continues to be a particularly divisive figure locally for his acquiesence to the oppressive Christianization campaign that swept through the Wollo region during this period.

8. The patterning of the saints to which a *tabot* was to be consecrated was highly variable, idiosyncratic, and almost reproachable when scrutinized. And while every locale most certainly has a St. Mary, St. Mikael, and St. Gabriel, the most pivotal intercessory figures in the Ethiopian Orthodox Christian worldview, this town of fifty thousand had two Arsema Mariam.

9. Officially called the Coordinating Committee of the Armed Forces, Police, and Territorial Army, referred to popularly as Derg (the Committee). During these years, religious activities were discouraged but not criminalized, so the Derg period does not connote categorical religious repression. As the examples provided here show (e.g., St. Gabriel Dessie), churches were lobbied and instituted as well as discouraged. The current constitution of the Federation of Ethiopia has an irreligious outlook (no state religion).

10. This urban condition presents parallels to Addis and Amhara zone developments (2010–2012), where to help finance the completion, building frames were constructed but only the first floor was occupied.

5. *Mahaber* and the Blessing

1. The reason that the bread in any religious ceremony is turned upside down is to memorialize the story of Abraham and Isaac at the altar (Gen 22:1–19),

imitating the action of Abraham making his son turn his head down (or upside down), so that he would not see what Abraham was about to do. The story encapsulates the act of sacrifice. The act of purity of heart and giving is what is being evoked even in the simplest offering, such as bread.

2. Baking your own bread represents a great demonstration of household labor (see du Boulay 2010, 152–55). Such deep symbolism, at least in Ethiopian cities, are less prescriptive, as one can buy ordinary loaves of bread for a birr (approximately 20 cents), light a candle for the saint of that day, and it becomes *tsebel tsadik* according to EOTC custom. This was commented on as a contemporary condition by one *mahaber* member, who was dismayed to see lines of women getting their onions chopped by machine on Easter weekend. "Our women aren't women anymore," he remarked.

3. *Ts'ewa mahabers* tended to be gender specific; as such, I was never invited to a *ts'ewa mahaber* that had men as members. I asked the Sellassie *mahaber* members why men were not made members. In their case, they claimed they had no closed gender policy, concluding that men were not interested in joining. With the other *ts'ewa mahabers*, this pattern was attributed to the fact that seats were inherited through mothers to daughters, fathers to sons.

4. Attending the service of the day is an integral part of nearly all *mahaber* events. The meal served is then sequentially correct according to church proscriptions. For example, on St. Michael's day, apart from the regular rubric of liturgical script, part of his hagiography is read from the Synaxarium (Senksar), and his miracles (*tamera*) and a homily on his life (*dersan*) are presented (Demeke 2011, 290).

5. The word itself is in reference to the day of rest, shabat (sebate, which is "seven" in Amharic). It is a point of theological confusion about whether Saturday *and* Sunday are honored as days of rest among Ethiopian Orthodox Christians (Fritsch 2001). It was decreed by Emperor Za'ra Yacob that Saturday is equal to Sunday, yet church councils in the late nineteenth century appear to overturn this interpretation. While there are certain church traditions that assert that Saturday is the day of observance of God's creation (see Seventh Day Adventists), this detail is diminished in the *senbete* gatherings, which always occur on Sundays.

6. Mequanent divides *mahabers* into secular and religious, profiling associations such as *iqubs* (lending associations), *geberres* (farming collectives), and *iddirs* (funerary organizations) all as examples of mutual assistance at the grassroots level. It is not my contention that *mahabers* must be of a religious purpose. However, my proposal to study the context of how collectives form and under what circumstances and influences they operate necessitates loosening the categories between secular and religious.

6. Movements of Sacred Promise

1. This book is well protected, and only select clergy are able to read from it, though one of its few copies is available at the British Library.

2. There is a separate monastery for women adjacent to the men's on the same grounds of the lakeside compound.

3. Women are not permitted to enter the church when they are menstruating. Wright (2004) presents the dilemmas of flesh and spirit among female monastics who lament being restricted from devoting their bodies fully in their path to renunciation.

4. The road to Gishen for many centuries was fortressed. Before its development as a church complex, the location of Gishen was a prison (pre–fifteenth century), where the local king locked up competitors to the throne, oftentimes his own kin.

Bibliography

Alter, Robert, and Frank Kermode, eds. 1990. *The Literary Guide to the Bible.* Cambridge, MA: Harvard University Press.
Ancel, Stéphane. 2005. "Mahbär et Sänbäte. Associations religieuses en Éthiopie." *Aethiopica* 8:95–111.
Ancel, Stéphane. 2011."The Centralization Process of the Ethiopian Orthodox Church. An Ecclesiastical History of Ethiopia during the 20th Century." *Revue d'Histoire Ecclésiastique* 106 (3–4): 497–520.
Ancel, Stéphane, and Éloi Ficquet. 2015. "The Ethiopian Orthodox Tewahedo Church (EO EC) and the Challenges of Modernity." In *Understanding Contemporary Ethiopia: Monarchy, Revolution, and the Legacy of Meles Zenawi*, ed. Gérard Prunier and Éloi Ficquet. London: Hurst & Co.
Antohin, A. 2019. "Preserving the Intangible: Orthodox Christian Approaches to Spiritual Heritage." *Religions* 10 (5): 1–12.
———. 2015. "Thinking with the Tabot: The Material Dimensions of Waiting in Addis Ababa." *Material Religions.* http://materialreligions.blogspot.com/2015/06/thinking-with-tabot-material-dimensions.html.
———. 2008. "Challenges of Being Orthodox in Russia: Education as Missionization in Magadan." MA thesis, University of Alaska Fairbanks.
Asad, Talal. 1993. *Genealogies of Religion: Discipline and Reasons of Power in Christianity and Islam:* Baltimore, MD: Johns Hopkins University Press.
Austin, J. L. 1962. *How to Do Things with Words.* Oxford: Clarendon.
Badone, Ellen. 1989. *The Appointed Hour: Death, Worldview, and Social Change in Brittany.* Berkeley: University of California Press.
Bakhtin, M. M. 1981. *The Dialogic Imagination: Four Essays.* Ed. Michael Holquist. Trans. Caryl Emerson and Michael Holquist. Austin: University of Texas Press.

Bajc, Vida, Simon Coleman, and John Eade. 2007. "Introduction: Mobility and Centring in Pilgrimage." *Mobilities* 2 (3): 321–29.

Bandak, Andreas. 2012. "Problems of Belief: Tonalities of Immediacy among Christians of Damascus." *Ethnos: Journal of Anthropology* 77 (4): 535–55.

Bandak, Andreas, and Tom Boylston. 2014. "The 'Orthodoxy' of Orthodoxy: On Moral Imperfection, Correctness, and Deferral in Religious Worlds." *Religion and Society: Advances in Research* 5:25–46.

Bateson, Gregory. 1936. *Naven*. Cambridge: Cambridge University Press.

Behar, Ruth. 1986. *Santa María del Monte: The Presence of the Past in a Spanish Village*. Princeton, NJ: Princeton University Press.

Berdyaev, Nikolai. 2012 [1952]. "The Truth of Orthodoxy." http://www.chebucto.ns.ca/Philosophy/Sui-Generis/Berdyaev/essays/orthodox.htm.

Berthomé, François, and Michael Houseman. 2010. "Ritual and Emotions: Moving Relations, Patterned Effusions." *Religion and Society: Advances in Research* 1:57–75.

Boulay, Juliet du. 2010. *Cosmos, Life, and Liturgy in a Greek Orthodox Village*. Ekdoseis: Denise Harvey.

Bowman, Glenn. 1991. "Christian Ideology and the Image of a Holy Land: The Place of Jerusalem Pilgrimage in the Various Christianities." In *Contesting the Sacred: The Anthropology of Pilgrimage*, ed. John Eade and Michael J. Sallnow. London: Routledge.

Boylston, Tom. 2018. *The Stranger at the Feast: Prohibition and Mediation in an Ethiopian Orthodox Christian Community*. Oakland: University of California Press.

———. 2012. "The Shade of the Divine: Approaching the Sacred in an Ethiopian Orthodox Christian Community." PhD diss., London School of Economics.

Briggs, Charles L., and Richard Bauman. 1992. "Genre, Intertextuality, and Social Power." *Journal of Linguistic Anthropology* 2 (2): 131–72.

Briggs, Philip. 2012. *Ethiopia: The Bradt Travel Guide*. Chalfont St. Peter: Bradt.

Budge, E. A. Wallis, trans. *Synaxarium: The Book of the Saints of the Ethiopian Orthodox Tewahedo Church*. Garland, TX: Ethiopian Orthodox Tewahedo Debre Meheret St. Michael Church.

Buitelaar, Marjo. 1993. *Fasting and Feasting in Morocco: Women's Participation in Ramadan*. Oxford: Berg.

Campbell, John Kennedy. 1964. *Honour, Family, and Patronage: A Study of Institutions and Moral Values in a Greek Mountain Community*. Oxford: Clarendon.

Cannell, Fenella, ed. 2006. *The Anthropology of Christianity*. Durham, NC: Duke University Press.

Caquot, A. 1955. "L'homélie en l'honneur de l'archange Ouriel (Dersâna Urâ'çl)." *Annales d'Éthiopie* 1 (1): 61–88.
Carroll, Timothy. 2018. *Orthodox Christian Material Culture: Of People and Things in the Making of Heaven*. London: Taylor and Francis.
———. 2017. "Theology as an Ethnographic Object: An Anthropology of Eastern Christian Rupture." *Religions* 8 (114): 1–21.
———. 2015. *Becoming Orthodox: Of people and Things in the Making of Religious Subjects*. London: University College London.
Chau, Adam Yuet. 2008. "The Sensorial Production of the Social." *Ethnos* 73(4): 485–504.
Christian, William A. 1996. *Visionaries: The Spanish Republic and the Reign of Christ*. Berkeley: University of California Press.
The Church of Ethiopia, a Panorama of History and Spiritual Life. 1970. Addis Ababa: Ethiopian Orthodox Church.
Coleman, Simon. 2000. *The Globalisation of Charismatic Christianity*. Cambridge: Cambridge University Press.
Coleman, Simon, and John Eade. 2004. *Reframing Pilgrimage: Cultures in Motion*. London: Routledge.
Constantinou, Eugenia Scarvelis. 2020. *Thinking Orthodox: Understanding and Acquiring the Orthodox Christian Mind*. Chesterton, IN: Ancient Faith.
Crummey, Donald. 1972. *Priests and Politicians: Protestant and Catholic Missions in Orthodox Ethiopia, 1830–1868*. Oxford: Clarendon.
Csoba DeHass, Medeia. 2009. "*Sugpiaq* Russian Orthodoxy—Conceptual Analogy in Religious Syncretism in Nanwalek Alaska." PhD diss., University of Alaska Fairbanks.
Damon, Anne. 2006. "Aqwaqwam ou la danse des cieux." *Cahiers d'Études Africaines* 182 (2): 261–90.
Daoud, Rev. Marcos, trans. 1991. *The Liturgy of the Ethiopian Church*. Kingston, Jamaica: Ethiopian Orthodox Church.
Demeke, Worku. 2011. "Yäsəwa Mahəbär: A Religious Association." *Ethiopian Review of Cultures* 14: 283–303.
Desai, Amit. 2010. "Dilemmas of Devotion: Religious Transformation and Agency in Hindu India." *Journal of the Royal Anthropological Institute* 16 (2): 313–29.
Donham, Donald. 1999. *Marxist Modern: An Ethnographic History of the Ethiopian Revolution*. Berkeley: University of California Press.
Donham, Donald, and Wendy James, eds. 2002. *The Southern Marches of Imperial Ethiopia: Essays in History and Social Anthropology*. Oxford: James Currey.

Driessen, Henk. 1984. "Religious Brotherhoods: Class and Politics in an Andalusian Town." In *Religion, Power, and Protest in Local Communities: The Northern Shore of the Mediterranean*, ed. Eric R. Wolf. Berlin: Mouton.

Durkheim, Emile. 1982. *The Rules of the Sociological Method and Selected Texts on Sociology and Its Method*. Ed. Steven Lukes. Trans. W. D. Halls. New York: Free Press.

———. 1965 [1915]. *The Elementary Forms of Religious Life*. New York: The Free Press.

Durkheim, Emile, and Marcel Mauss. 1969. *Primitive Classification*. 2nd ed. London: Cohen & West.

Ethiopian Orthodox Tewahedo Church. 1997. "Today's Ethiopia Is Ethiopia of the Holy Scriptures, History and Antiquity." Addis Ababa.

Engelhardt, Jeffers. 2010. "The Acoustics and Geopolitics of Orthodox Practices in the Estonian-Russian Border Region." In *Eastern Christians in Anthropological Perspectives*, ed. C. Hann and H. Goltz. Berkeley: University of California Press.

Evans-Pritchard, E. E. 1956. *Nuer Religion*. Oxford: Clarendon.

Evdokimov, Paul. 2011. *Orthodoxy*. Hyde Park, NY: New City Press.

Fabian, Johannes. 1995. "Ethnographic Misunderstanding and the Perils of Context." *American Anthropologist* 97 (1): 41–50.

Feld, Steven. 1990. *Sound and Sentiment: Birds, Weeping, Poetics, and Song in Kaluli Expression*. Philadelphia: University of Pennsylvania Press.

Felman, Shoshana. 2003. *The Scandal of the Speaking Body: Don Juan with J. L. Austin, or Seduction in Two Languages*. Stanford, CA: Stanford University Press.

Fernandez, James, John Blacking, Alan Dundes, Munro S. Edmonson, K. Peter Etzkorn, George G. Haydu, Michael Kearney, et al. 1974. "The Mission of Metaphor in Expressive Culture [and Comments and Reply]." *Current Anthropology* 15 (2): 119–45.

Fernandez, James W. 1991. *Beyond Metaphor: The Theory of Tropes in Anthropology*. Stanford, CA: Stanford University Press.

Ficquet, Eloi. 2002. "Du barbare au mystique: Anthropologie historique des recompositions identitaires et religieuses dans le Wallo." Paris: EHESS.

Florensky, P. A. 2002. *Beyond Vision: Essays on the Perception of Art*. Trans. Nicoletta Misler. London: Reaktion.

Fortescue, Adrian. 1913. *The Lesser Eastern Churches*. London: Catholic Truth Society.

Freeman, Dena. 2012. "Development and the Rural Entrepreneur: Pentecostals, NGOs, and the Market in the Gamo Highlands, Ethiopia." In *Pentecostalism and Development: Churches, NGOs, and Social Change in Africa*, ed. Dena Freeman. New York: Palgrave Macmillan.

Freeman, Susan Tax. 1987. "Egalitarian Structures in Iberian Social Systems: The Contexts of Turn-Taking in Town and Country." *American Ethnologist* 14 (3): 470–90.

Fritsch, Emmanuel. 2001. *The Liturgical Year of the Ethiopian Church: The Temporal: Seasons and Sundays*. Master Printing Press.

Fritsch, Emmanuel, and Michael Gervers. 2007. "Pastophoria and Altars: Interaction in Ethiopian Liturgy and Church Architecture." *Aethiopica* 10:7–51.

Gascon, Alain, and Bertrand Hirsch. 1992. "Les espaces sacres comme lieux de confluence religieuse en Ethiopie." *Cahiers d'Études Africaines* 128 (32–34): 689–704.

Gates, Henry Louis, Ben Goold, Nicola Colton, and Nick Godwin. 1999. *Wonders of the African World*. Parts 3–4. Alexandria, VA: PBS Home Video.

Gebrekidan, Fikru Negash. 2015. "Ethiopia in Black Studies from W. E. B. Du Bois to Henry Louis Gates, Jr." *Northeast African Studies* 15, no. 1: 1–34.

Girma, Mohammed. 2012. *Understanding Religion and Social Change in Ethiopia: Toward a Hermeneutic of Covenant*. New York: Palgrave Macmillan.

Habtemichael, Kidane. 2003. "Eucharist." In *Encyclopaedia Aethiopica*, ed. Siegbert Uhlig, vol. 2. Wiesbaden: Harrassowitz.

Haile, Getachew. 1988. "A History of the Tabot of Atronəsä Maryam in Amhara (Ethiopia)." *Paideuma* 34:13–22.

Hancock, Graham. 1997. *The Sign and the Seal: A Quest for the Lost Ark of the Covenant*. London: Arrow.

Handelman, Don. 2004. "Introduction: Why Ritual in Its Own Right? How So?" *Social Analysis: The International Journal of Social and Cultural Practice* 48 (2): 1–32.

Hanks, William F. 1987. "Discourse Genres in a Theory of Practice." *American Ethnologist* 14 (4): 668–92.

Hann, Chris, and Hermann Goltz, eds. 2010. *Eastern Christians in Anthropological Perspective*. Berkeley: University of California Press.

Harding, Susan Friend. 2000. *The Book of Jerry Falwell: Fundamentalist Language and Politics*. Princeton, NJ: Princeton University Press.

Hart, Laurie Kain. 1992. *Time, Religion, and Social Experience in Rural Greece*. Lanham, MD: Rowman & Littlefield.

Heldman, Marilyn E. 1994. *The Marian Icons of the Painter Frç Seyon: A Study in Fifteenth-Century Ethiopian Art, Patronage, and Spirituality*. Orientalia Biblica et Christiana 6. Wiesbaden: Harrassowitz.

Hénaff, Marcel, and Jean-Louis Morhange. 2010. *The Price of Truth: Gift, Money, and Philosophy*. Stanford, CA: Stanford University Press.

Herzfeld, Michael. 1990. "Pride and Perjury: Time and the Oath in the Mountain Villages of Crete." *Man* 25 (2): 305–22.

———. 1987. *Anthropology through the Looking-Glass: Critical Ethnography in the Margins of Europe*. Cambridge: Cambridge University Press.

Hirschkind, Charles. 2006. *The Ethical Soundscape: Cassette Sermons and Islamic Counterpublics*. New York: Columbia University Press.

Houseman, Michael, and Carlo Severi. 1998. *Naven, or, The Other Self: A Relational Approach to Ritual Action*. Leiden: Brill.

Humphrey, Caroline, and James Laidlaw. 1994. *The Archetypal Actions of Ritual*. Oxford: Clarendon.

Jackson, Michael. 2005. *Existential Anthropology: Events, Exigencies, and Effects*. New York: Berghahn.

Jiménez, Alberto Corsín. 2011a. "Trust in Anthropology." *Anthropological Theory* 11 (2): 177–96.

Joseph, Miranda. 2002. *Against the Romance of Community*. Minneapolis: University of Minnesota Press.

Kan, Sergei. 1985. "Russian Orthodox Brotherhoods among the Tlingit: Missionary Goals and Native Response." *Ethnohistory* 32 (3): 196–222.

Kane, Thomas Leiper. 1990. *Amharic–English Dictionary*. Wisebaden: O. Harrassowitz Verlag.

Kapferer, Bruce. 2004. "Ritual Dynamics and Virtual Practice: Beyond Representation and Meaning." *Social Analysis: The International Journal of Social and Cultural Practice* 48 (2): 35–54.

Kaplan, Steven. 2008. "Finding the True Cross: The Socio-Political Dimension of the Ethiopian *Mesqel* Festival." *Journal of Religion in Africa* 38:447–65.

Keane, Webb. 2014. "Rotting Bodies: The Clash of Stances toward Materiality and Its Ethical Affordances." *Current Anthropology* 55:312–21.

———. 1994. "The Value of Words and the Meaning of Things in Eastern Indonesian Exchange." *Man* 29 (3): 605–29.

Kebede, Messay. 2003. "Eurocentrism and Ethiopian Historiography: Deconstructing Semitization." *Journal of Ethiopian Studies* 1 (1): 1–19.

Kur, Stanislaw, and Denis Nosnitsin. 2007. "Kidan." In *Encyclopaedia Aethiopica*, vol. 3, ed. Siegbert Uhlig. Wiesbaden: Harrassowitz.

Lakoff, George, and Mark Johnson. 1980. *Metaphors We Live By*. Chicago: University of Chicago Press.

Lee, Ralph. 2011. "Symbolic Interpretations in Ethiopic and Ephremic Literature." PhD diss., SOAS, University of London.

Levine, Donald. 1965. *Wax and Gold: Tradition and Innovation in Ethiopian Culture*. Chicago: University of Chicago Press.

———. 1974. *Greater Ethiopia: The Evolution of a Multiethnic Society*. Chicago: University of Chicago Press.

The Liturgy of the Ethiopian Orthodox Church. 2010. Addis Ababa: Tensae Publishing House.
Lossky, Vladimir. 1974. "Tradition and Traditions." In *In the Image and Likeness of God.* Crestwood, NY: St. Vladimir's Seminary Press.
Luehrmann, Sonja, ed. 2018. *Praying with the Senses: Contemporary Orthodox Christian Spirituality in Practice.* Bloomington: Indiana University Press.
Mahmood, Saba. 2004. *Politics of Piety: The Islamic Revival and the Feminist Subject.* Princeton, NJ: Princeton University Press.
Makris, G. 2007. *Islam in the Middle East: A Living Tradition.* Oxford: Blackwell.
Marcus, Cressida. 2001. "The Production of Patriotic Spirituality: Ethiopian Orthodox Women's Experience of War and Social Crisis." *Northeast Africa Studies* 8 (3): 179–208.
———. 2008. "Sacred Time, Civic Calendar: Religious Plurality and the Centrality of Religion in Ethiopian Society." *International Journal of Ethiopian Studies* 3 (2): 143–75.
Marcus, G., and E. Saka. 2006. "Assemblage." *Theory, Culture and Society* 23 (2–3): 101–9.
Marrassini, Paolo. 2007. "Kebre Negest." In *Encyclopaedia Aethiopica*, vol. 3, ed. Siegbert Uhlig. Wiesbaden: Harrassowitz.
Mauss, Marcel. 1990. *The Gift: The Form and Reason for Exchange in Archaic Societies.* London: Routledge.
McGuckin, John Anthony, ed. 2010. *Encyclopedia of Eastern Orthodox Christianity.* Chichester: John Wiley & Sons.
Mittermaier, Amira. 2012. "Dreams from Elsewhere: Muslim Subjectivities beyond the Trope of Self-Cultivation." *Journal of the Royal Anthropological Institute* 18 (2): 247–65.
Mequanent, Getachew. 1988. "Community Development and the Role of Community Organizations: A Study in Northern Ethiopia." *Canadian Journal of African Studies* 32 (3): 494–520.
———. 1996. "The Role of Informal Organizations in Resettlement Adjustment Process: A Case Study of Iqubs, Idirs and Mahabers in the Ethiopian Community in Toronto." *Refuge: Canada's Journal on Refugees* 15 (3): 30–39.
Mihretie, Kindeneh Endeg. 2015. "Addis Ababa Public Space: An Arena for Religious Rivalry." *Horn of Africa Bulletin* 26 (2): 4–8. http://life-peace.org/wp-content/uploads/2015/04/Horn-of-Africa-Bulletin-March-April-2015.pdf.
Miyazaki, Hirokazu. 2000. "Faith and Its Fulfillment: Agency, Exchange, and the Fijian Aesthetics of Completion." *American Ethnologist* 27 (1): 31–51.
Molinie, Antoinette. 2004. "The Revealing Muteness of Rituals: A Psychoanalytical Approach to a Spanish Ceremony." *Journal of the Royal Anthropological Institute* 10:41–61.

Moore, Sally Falk. 1987. "Explaining the Present: Theoretical Dilemmas in Processual Ethnography." *American Ethnologist* 14 (4): 727–36.

Morinis, Alan. 1992. *Sacred Journeys: The Anthropology of Pilgrimage*. New York: Greenwood.

Mosse, David. 2006. "Collective Action, Common Property, and Social Capital in South India: An Anthropological Commentary." *Economic Development and Cultural Change* 54 (3): 695–724.

Munn, Nancy. 1992. "The Cultural Anthropology of Time: A Critical Essay." *Annual Review of Anthropology* 21:93–123.

Naumescu, Vlad. 2018. "Becoming Orthodox: The Mystery and Mastery of a Christian Tradition." In *Praying with the Senses: Contemporary Eastern Orthodox Spirituality in Practice*, ed. Sonja Luehrmann. Bloomington: Indiana University Press.

———. 2007. *Modes of Religiosity in Eastern Christianity: Religious Process and Social Change in Ukraine*. Munster: Lit Verlag.

Newman, Deena. 1998. "Prophecies, Police Reports, Cartoons and Other Ethnographic Rumors in Addis Ababa." *Etnofoor* 11 (2): 83–110.

Nielsen, Morten. 2011. "Futures Within. Reversible Time and House-Building in Maputo, Mozambique." *Anthropological Theory* 11 (4): 397–423.

Nixon, Lucia. 2006. *Making a Landscape Sacred: Outlying Churches and Icon Stands in Sphakia, Southwestern Crete*. Oxford: Oxbow.

Orsi, Robert A. 1985. *The Madonna of 115th Street: Faith and Community in Italian Harlem, 1880–1950*. New Haven, CT: Yale University Press.

Østebø, Terje. 2013. "Islam and State Relations in Ethiopia: From Containment to the Production of a 'Governmental Islam.'" *Journal of the American Academy of Religion* 81 (4): 1029–60.

Ott, Sandra. 2009. "Blessed Bread, 'First Neighbours' and Asymmetric Exchange in the Basque Country." *European Journal of Sociology* 21 (1): 40–58.

Pankhurst, Alula. 1994. "Reflections on Pilgrimages in Ethiopia." In *New Trends in Ethiopian Studies: Papers of the 12th International Conference of Ethiopian Studies*.

Panofsky, Erwin. 1991. *Perspective as Symbolic Form*. Trans. Christopher S. Wood. New York: Zone.

Paxson, Margaret. 2005. *Solovyovo: The Story of Memory in a Russian Village*. Washington, DC: Woodrow Wilson Center Press.

Pitt-Rivers, Julian. 2011 [1992]. "The Place of Grace in Anthropology." *HAU: Journal of Ethnographic Theory* 1 (1): 423–50.

Persoon, Joachim. 2010. "The Planting of the Tabot on European Soil: The Trajectory of Ethiopian Orthodox Involvement with the European Continent." *Studies in World Christianity* 16 (3): 320–40.

Pesman, Dale. 2000. *Russia and Soul: An Exploration*. Ithaca, NY: Cornell University Press.
Pruess, James B. 1992. "Sanctification Overland: The Creation of a Thai Buddhist Pilgrimage Center." In *Sacred Journeys: The Anthropology of Pilgrimage*, ed. Alan E. Morinis. Westport, CT: Greenwood.
Raes, Alphonse. 1951. "Antimension, Tablit, Tabot." *Proche-Orient Chretien* 1:59–70.
Rappaport, Roy A. 1999. *Ritual and Religion in the Making of Humanity*. Cambridge: Cambridge University Press.
———. 1979. "Obvious Aspects of Ritual." In *Ecology, Meaning, and Religion*, 173–221. Berkeley, CA: North Atlantic Press.
Robbins, Joel. 2010. "On Imagination and Creation: An Afterword." *Anthropological Forum: A Journal of Social Anthropology and Comparative Sociology* 20 (3): 305–13.
———. 2007. "Continuity Thinking and the Problem of Christian Culture: Belief, Time, and the Anthropology of Christianity." *Current Anthropology* 48 (1): 5–38.
———. 2003. "On the Paradoxes of Global Pentecostalism and the Perils of Continuity Thinking." *Religion* 33 (3): 221–31.
Said, Edward W. 1994 [1978]. *Orientalism*. New York: Vintage.
Sahlins, Marshall. 1976. *Culture and Practical Reason*. Chicago: University of Chicago Press.
Schieffelin, Edward L. 1985. "Performance and the Cultural Construction of Reality." *American Ethnologist* 12 (4): 707–24.
Scott, William. 2004. "The Ethiopian Ethos in African American Thought." *International Journal of Ethiopian Studies* 1 (2): 40–57.
Shelemay, Kay Kaufman, and Peter Jeffery. 1994. *Ethiopian Christian Liturgical Chant: An Anthology*. Madison, WI: A-R Editions.
Shenoda, Anthony. 2012. "The Politics of Faith: On Faith, Skepticism, and Miracles among Coptic Christians in Egypt." *Ethnos: Journal of Anthropology* 77 (4): 477–95.
Shevzov, Vera. 2006. "Between 'Popular' and 'Official': Akafisty Hymns and Marian Icons in Late Imperial Russia." In *Letters from Heaven: Popular Religion in Russian and Ukraine*, ed. John-Paul Himka and Andriy Zayarnyuk. Toronto: University of Toronto Press.
Smith, Anthony D. 2003. *Chosen Peoples*. Oxford: Oxford University Press.
Spencer, Diana. 2003. *The Woman from Tedbab*. Surrey: Elizabeth Horne.
Stewart, Charles. 2012. *Dreaming and Historical Consciousness in Island Greece*. Cambridge, MA: Harvard University Press.
———. 1991. *Demons and the Devil: Moral Imagination in Modern Greek Culture*. Princeton, NJ: Princeton University Press.

Strhan, Anna. 2013. "Christianity and the City: Simmel, Space and Urban Subjectivities." *Religion and Society: Advances in Research* 4:125–49.

Summary and Statistical Report of the 2007 Population and Housing Census. Addis Ababa: Federal Democratic Republic of Ethiopia Population Census Commission, 2008. https://web.archive.org/web/20120214221803/http://www.csa.gov.et/pdf/Cen2007_firstdraft.pdf.

Taft, Robert F. 1986. *The Liturgy of the Hours in East and West: The Origins of the Divine Office and Its Meaning for Today.* Collegeville, MN: Liturgical Press.

Taiwo, Olufemi, ed. 2000. "West Africa Review: Editorial Introduction." *Black Scholar* 30, no. 1: 2–4.

Tamrat, Taddesse. 1984. "Feudalism in Heaven and on Earth: Ideology and the Political Structure in Medieval Ethiopia." In *Proceedings of the Seventh International Conference of Ethiopian Studies, University of Lund, 26–29 April, 1982*, ed. Sven Rubenson. Addis Ababa: Institute of Ethiopian Studies.

———. 1972. *Church and State in Ethiopia, 1270–1527.* Oxford: Clarendon.

Terpstra, Nicholas. 2000. *The Politics of Ritual Kinship: Confraternities and Social Order in Early Modern Italy.* Cambridge: Cambridge University Press.

Tilson, Dana, and Ulla Larsen. 2000. "Divorce in Ethiopia: The Impact of Early Marriage and Childlessness." *Journal of Biosocial Science* 32 (2): 355–72.

Tugendhaft, Aaron. 2013. "Paradise in Perspective: Thoughts from Pavel Florensky." *KRONOS Metafizyka–Kultura–Religia.* http://www.kronos.org.pl/index.php?23151,469.

Turner, Victor, and Edith Turner. 1978. *Image and Pilgrimage in Christian Culture: Anthropological Perspectives.* New York: Columbia University Press.

Turner, Victor W. 1974. *Dramas, Fields, and Metaphors: Symbolic Action in Human Society.* Ithaca, NY: Cornell University Press.

Ullendorff, Edward. 1968. *Ethiopia and the Bible.* London: Published for the British Academy by the Oxford University Press.

United Nations Office for the Coordination of Humanitarian Affairs (OCHA). 2010. "Humanitarian Response Fund Ethiopia: Annual Report." https://docs.unocha.org/sites/dms/Documents/Ethiopia%20ERF%202010.pdf.

United States Department of State. 2014. "2007 Report on International Religious Freedom—Ethiopia." http://www.refworld.org/docid/46ee675c6e.html.

Wagner, Roy. 2001. *An Anthropology of the Subject: Holographic Worldview in New Guinea and Its Meaning and Significance for the World of Anthropology.* Berkeley: University of California Press.

---. 1986. *Symbols That Stand for Themselves*. Chicago: University of Chicago Press.
---. 1974. *The Invention of Culture*. Chicago: University of Chicago Press.
Walzer, Michael. 1985. *Exodus and Revolution*. New York: Basic Books.
Ware, Bishop Kallistos. 1995 [1979]. *The Orthodox Way*. Crestwood, NY: St. Vladimir's Seminary Press.
Weber, Max. 1964. *The Theory of Social and Economic Organization*. Ed. Talcott Parsons. New York: Collier MacMillan.
Weinfeld, Moshe. 1977. "Berith." In *Theological Dictionary of the Old Testament*, ed. G. Johannes Botterweck, H. Ringgren, and Heinz Josef Fabry. Grand Rapids, MI: Eerdmans.
Williams, Ron G., and James W. Boyd. 1993. *Ritual Art and Knowledge: Aesthetic Theory and Zoroastrian Ritual*. Columbia: University of South Carolina Press.
Wolde-Mariam, Mesfin. 1991. *Suffering under God's Environment: A Vertical Study of the Predicament of Peasants in North-Central Ethiopia*. Berne: African Mountains Association, Geographica Bernensia.
Wondmagegnehu, Aymro, and Joachim Motovu. 1970. *The Ethiopian Orthodox Church*. Addis Ababa: Ethiopian Orthodox Mission.
Wright, Marta. 2004. "Mary in Contemporary Ethiopian Orthodox Devotion." In *The Church and Mary: Papers Read at the 2001 Summer Meeting and the 2002 Winter Meeting of the Ecclesiastical History Society*, ed. R. N. Swanson. Suffolk: Boydell.
Yesehaq, Abune. 1989. *The Ethiopian Tewahedo Church: An Integrally African Church*. New York: Vantage.

Index

Abba (mark of respect), 161
Abyssinia, 24–25
Addis Ababa, Ethiopia, 1, 14–15, 25, 63, 73, 76, 97, 111
Aedesius, 4
aesthetics, Orthodox, 9
African Unity, 25
agape symbolism, 105
Ahmed, Abiy, 154
akafisty (hymn), 36
alcoholic drink. See *t'ela*
almsgiving, 144–46; "in the name of" (*see* vows); *yene beete* ("one like me"), 99, 163
Alter, Robert, 34
American Bible Society, 31
Amhara, 167n1; billboard of attraction in, *136*
Amlak, Yekuno, 24
anticlericalism, 113–17
antimension, 7
Apostolic of Church Fathers, 34
aqwaqwam (prayer), 42, 45, 47–53, *52*, 60, 132, 161
architecture, church, 8
Aregawi (Abune) (saint), 6, 7, 108
ark housed in the sanctuary. See *tabot*
Ark of the Covenant. See *Tabota Tsion*
ark planting. See *tabot tekele*
Arseima Mariam Church, 75, 79, 170n3
Asfa Wossen (Crown Prince), viii
"association." See *mahaber*
Axumite kingdom, 6

bahetawi (hermit), 97, 161
Bajc, Vida, 134

bale habtoch (benefactors), 97
Bandak, Andreas, 36, 58
Basil the Great (Saint), 12–13
Battle of Adwa, 28, 72
benefactors. See *bale habtoch*
benefactorship, 146
Berdyaev, Nikolai, 117
bereket (blessing), 100, 161
bete kristiyan, 55, 64, 161
bete meqdes (sanctuary), 1, *40*, 46, 61, 66, 161
Bible, 169n4; Book of John, 32; Book of Luke, 32; Book of Mark, 32; Book of Matthew, 32, 65; Book of Psalms, 49, 61; New Testament, 34; Old Testament, 27, 33, 34, 50, 111, 167n3
Birth of Mary. See Lideta
Black liberation ideologies, 72
blessing. See *bereket*
Blue Nile, 90
Boulay, Juliet du, 13, 94, 96
Bourdieu, Pierre, 152
Bowman, Glenn, 130
Boyd, James W., 64
Boylston, Tom, 36, 115, 116, 132
bread, 170n1; baking, *107*, 171n2
Buddhism, Sri Lankan, 64

call to prayer, 57
Campbell, John, 96
cantor. See *debtera*
Carroll, Timothy, 33, 115
Catholics, 4, 91, 110, 113–15, 142, 149, 165n3; folklore, 137; Italian, 102
chalice. See *ts'ewa*
chant. See *zema*

chanting of liturgical poetry. See *qene mahelet*
charisma, 95–96
"chosen people," 22, 24, 96
Christmas, 13
chromolithographs, 60
"Chronicles of the Cross." See *Meshafe Tefut*
churches-in-progress, 87–91
Church of Alexandria, 4, 125
Church of Egzeiabher Ab', 126, *126*, 130, 132, 135
Church of Mary of Zion (Axum), 22
Coleman, Simon, 134
commemoration, culture of, 97
commensality, 69–70, 115
"common believers," 15, 151
communion. See *qurban*
Constantine (Emperor), 125
Constantinople, 125
cosmic habitus, 64
Council of Chalcedon, 5
Counter-Reformation, 114
counting of rosary beads. See *mekuteria*
covenant. See *kidan*; specific topics
Covenant of Mercy. See *Kidane Meheret*
covenant refractions, 3, 10–14, 21, 36, 136; elaboration, 35–36 (hologram and, 42; patterns of, 3, 21)
COVID-19 pandemic, 155
cross. See *meskel*
crowning the ark. See *tabot negs*
cultural value, 20
culture: of commemoration, 97; of offering, 105. See also devotional culture
Cyriacus the Child. See Kirkos lij

Debre Damo, 6
Debre Libanos, 121
debtera (cantor), 45, 52, 161
Derg, 170n9; Derg era, 88, 94, 118; Coordinating Committee of the Armed Forces, Police, and Territorial Army, 170n9; Ethiopian Peoples' Revolutionary Democratic Front (EPRDF), 118, 154; Ethiopian revolution (1974), 153
Dersane Uriel (The Homily of St. Uriel), 79–80, 128
Dessie, Ethiopia, 3, 6, 46, 85, 116, 120; devotional culture in, 14–15; Medhane Alem Church, 57; postrevolutionary history of, 73–77; St. Gabriel Church in, 41
deterritorialization, of church, 64–67
devotional culture, 50, 89, 96, 114, 120, 149–50, 153; covenant refractions and, 3, 13; cultural norms, ix, 67, 70; first pilgrimages in, 137;

lay engagement and, 9; liturgical space/time in, 32; as lived religion, 14–20; patterns of elaboration in, 21; *tabot* and, 34, 38, 54
Divine Liturgy. See *qidase*
Durkheim, Emile, 7, 48, 152; collective effervescence, 7

Easter, 13, 61
East Harlem, 102, 142
ecumenical councils, 5
educational campaigns. See *zemecha*
Egyptian Orthodox Church, 4; Coptic, 4, 24, 165n2
elders. See *shemageles*
Eleni (Queen), 125–28
Emebetachin ("Our Lady"), 1, 18
empiricism, faith and, 28–29
EOTC. See Ethiopian Orthodox Tewahedo Church
EPRDF. See Derg: Ethiopian Peoples' Revolutionary Democratic Front
Eritrea, 153–54
Ethiopia and the Bible (Ullendorff), 27–28
Ethiopian exceptionalism, 54; consciousness, local, 21
Ethiopian Orthodox Tewahedo Church (EOTC), vii, 8, 13, 95, 127, 149–52, 169n4; demographic shifts in, 73; formation of, 4; "Today's Ethiopia Is Ethiopia of the Past," 31; *yenefs abbat* ("father of the soul"), 163
Ethiopian Pentecostal Christians, 34
ethnic federalism, 11, 154
Eucharist, 19, 32, 55, 61–62, 109, 165n4, 169n2
Eurocentric paradigm, 167n4
exceptionalism, 21, 22–27, 37, 54

faith: empiricism and, 28–29; miracles as testing, 137–39
Farensai Abo Church, 109
farming collectives. See *geberres*
Farrakhan, Louis, 29
fast. See *ts'om*
fast of the Flight of the Holy Family. See Tsige tsom
feast-day celebrations, 6, 8–9, 33
"feast of Epiphany." See *Timqet*
Fetha Negest (Law of the Kings), 34
fitat (prayer for the deceased), 98, 161
Florensky, Pavel, 53
Freeman, Dena, 105
funerary organizations. See *iddirs*

Gabriel (Saint), 8
Garvey, Marcus, 29

Index

Gates, Henry Louis, Jr., 29, 30
geberres (farming collectives), 171n6
gedl (hagiography), 131, 161
Ge'ez (liturgical language), 2, 49, 58
Genete Le Yesus (Heaven of Jesus Church), 97
George (Saint), 142
Gerar Amba, 88
Gezachew, 65, 66, 67
Girma, Mohammed, 11, 81, 146
Gishen Mariam, viii, 15,19, 120, 126–27, 129–37, 147, 172n4
Glory of the Kings. *See* Kebre Negest
Good Friday. *See* Seklet
Good News Bible, 31
grace, 95, 134
"grain students." See *kolo tamariwoch*
grass reeds. See *qetema*
Greece, 60, 87, 94, 96, 133
Greek mythology, 69
Greek Orthodoxy, 9, 13, 16, 33
Gugsa, Dejazmatch, 74

hagiography. See *gedl*
Haile, Getachew, 167n1, 170n3
Haile Sellassie I (emperor), viii, 4, 14, 25, 27, 72
Hanks, William F., 73
Harrar, Ethiopia, 74
Hawas (Abba), 129
Haymanot Abew ("Faith of the Fathers"), 34, 150
head cantor. See *merigeta*
Heaven of Jesus Church. *See* Genete Le Yesus
Hebrew Bible, 34
hermit. See *bahetawi*
hierarchy, 115
Hig (law), 161
Hinduism, 133, 143
HIV, 77
hologram, 42, 167n4
holy. *See qeddest*
Holy Communion, 7, 32
Holy Spirit, 29, 106, 152
Holy Tradition, 12–13, 19, 21, 34–36, 147; Church Tradition, 150; cultural adaptation, 154
Holy Week, 58, 61, 106; Holy Friday, 62, 71; Holy Saturday, 46; Holy Thursday (*see* Tselot Hamus)
The Homily of St. Uriel. *See* Dersane Uriel
honorary association. See *senbete*
honorary feast. See *zikir*
Horn of Africa, 156
Horologion. *See* Liturgy of the Hours

Hudadae (Lent), 58, 62, 66–67, 71, 161
Humphrey, Caroline, 59, 133
hymns. See *akafisty*; *mizmur*

icons, 60
iddirs (funerary organizations), 171n6
identity, 20; local, 46; local parish, 8; national, 6; political, 116, 154; religious, 155
immanence, material reality of, 49–53
individualism, 54, 115, 117
invention, 35–36
Invention of Tradition (Hobsbawn and Ranger), 35
iqubs (lending associations), 171n6
Islam, 16, 54, 58, 75–76, 77, 154
Italian Catholics, 102
Italy, 25, 72

Jan Meda, 83–84
Joseph, Miranda, 116
Judaism, 27–28, 34, 166n3

kalkidan ("word of Promise"), 39, 161
Kaluli song, 53
Kan, Sergei, 114
Kana ze Galila, 168n6
Kapferer, Bruce, 63
Kebede, Messay 27, 28, 167n4
kebele (governmental association), 41, 95, 161
Kebre Negest (Glory of the Kings), 22–25, *23*, 36–37, 80
kidan (covenant), 22, 161
Kidane, Habtemichael, 32
Kidane Meheret (Covenant of Mercy), 33, 37, 85, 90
kin relationships, 19
kinship: *bete Abraham* ("house of Abraham"), 124, 161; ideologies of, 84; normative, 96; ritual, 96; spiritual, 96–97, 103
Kirkos lij (Cyriacus the Child), 77–78, 87
kolo tamariwoch,144
Koran, 75

Laidlaw, James, 59, 133
Lalibela, 25, 30, 136, 138
Law of the Kings. *See* Fetha Negest
law of the *tabot*. See *tabot hig*
lay engagement, templates of, 7–10, 17, 152
League of Nations, 25
legends, *tabot*, 81–91
lending associations. See *iqubs*
Lent. See *Hudadae*
leqso (mourning house), 18, 67–70, 161
Levine, Donald, 12, 51

Levites, 49
Lideta (Birth of Mary), 90
liturgical calendar, 5, 8–9, 15, 18, 46, 63; Feast of the Holy Cross, 9; Feast of the Holy Resurrection, 8; Feast of the Nativity of Jesus, 8, 13
liturgical context, covenant in, 32–36; Last Supper of Jesus Christ, 32
liturgical language. *See* Ge'ez
liturgical materialities, 60–64
liturgical space/time, 32–33, 56–60, 62
liturgical stances, refraction of, 67–70
liturgy of the Hours. *See sa'atat*
Liturgy of the Hours (Horologion), 168n3
Lord's Prayer, 99

mahaber ("association"), 10–11, 15, 19, 68, 93, 162; anticlericalism and Orthodox autonomy, 113–17; brotherhood, 10; "charismatic collectives," 98; conclusion, 118; family's sacred history and, 96–101; role-playing, 112; *senbete* and parish development, 109–13; sisterhood, 10; spiritual kindred and, 94–96; traveling household and, 102–9; *ts'ewa mahaber*, 102–3, 108, 112
mahaber lij (kid), 108
mahelet (matins), 162
malaria, 77
Marxism-Leninism, 118
Mary (Saint), 8, 36; Lideta, 90; Tamera Mariam, 66
masqedes (worship), 55
material ecology, Orthodox, 9
materiality, 41; liturgical, 60–64
Matias (Abune) (Patriarch), 154
matins. *See mahelet*
Mauss, Marcel, 93
Medhane Alem (Dessie), 57, 85, 87
Medhane Alem Church (Addis Ababa), 86, 97–98, 112,129
media: devotional, 63; visual, 47
Mefekeria Seb (Abba), 87–89
memhir (teacher), 162
Memhir Eshetu (deacon), 127, 128
Menelik I, vii, 2, 22, 28, 72
Menelik II, 25, 80
menokse (monk or nun), 162
Mequanent, Getachew, 111
merigeta (head cantor), 43, 52
mesalem, 16, 33, 56, 57, 61, 162
Meshafe Tefut, 131–32
meskel (cross), 125, 162
mesob (woven basket), 104, 162

metanoia, 33
Mezgeba Tselot (registry of prayers), 61
Michael (Saint), 8
miracles. *See tamerat*
miracles, as testing faith, 137–39
Miracles of Mary. *See* Tamera Mariam
mist' ir (sacrament, "mystery"), 162
mizmur (hymns), 6–7, 123–24, 162,
mizmur Dawit (Songs of David), 61
monk. *See menokse*
Moses, 1, 22, 166n6
mourning house. *See leqso*
Munn, Nancy, 60; cultural governance, 60
Muslims. *See* Islam
mutual-aid societies, 10–11, 150
mythology, Greek, 69

national exceptionalism, 24
national identity, 6
Nation of Islam, 29
Nations and Nationalism, 35
Natnael, 135–36
Negest Eleni, 127, *127*
Negus Mikael, 86
net'ela (white cotton cloth), 162
"new Jerusalem," 2, 25
New Testament, 34
Nile (river), 2
normative kinship, 96
nun. See *menokse*

obligation, 69
offering, culture of, 105
Old Kingdom of Egypt, 27
Old Testament, 27, 33, 34, 50, 111, 167n3
Organization of African Unity (African Unity), 25
Orientalism (Said), 31
Orientalist scholarship, 27
Oriental Orthodox churches, 5
Oromia, 154
Orsi, Robert A., 102, 142
Orthodox autonomy, 113–17
Orthodox Christianity. *See specific topics*
"our duty." *See giddeta*
"Our Lady." *See Emebetachin*

painting studio. See *s' il bet*
Pan-Africanism, 25
Panagia Protothronos, 87
Panovsky, Erwin, 50
paradigmatic thinking, 124
parish development, 109–13
Passion of Christ, 50

Patriarchate of Alexandria, 4
Patriots Day, 112
patterns of elaboration, 3, 21
Paulos (Patriarch), 30, 129, 166n3
Paxson, Margaret, 10
peace talks, 111
Pentecostal Christians, 58, 154, 169n4
pilgrimage, 119–23; almsgiving and, 144–46; conclusion, 146–47; Gishen, 15, 125–26, 129–37, 147, 172n4; holographic relic and, 124–37; *menfesawi guzo* ("spiritual journey"), 119, 162; miracles as testing faith in, 137–39
vows as tradition making, 139–43
Pitt-Rivers, Julian, 95
pledges, as fundraising technique, 90
pollution, 132
popular devotion, 102
post-Enlightenment thought, 129
prayer. See *aqwaqwam*; *tselot*
prayer for the deceased. See *fitat*
preaching. See *sebket*
prescriptive ontology, 133
prostration. See *mesged*; *Segdet*
Protestants, 4, 149, 165n3
Psalm 68, 29
Psalms, Book of, 49, 61
public sphere, 57–58, 76
puja, 59, 133

qeddest (holy), 1, *40*
Qedus Kirkos, 78
qene mahelet (chanting of liturgical poetry), 1, *40*
qetema (grass reeds), 162
qidase (Divine Liturgy), 9, 12, 56–59, 62–63, 120, 162
qirs (relic, treasure), 162; relic of the True Cross, 19, 124–27, 135, preservation, of relics, 136
qolo temariwoch (students of traditional Church education), 162
qurban (communion), 18, 32, 55, 162; Holy Eucharist, 62

Raiders of the Lost Ark (film), 28
Rappaport, Roy A., 9, 56
Ras Kassa, 101
Ras Mekonnen, 74
Rastafarianism, 25–26
reciprocity, 69, 94
registry of prayers. *See* Mezgeba Tselot
relic. See *qirs*
religion. See *haymanot*

religious exceptionalism, 21, 24
religious identity, 155
Renaissance Dam, 90
Renaissance Europe, 114
"restoration of the Solomonic dynasty," 24
ritual, 41; common, 58
ritual kinship, 96
ritual praxis, *86*
Robbins, Joel, 119; innovation, traditions of, 119
Russia, 10, 36, 60, 133, 155
Russian Orthodox Church, 15, 95

sa'atat (liturgy of the Hours), 13, 57, 59, 65, 162
Sabbath, 34, 63
sacrament. See *mist'ir*
sacred indwelling, 53
sacred speech, 101
St. Gabriel Church (Dessie), 41, 73–74, 89
St. Gabriel's Sunday School, *45*, 121
St. Mikael's Church (Addis Ababa), 82–83, *83*
sanctuary. See *bete meqdes*
Savior of the World. *See* Medhane Alem
Schieffelin, Edward L., 41
sebket (preaching), 162
Segdet (prostration), 61, 162
Seklet (Good Friday), *59*
Sellassie (Trinity) Church (Dessie), 75
semenaworq ("wax and gold"), 51
Semitization thesis, 27–28
senbete (honorary association), 109–13, *113*, 162
shai/buna, 101, 162
Sheba (Queen), vii, 22, 27, 31
shebsheba, 46, 52
Shelemay, Kay Kaufman, 51
shemageles (elders), 111
Shenoda, Anthony, 137
Shevzov, Vera, 36
The Sign and the Seal, 28, 30
s'il bet (icon or painting studio), 74
s'let (vow), 139–43, 162
social mobilization, 72
Solomon (King), vii, 22, 27
Songs of David. See *mizmur Dawit*
South Africa, 24
Soviet Union, 95
space/time, 141; liturgical, 32–33, 56–60, 62;
Spain, 91, 106, 114
spiritual challenge, 139
"spiritual heritage," 35
spiritual kinship, 10, 94–97, 103
spiritual retreat. See *subaye*
Stations of the Cross, 127
Stewart, Charles, 129

students of traditional Church education. See *qolo temariwoch*
subaye (spiritual retreat), 145, 162
symbolism, agape, 105
Synaxarium, 33
Syrian Orthodoxy, 36

tablet. See *tselat*
tabot (ark housed in the sanctuary), 6–8, 11, 18–19, 33, 38, 60, 151, 162; complicated definition of, 39–43; conclusion, 54; *dabbaloch* (roommate), 77; directions of movements, 44; divine presence, 38, 48; Exodus 25:10–22, 7; immanence and, 49–53; legends, 81–91; listening to, 85–87; local identity, 8, 46; political framing of action, 77–81; provenance of, 73–77, 76; ritual praxis and, 86; Timqet as action, 43–49
Tabota Tsion (Ark of the Covenant), vii, 1, 7, 11, 22, 24, 28, 30, 73, 166n1
tabot hig (law of the *tabot*), 74, 162–63
tabot negs (crowning the ark), 39, 74, 162, 163
tabot tekele (ark planting), 162, 163
Tamera Mariam (Miracles of Mary), 66
tamerat (miracle), 122, 163
teacher. See *memhir*
Teachings of Church Fathers, 12
tea/coffee money. See *shai/buna*
tej bet (traditional honey wine bar), 41
Tekle Haymanot (Saint), 169n5
t'ela (alcoholic drink), 99, 104, 121, 163
Teleyayen River, 138
temesgen (thanksgiving), 3, 16, 55, 124, 138–39
Ten Commandments, 39–40, 50
Terpstra, Nicholas, 113–14
test. See *fet'ena*
Tewodros II, 4
Tezekere, 58
thanksgiving. See *temesgen*
Theotokos (Mother of God), 61
Tigray, 153–54
Timqet ("baptism"), 3, 18, 29, 38, 42, 150, 163; baptism of Christ, 167n3; as *tabot* action, 43–49
Ti'ta Mikael,110
"Today's Ethiopia Is Ethiopia of the Past" (treatise), 31
tradition: Church Tradition, 150; Holy Tradition, 12–13, 19, 21, 34–36, 147; of innovation, 119
traditional honey wine bar. See *tej bet*
traditionalism, 54, 103

tradition making, vows as, 139–43
treasure. See *qirs*
Trinitarian formula, 39
True Cross, relic of, 19, 124–27, 135
ts'ebel ts'adik, 143, 163
tselat (tablet), 40, 163
tselot (prayer), 163
Tselot Hamus (Holy Thursday), 88
ts'ewa (chalice), 102–6, *104*, 108, 110, 163
ts'ewa mahaber, 102–3, 108, 112
Tsige tsom (fast of the Flight of the Holy Family), 99
ts'om (fast), 8–9, 58, 62, 67, 71, 163
Turner, Edith, 137
Turner, Victor, 137

Ukraine, ix, 155
Ullendorff, Edward, 27, 49, 111
Understanding Religion and Social Change in Ethiopia (Girma), 11
United States, viii, 24, 156
Uriel (Saint), 170n4

veneration, 8, 60–61, 133, 166n7; Ethiopian Orthodox, 4–7
vigil service. See *wazema*
virtual space, 96
visual media, 47
vitality, Ethiopian Orthodox, 4–7
vital symbiosis, 13
vows(*s' le*), 144, 162

Wagner, Roy, 42, 167n4
Wax and God (Levine), 12
"wax and gold." See *semenaworq*
wazema, 43, 44, 163, Christmas eve, 46
white cotton cloth. See *net'ela*
Williams, Ron G., 64
Wittgenstein, Ludwig, 137
Wollo, Archbishop of, 128
Wollo University, 120
Wolloye Muslims, 75
women, 68, 103, 132, 151, 172n3
Wonders of the African World (Gates), 29
World Bank, 116
World Council of Churches, 5
worship. See *masqedes*
woven basket. See *mesob*
Wright, Marta, 172n3

Yared (Saint), 49, 50, 169n5
Yemezgib Tselot, 61
Ye Muse Kidan (Sinai covenant), 37
Yesehaq (Abune), 24

Yesus Church (Addis), 84
Yordanos (Jordan) river, 45
YouTube, 155

Za'ra Yacob (King), 34, 125

zema (chant), 49, 58
zemecha (educational campaigns), 118
Zenawi, Meles, 169n7
zikir (honorary feast), 94, 97–98, 101, 129, 163

Alexandra Edjigaheu Sellassie Antohin is an independent researcher and holds an academic affiliation with the George Washington University. A former Postdoctoral Fellow at the Truman Institute at Hebrew University of Jerusalem, Alexandra has published widely on topics related to Orthodox Christianity.

ORTHODOX CHRISTIANITY AND CONTEMPORARY THOUGHT

SERIES EDITORS
Aristotle Papanikolaou and Ashley M. Purpura,

Alexandra Sellassie Antohin, *The Covenant's Veil: Ethiopian Orthodox Tradition of Elaboration*

Sarah Bakker Kellogg, *Sonic Icons: Relation, Recognition, and Revival in a Syriac World*

A. G. Roeber, *Orthodox Christianity and the Rights Revolution in America*

Bryce E. Rich, *Gender Essentialism and Orthodoxy: Beyond Male and Female*

Kristina Stoeckl and Dmitry Uzlaner, *The Moralist International: Russia in the Global Culture Wars*

Sarah Riccardi-Swartz, *Between Heaven and Russia: Religious Conversion and Political Apostasy in Appalachia*

Thomas Arentzen, Ashley M. Purpura, and Aristotle Papanikolaou (eds.), *Orthodox Tradition and Human Sexuality*

Christina M. Gschwandtner, *Welcoming Finitude: Toward a Phenomenology of Orthodox Liturgy*

George E. Demacopoulos, *Colonizing Christianity: Greek and Latin Religious Identity in the Era of the Fourth Crusade.*

Pia Sophia Chaudhari, *Dynamis of Healing: Patristic Theology and the Psyche*

Brian A. Butcher, *Liturgical Theology after Schmemann: An Orthodox Reading of Paul Ricoeur.* Foreword by Andrew Louth.

Ashley M. Purpura, *God, Hierarchy, and Power: Orthodox Theologies of Authority from Byzantium.*

Aristotle and George E. Demacopoulos (eds.), *Faith, Reason, and Theosis*

Aristotle Papanikolaou and George E. Demacopoulos (eds.), *Fundamentalism or Tradition: Christianity after Secularism*

George E. Demacopoulos and Aristotle Papanikolaou (eds.), *Christianity, Democracy, and the Shadow of Constantine.*

George E. Demacopoulos and Aristotle Papanikolaou (eds.), *Orthodox Constructions of the West.*

George E. Demacopoulos and Aristotle Papanikolaou (eds.), *Orthodox Readings of Augustine* [available 2020]

John Chryssavgis and Bruce V. Foltz (eds.), *Toward an Ecology of Transfiguration: Orthodox Christian Perspectives on Environment, Nature, and Creation.* Foreword by Bill McKibben. Prefatory Letter by Ecumenical Patriarch Bartholomew.

Lucian N. Leustean (ed.), *Orthodox Christianity and Nationalism in Nineteenth-Century Southeastern Europe.*

Georgia Frank, Susan R. Holman, and Andrew S. Jacobs (eds.), *The Garb of Being: Embodiment and the Pursuit of Holiness in Late Ancient Christianity*

John Chryssavgis (ed.), *Dialogue of Love: Breaking the Silence of Centuries*. Contributions by Brian E. Daley, S.J., and Georges Florovsky

A. G. Roeber, *Orthodox Christians and the Rights Revolution in America*

Ecumenical Patriarch Bartholomew, *In the World, Yet Not of the World: Social and Global Initiatives of Ecumenical Patriarch Bartholomew*. Edited by John Chryssavgis. Foreword by Jose Manuel Barroso

Ecumenical Patriarch Bartholomew, *Speaking the Truth in Love: Theological and Spiritual Exhortations of Ecumenical Patriarch Bartholomew*. Edited by John Chryssavgis. Foreword by Dr. Rowan Williams, Archbishop of Canterbury.

Ecumenical Patriarch Bartholomew, *On Earth as in Heaven: Ecological Vision and Initiatives of Ecumenical Patriarch Bartholomew*. Edited by John Chryssavgis. Foreword by His Royal Highness, the Duke of Edinburgh.

www.ingramcontent.com/pod-product-compliance
Lightning Source LLC
Chambersburg PA
CBHW020410080526
44584CB00014B/1254